How to cope with a Fatal Illness

THE RATIONAL MANAGEMENT OF DEATH AND DYING

BY ALBERT ELLIS, PH.D.
MICHAEL ABRAMS, PH.D.

Barricade Books Inc.
New York

Published by Barricade Books Inc.
61 Fourth Avenue
New York, NY 10003

Printed in the United States of America.

Library of Congress Cataloging-in-Publication Data

Abrams, Michael
    How to cope with a fatal illness / by Michael Abrams, Albert Ellis.
        p.   cm.
    ISBN 1-56980-005-7 : $14.95
        1. Death—Psychological aspects. 2. Terminally ill—Psychology.
    3. Rational-emotive psychotherapy.   I. Ellis, Albert.   II. Title.
    BF789.D4A27   1994
    155.9'37—dc20   93-45551
                                                                 CIP

First printing

The authors would like to thank Ellyn O'Neill for her excellent work in indexing both
this book and *The Art and Science of Rational Eating*.

Contents

end. Odd? Yes, statistically. But some "odd" people really do achieve this "strange" state.

At the other extreme, some people, the minute they hear that they have only a limited time to live, even if that limit is diagnosed at five to ten years, immediately make themselves completely miserable, stop themselves from having any—yes, *any*—enjoyment, and think only of the horror of it all until they finally pass away. Between these two extremes, the majority of death-notified individuals sometimes suffer emotionally and sometimes do not; often they are depressed or panicked and just as often are calm and lighthearted. Sometimes they are inert and ineffective and at other times they are active and productive.

The wide range of feelings and behaviors that afflict or enhance the remaining days of people with fatal ailments clearly proves that, when faced with grim reality, people show infinite variety. Obviously, they have some *choice* in how they take and react to the news that their life span is now distinctly limited. All, no doubt, react in one way or another. But some react poorly and some magnificently. Quite a choice!

Similarly, the relatives and close friends of fatally afflicted people can feel almost any emotion, ranging from complete horror and constant anguish to calmness, acceptance, and sometimes real companionship and enjoyment of many fine hours with their about-to-die intimates.

Do people really have a *choice* of how they can feel and behave when they themselves or one of their close associates is in the process of dying? Of course they do—as thousands of years of recorded history have shown. They always did have this choice; and since the growth of psychotherapy, self-help groups, therapeutic workshops, and written and recorded self-help materials, they have a much wider choice in this respect today.

Why is this so? The answer to this question was given many years ago by several ancient philosophers, including Confucius, Lao-Tse, Gautama Buddha, Epicurus, Zeno of

Cytium, Seneca, Epictetus, and Marcus Aurelius. These thinkers and teachers had many different views, but they tended to agree on one major point: Humans, contrary to the views of Sigmund Freud and his psychoanalytic followers, do not usually *get* emotionally upset because of the unfortunate circumstances of their lives. No. These sad circumstances, as well as their early experiences and genetic tendencies, importantly *influence* them to prefer this and to hate that, to seek out many "pleasures" and to avoid many "pains." True. Because practically all of us are *born* gullible and teachable, and therefore frequently—though not *always*—accept the notions of "good" and "bad," "enjoyable" and "unenjoyable" feelings and behaviors that our parents and our culture indoctrinate into our heads and our hearts. We therefore largely *learn* our tastes and distastes, and we partly *learn* to enjoy living and to abhor dying.

But not *completely!* Even in our somewhat homogenized American society, some of us are indifferent to or hate baseball, TV, and apple pie. For we can think and value (and disvalue) for ourselves, even though we commonly lazily refuse to do so. Moreover, as the ancient philosophers and teachers often taught and as more modern thinkers have frequently agreed, we can choose to upset ourselves or *not* upset ourselves when bad things happen in our lives. As Epictetus nicely put it two thousand years ago, "People are disturbed not by the things that happen to them but by their view of these things." Even if dying and death happen to them? Yes, even then.

"Are you trying to tell me," you, the reader of this book, may ask with some degree of astonishment, "that even if I suddenly find myself stricken with AIDS, with fatal cancer, with a rapidly failing heart, or with some other death-dealing affliction, I can *choose* to upset myself or not upset myself about this fatal blow?"

"Yes, you obviously have that choice," we firmly reply. "As we noted above, not everyone with a deadly disease upsets herself or himself. Most do, many don't. So you obviously have a choice!"

"But *how?* How do I choose my feelings when I am faced—which I hope I shall never be!—with the grimmest of reapers?"

"By acquiring, as so many others have done, an accepting, nondisturbing *philosophy*. For you largely feel the way you think; and there are several major philosophies or attitudes that you can take that will nicely pull you through—and we might say, literally pull you through death's door."

"Several?"

"Yes, several, as we shall show a little later on."

"You mean that I even have a choice of which philosophies to choose to get myself off death's nasty hook?"

"Yes, a real choice. But not a choice of completely avoiding death. That, alas, will come to you, as to all of us, sooner or later. Your real choice is how and when to create certain feelings and actions that will help you much better to *deal with* unavoidable death."

"So I really can choose an accepting, nonhorrifying philosophy?"

"You definitely can. But there's one catch: To *feel* this philosophy and to *use* it effectively, you damned well better *believe* it. No namby-pamby half-belief, no amount of wishy-washy parroting of any good belief—none of that will do. Just as you now may hold needlessly upsetting beliefs about many things, including approaching death, you are probably going to have to strongly and persistently hold powerfully healthy, nondisturbing beliefs. No namby-pambyism—as those ancient philosophers we mentioned above pointed out."

"I see. But what about my loved ones? I really might be able to have a good attitude if I were faced with impending death, because I can usually take care of myself even in bad circumstances. But what about the people I especially love and take joy in being with? My mother and father, for instance, or my mate, or heaven forbid, one of my children.

How could I stubbornly refuse to make myself miserable—as one of your books advises—if I knew that they were about to suffer through a painful dying process and then be snuffed out entirely?"

"Not easily!" we assure you. "Watching and caring for someone who is most probably dying is really much to cope with. But, again, as relatives and friends have shown over the centuries, a good philosophy of coping will distinctly help."

"Meaning exactly what? *What* good, sensible philosophy are you talking about?"

"Not one, but several. Sanely coping with death, your own or a loved one's, includes a number of self-helping ideas. In this book, we shall describe several good possibilities, some elegant and some not so elegant. All of them, for one person or another, can work. But we shall recommend some of them more than others and show why they work better for more people more of the time. Especially, we shall show you how to use the theory and practice of Rational Emotive Behavior Therapy (REBT)."

"REBT? What the devil is that?"

"Read on!"

2

Rational Emotive Behavior Therapy and the Acceptance of Fatal Illness

Rational Emotive Behavior Therapy (REBT) was born when I (AE) became disillusioned in 1953 with psychoanalysis, after practicing it and psychodynamic-oriented therapy for ten years. But having some genes for efficiency, while poor Sigmund Freud and most other analysts seem to have strong genes for inefficiency, I saw that psychoanalysis is startlingly ineffective. So I went back to philosophy, which had been my main hobby from the age of sixteen onward, and welded it, for the first time in modern psychotherapeutic history, to behavior therapy.

Why did I value behavior therapy, when psychoanalysis treats it as a rotten stepchild and almost completely neglects it? Because I had used it very successfully on myself, as I have reported elsewhere, at the age of nineteen.[1] At that time, I had a public speaking phobia and never spoke in public if I could possibly cop out and avoid doing so. But, following the desensitizing procedures of the pioneering behaviorist, John B. Watson, I forced myself—very uncomfortably—to speak and speak in public until I saw—and felt—that nothing terrible would happen if I spoke poorly. Encouraged by this new attitude, I applied it to encountering women, with whom I often flirted but was phobic about actually approaching. I forced myself to ask a hundred of

7

them for a date, had no success at first, but completely got over my fear of encountering them. For once again, I saw—and *felt*—that rejection wasn't *awful* and *horrible*, but only damned inconvenient. In regard to both public speaking and encountering women, I made almost a hundred percent change: My phobias vanished and I actually began to *enjoy* picking up women and public speaking.

So because behavior therapy was so useful to me, I welded it to philosophic, or cognitive, therapy to create REBT in 1955, and I thereby started the now very popular cognitive behavior therapy (CBT) movement. The cognitive part, as I implied above, I mainly took from philosophers—though a few psychotherapists, such as Paul Dubois and Alfred Adler, also partly saw it too.[2] I added to these thinkers by formulating the now famous—though originally scoffed at and neglected—ABC theory of human neurosis. This theory holds that humans almost invariably have strong goals (G) and values, and that these often are blocked or thwarted at point A (Activating Event or Activating Experience). Thus, you strongly desire or have the Goal (G) of being successful and winning the approval of people you favor, and you fail at an important project and get disapproved. Your failing and being disapproved we call A, your negative Activating Experience or Adversity.

When A is negative (against your interests) or bad (worse than you want it to be) you have two main choices at C (your emotional and behavioral Consequence) which follows A: (1) You can make yourself feel appropriately or self-helpingly sorry, regretful, or disappointed and thereby encourage yourself to change A. Or if you cannot change A (Adversity) you can choose to accept it and to live reasonably happily in spite of it. (2) You can make yourself inappropriately or self-defeatingly panicked, depressed, enraged, self-damning, or self-pitying, refuse to accept A (Adversity), behave dysfunctionally about it, and make it and your whole life much more miserable than it would otherwise be.

How do you make this choice of reacting (at C) to the

unfortunate events (A) that happen or that you make happen, to you? Mainly, says REBT, by choosing, consciously or unconsciously, thoughts or self-statements at B, your Belief System. For at B you usually first have a sensible, rational Belief (rB), which you hold as a *preference.* Such as: "I don't like failing and being rejected at point A. I wish I had succeeded and got accepted. How annoying and frustrating! But it's obviously not the end of the world and I can live fairly happily in spite of this Adversity."

If, says REBT, you would *only* stay with this preferential Belief and *never* go beyond it, you would have a hard time really upsetting yourself about anything. Because a preferential sentence includes an underlying, realistic *but:* "I would *like* success very much, *but* it doesn't *have to* occur the way I'd like it to happen." Or: "I *hate* failure *but* if it occurs and I can't change it, I'll accept its pain and live with it as best I can." If you strongly *believe* these philosophies and not merely unconvincingly parrot them, you will still feel (at C) appropriately and self-helpfully sorry and regretful about your frustrating A, but you will not feel very disturbed and act neurotically about it. You will *cope* with it instead of *horrifying yourself* about it.

On the other hand, if exactly the same unfortunate Activating Event or Adversity (A) occurs, and you construct a philosophy or Belief (B) about it that is absolutely demanding, or completely needy, you almost always will needlessly upset yourself about it. Thus, if you strongly tell yourself, "I *absolutely should not* have failed and got myself rejected and because I did what I *utterly must not do,* it's *awful* and I'm *no good* for bringing about that terrible Adversity!" you will almost always feel—that is, *make yourself* feel—panicked, depressed, or self-hating at point C (Consequence). Yes, says REBT, you have a real choice. Not often about what happens to you at A. But how you *react* to A at point B, and how you largely *create,* with your Beliefs, your feelings and your behaviors at C?

"Really?" you may ask. "No matter *what* happens to me

at point A, I can *still* make myself feel appropriately sorry and regretful instead of self-defeatingly horrified and depressed at point C?[3] That seems too much. Isn't that an exaggerated view?"

"Well, yes. Slightly exaggerated. But not as much as you'd think. Suppose, as Bertrand Russell once objected, you were forced to spend a night in a raging storm in sub-zero weather while you were wearing only a few rags? Could you then only make yourself feel calm and serene or somewhat sorry or regretful? Technically, yes, because a few people have at times accomplished such a feat; and a few Asian gurus and Western practitioners (like Harry Houdini) have been able to control their bodily sensations so well that they almost eliminate pain and are therefore able to handle it beautifully. A few. But the rest of us are far from being able to do this."

"See! Just as I was predicting!"

"Yes. But hold on. While we normal humans cannot very well face *any* physical problem, like intense pain, and make ourselves feel calm or undisturbed, we often *can* do so when we are confronted with severe Adversities, such as poverty, loss of a loved one, serious disease, and even death. We don't *easily* conquer such A's and come up with appropriate negative feelings. But with persistent hard work and straight thinking, we can arrange to do so. Not always, of course. But quite often."

"We can? Precisely how?"

"We shall show you several inelegant and elegant ways to do this throughout the book. Elegant methods of finding emotional well-being in spite of real Adversities are realistic, logical, and long lasting. Less elegant ways sometimes work but are often unrealistic, illogical, and short lasting. But let us first get back to outlining some of the main therapeutic theories and practices of Rational Emotive Behavior Therapy (REBT)."

"Good! I am eager to hear about them."

When REBT was founded in 1955, it soon became

clear that people rarely create serious emotional trouble for themselves if they firmly stay with their *preferences* and *wishes*. If, for example, you only *prefer* to dress well, and you actually dress below your standards, you usually think, "I am not behaving as I *preferably* should, and that's wrong and deplorable, so I'd better change my ways and act more desirably." You then, according to REBT, feel *appropriately* or *healthfully* sorry and disappointed but not, usually, self-defeatingly depressed and panicked. It is mainly when you *absolutely demand* to do well and command, "I *positively must* dress exceptionally well!" that you make yourself—yes, *make* yourself—neurotic.

REBT acknowledges that you take *some* of your imperative musts from your parents and culture (because you are born gullible) but points out that you usually *construct* or *manufacture* many of them yourself. Why? Because, as a human, you have a strong innate tendency to take almost any of your strong *desires,* however you arrive at them, and raise them into *dire necessities.* This kind of constructing seems to be a normal and common part of your nature.

You are born and reared, in fact, with two opposing predispositions. First, the constructive one of observing your behavior and that of other people, of discovering when you and they act "badly"—meaning, against your Goals (G) and preferences—and then *changing* the ways you behave and trying to change the ways they behave. If you construct "good" thoughts and behaviors, you arrange to get more of the things you want and less of the things you don't want, and thereby make yourself happy—or, at least, happi*er* than you otherwise would be. Thus, you have natural self-changing or *self-actualizing* tendencies.[4]

Fine! But, as we have been pointing out, you *also* have innate and acquired *self-defeating* tendencies: to take your Goals and desires and to foolishly raise them to godlike, grandiose *demands* and *commands.* Your three basic or core demands, by which you often disturb yourself (and help disturb others), are:

1. *"I* must practically always, under all conditions, perform well and be approved by significant others;
   and if I don't perform as well as I, or be approved
   as much as I, *absolutely must,* I am a pretty worthless, inadequate *person!"* This unrealistic and illogical *must* helps you make yourself anxious, panicked,
   depressed, and self-hating and leads to behaviors
   like inhibition, withdrawal, and lack of assertion.
2. *"You* (other people) *absolutely must* treat me
   kindly, fairly, and lovingly at practically all times;
   and if you don't treat me as well as you *must,* you
   are *rotten people* and deserve to be damned and
   punished!" This quite unrealistic and illogical *must*
   often leads you to make yourself angry, furious, and
   wishfully homicidal and creates behaviors like vindictiveness, feuds, wars, terrorism, and genocide.
3. "The conditions and circumstances under which I
   live *absolutely must* be comfortable, pleasurable,
   and free from serious hassles; and if they are not as
   they *must* be, it's *awful,* I *can't stand it,* and my life
   is really rotten and hopeless!" This unrealistic and
   illogical *demand* often leads to feelings of low frustration tolerance and depression and to behaviors
   such as procrastination, addiction, and withdrawal.[5]

If you (or anyone else) frequently have one or more of
these grandiose demands—and thereby are addicted to what
REBT calls *mus*turbation—you will tend to lead a pretty
miserable life. If you frequently have all three—as much of
the human race has—watch it! Your chances for steady pro-
ductiveness and happiness are slim. Even if you, because of
your talents, *do* well, you will rarely *feel* well.

How do these three major absolutist, dogmatic musts—
and the scores of specific irrational Beliefs (iB's) that stem
from them—relate to you or your loved ones having a fatal
disease? Very closely! If you *must* perform well and be lovable and you have a life-threatening disability, you will prob-

ably put yourself down and make yourself panicked and depressed. If you think that others *have to* be kind and considerate to you, and they avoid you or do not treat you as well as they presumably *must,* you will probably make yourself incensed. If you really believe that the conditions of your life *have got to be* comfortable and easy, and your ailment makes them very hard, you will surely make yourself very miserable.

"Yes, I can see that," you say. "But even without my having any of these foolish *demands,* wouldn't my fatal disease—or that of my close friends and relatives—*still* make me angry and depressed?"

"No, it really wouldn't. Such a very bad condition would almost certainly help you to feel very sad, disappointed, frustrated, and displeased. But unless you then *added,* in your own philosophy, the *demand* that you *absolutely must not* experience sad, disappointing, frustrating, and displeasing Activating Events (A's), such as your or your friend's fatal disease, you would most probably not make yourself *highly disturbed* about such an ailment."

"So if I use REBT, and surrender all my *absolutist musts* about myself, about other people, and about the world, I can *then* really accept and live much better with my or my close associate's fatal affliction."

"In a word: Yes."

"And, specifically, I can do that by using what precise REBT methods?"

"By using many that we shall soon elaborate. But first, in the next few chapters, let us consider some less elegant, non-REBT methods, that you can use to deal with fatal ailments and show how they all to some extent work but why they have their distinct limitations and are therefore inelegant."

Before we go on to the next chapter let us present one of the early cases that showed how a client could use REBT to profoundly change his philosophy about dying. Ron was an almost perfect specimen of the All-American Male, who won swimming races from the age of five, was easily the best athlete in his high school, and starred in baseball, football, and wrestling in college. Being so talented, and winning great popularity, he had enormous achievement confidence and distinctly liked himself because he was so accomplished.

Unfortunately, Ron was overconfident about learning how to ski, rushed on to risky slopes long before he should have tried them, broke his spine in an accident he foolishly brought on, suffered from a series of infections following several operations, and acquired an impaired immune system which could well prove fatal.

Ron suffered from devastating depression and self-hatred. His self-esteem, which was based largely on his athletic prowess and fame, was entirely gone. Even worse, he loathed himself because he knew that he had brought on his afflictions by his own stupid risk-taking and that he could still have been his old athletic self if he had been sensible about his skiing.

After several months of Rational Emotive Behavior Therapy, in the course of which he refused to Dispute (at point D) his irrational Beliefs (iB's) and kept insisting that he *absolutely should not* have taken such foolish skiing risks and that he was a cripple with a wasted life, Ron still felt completely worthless. His therapist, who at the time was being supervised at the Institute for Rational-Emotive Therapy in New York, was herself feeling discouraged, but she persisted in showing Ron that no matter how foolishly he had acted and no matter how useless his life now was from an athletic standpoint, his worth *as a person* was not dependent on his good accomplishments, nor did it depend on his acting wisely and sanely in regard to skiing or anything else.

Ron fought like hell against this REBT philosophy and kept insisting that with *such* foolishness as his and with the *enormous* waste of his life he had brought on, he really *was* an idiot and a worthless person. For session after session his therapist tried to show him otherwise—and still failed. Then, to her surprise, Ron finally got it. When he was most depressed about having another complicated operation and he was sure that this time he would not survive it, and when his therapist still insisted that, despite his sad condition, Ron had a *choice* of making himself utterly miserable or merely very concerned and sad, he was able to report, just before he entered the hospital again, "I've been doing some tall thinking, and I see that you're right. My physical *condition* is certainly bad and I hate *it*. But I *do*, as you keep saying, have a choice. I can lament about my condition or about *me*, myself. It, my condition, is certainly bad, but I *am* not it. I am a *person who* behaved very stupidly and badly. But I am not a *bad, rotten person!* I'm now really beginning to see the difference."

Ron kept working on his new philosophy in the hospital, got through the operation successfully, and returned to therapy to keep working on it. He never recovered his physical health completely but he lived fairly happily, went back to his work as an accountant, and remained physically limited. But not self-hating and depressed. His therapist, encouraged by Ron's dramatic change, now confidently uses REBT with other seriously afflicted clients. So do the authors of this book.

Notes to Chapter 2

1. Dryden & Ellis, 1989; Ellis, 1972d, 1988a, 1989, 1990a, 1990c; Warga, 1989.

2. Adler, 1927, 1929; Dubois, 1907; Ellis, 1989.

3. Ellis, 1957, 1958a, 1962, 1971, 1973b, 1985c, 1988a.

4. Ellis, 1962, 1988a, 1990a, 1990b, 1990d, 1991a, 1991f; Ellis & Dryden, 1987, 1990, 1991.

5. Ellis, 1962, 1976b, 1978, 1979a, 1979d, 1980a, 1987a, 1988a, 1991c, 1991h, 1992a; Ellis, Abrams & Dengelegi, 1992; Ellis & Dryden, 1987, 1990, 1991; Ellis & Grieger, 1977, 1986; Ellis & Harper, 1975; Ellis & Knaus, 1977; Ellis, McInerney, DiGiuseppe & Yeager, 1988; Ellis & Velten, 1992; Ellis & Whiteley, 1979; Hauck, 1974.

3

Some Inelegant Methods of Coping with Fatal Illness

"God's Will Be Done"

One of the inelegant methods you can use to cope better with AIDS, intractable cancer, or any other fatal disease, is to strongly hold the Belief, "God's will be done." If you just get yourself to firmly believe this widely held Belief, you can face almost any Adversity, including impending death.

"I see. You may be right about that. But why, if it sometimes works, is this philosophy inelegant?"

"For several reasons that we shall now discuss."

The most obvious problem in allaying death anxiety through belief in God is that you may not believe in God, or any other greater power. Suppose you do believe in a supreme being, it does not follow that you assume that your illness is a result of God's will. Many, including the deist founders of the United States, viewed God as the primal force behind the universe. But they concluded that, once created, the universe and all of its inhabitants were on their own.

A very natural response to the suffering involved in a life-threatening illness is anger at the unfairness of being among the minority of people who are so afflicted. This implies that God's will is either unfair or that God is uninterested in you or is too weak to save you from the evil forces that bring on your fatal ailment. How frightening it can be to put all of your faith in a God that is too weak to save you from serious Adversity. Or, if you believe that it is indeed God's will that makes you sick, you will tend to be very angry at God.

This dilemma exemplifies what we mean when we speak of inelegant solutions to fatal ailments. Trying to accept your illness because it is "God's will" may well create more, and sometimes circular, problems for you. For example, "I accept my illness, because it is God's will, but then I have to work at accepting God's will. If I cannot accept God's will as fair, then I cannot accept my illness." And so on.

Whenever you adopt or invent a philosophy that relies on God or some other supernatural force, you will probably always have serious doubts about it because you can never validate or falsify it. To do so, *you* would have to be supernatural and thereby observe and talk to your God to really prove that He or She exists. But you are, obviously, a nongodlike, limited *human*. Therefore, you will tend to have serious doubts about the truth of your God-involved philosophy, and can easily become disillusioned with it.

Thus, if you tell yourself, "I have AIDS or fatal cancer, but I can accept it and not unduly upset myself about it because God's will be done," you will then tend to be doubtful and skeptical and think, "But suppose there *is* no God?" or "Suppose God exists but is deliberately punishing me for my misdeeds?" Or you may think, "What if the Devil, this time, has won out over God and will see that I am damned and punished for eternity?" So your acceptance of your fatal affliction through your believing in God's will is a risky kind of acceptance and you would be better off if you replaced it with the kind of untheological acceptance described later in this chapter.

Instead of believing, "God's will be done," you can much more realistically believe, "Whatever shall be, obviously shall be. If my destiny (or my friend's destiny) is to die soon of a fatal disease, that's the way it indubitably is. So I'd better fully *accept it* even though I'll never *like it.* Tough! But that's the way it is!"

Kevin, an agnostic, was stricken with AIDS and at first was desperate and depressed until a religious friend convinced him to believe in God and he started to tell himself, "God's will be done." He felt much better at first, but as he saw that one of his friends after another was stricken with AIDS, and that almost everyone he knew in New York had several friends or relatives who also were dying or had died of AIDS, and when he realized that a good many other young people had fatal diseases which they had done nothing to bring on, he decided that if there was a God, He or She must be a sadist. So he went back to being an agnostic and changed his core philosophy to: "God, if there is one, only helps those who help themselves. So, although having AIDS is the worst thing that ever happened to me, I am determined to accept it, to live with it as long as I can, and to stop demanding that it not exist. What shall be, shall be. Too damned bad—but it's not awful!"

Devout Belief in Immortality

Another philosophy that many use to stave off their apprehension about dying is to simply contradict it by saying, "I am sure that this is not our only existence but that we humans, including myself, are immortal and that I will have a continuing existence and can therefore bear dying in this existence." This philosophy, if you truly convince yourself of it, may help you cope with impending death. But it has its great weaknesses!

The most compelling argument against this ideal is that there is no evidence that we humans are immortal and that our souls or spirits last forever. All existing evidence is against this theory, as not a single human, of all the billions that have existed since man and woman first evolved, has ever come back to earth after death, or otherwise proven his or her continuing existence. Many persons, such as Harry

Houdini, have prearranged signals to show their loved ones on earth that they are still alive after death; but not one of them has come through with these signals. In fact, no proponents of the paranormal have any verifiable successes, with the sad exception of their profiting from their exploitation of gullible people.[1]

As Sigmund Freud and many other psychologists have shown, people who devoutly believe in personal immortality are in effect deluding themselves because they abhor so much the thought of dying (especially prematurely and painfully) that they dream up an afterlife. However, creating an afterlife to offset the pain in this current life only leads to more problems. You can only guess what it actually may be like if it exists. Will you go to Heaven—or to Hell? Will you be rewarded for the good life you have lived—or eternally punished for your sins? Even if you are not roasted in Hell for an eternity, will you come back, in your afterlife as *yourself* or as an entirely different person? Who can say? How do you know?

If you believe that only your good deeds in this life will make you successful, enjoying, and fit for Heaven in your hereafter, then you will have to watch yourself closely in this life and make *sure* that you do not do "evil" things. But suppose, being a fallible human, you *do* act badly in this life. Then what? Or suppose you act very well, give up most earthly enjoyments—such as sex and eating gourmet foods—and there *is* no afterlife. *Then* what? How can you be sure about what to do in this one life that you *know* truly exists to *ensure* a "good" afterlife? You *can't* be sure.

You may believe that your body and your present *self* or *personhood* undoubtfully die but that your *soul, spirit,* or *essence* is immortal and continues to exist. Perhaps so. But, if you are really thinking about this, you may easily realized that your *soul* or *spirit* may well *not* exist—and, like the concept of God or a Higher Power—cannot be falsified or verified. Even if it does possibly exist, your existing forever as a disembodied soul or spirit may be a consoling thought, especially when you have a fatal illness, but—you'd better face it—how is this soul or spirit going to enjoy itself eating, drinking, copulating, or participating in art, music, or literature? Not very easily!

When you are able to accede to death only because you positively accept that you will be born again or will live forever in some other way you are being blindly optimistic or Pollyannaish. Yes, this form of denial can make you feel better in the short run. But it carries with it certain risks. Relying on personal immortality requires that you accept a monumental premise on very little evidence. Even the Judeo/Christian bible is equivocal on the nature and promise of personal immortality, and the holy books of the eastern religions often don't support it. Thus, using this approach is the same as saying: "My personal demise is horrible and terrible, but I can accept it if I won't really die!" But since you cannot be sure you won't really die, you are left with: "My personal death is horrible and terrible!" We suggest that you more realistically and logically believe, "I cannot know for sure what happens after my death, but I have reason to believe that it will not be the least bit disagreeable. Without my having any reason to dread it, viewing it as horrifying makes no sense at all!"

As we noted before in the case of dying individuals who believe in God and in the philosophy that God's will be done, if you believe in immortality, and there is no evidence that it does exist and much reason to believe that it does not, you will tend to be skeptical that immortality does exist, and will probably keep anxiously worrying about whether or not it really does. At times you will probably think, "My firm belief in immortality may well be false and I may just be kidding myself about it." You will then lose your temporary lack of anxiety about dying and may be more anxious than ever. Again, your questionable belief in immortality may prevent you from working on the belief that death really is final. You can *still* accept it and not unduly upset yourself about it. Several studies have demonstrated that death anxiety is not reduced by religious beliefs.[2] Some researchers have found that religiosity can even worsen fears about death.[3] Why? Probably because people prone to anxiety often seek through religion a certainty about an afterlife that religion refuses to guarantee. Religion at best holds out the possibility of some type of existence after death, but no one is promised heaven.

Thus, thinking in a Pollyannaish manner about death or other adversities usually makes you *more* neurotic than you otherwise would be. This is true of most phobic and defensive reactions. If, for example, you are phobic about trains or elevators, and you therefore avoid going in them, you will experience a drop in anxiety each time you stay away from them. But you are really telling yourself, every time you withdraw, "It *would* be terrible if I risked going on a train or elevator!" So your anxiety is *temporarily* alleviated, but is *raised* in the long run. Similarly, if you are Pollyannaishly sure you will be immortal, your anxiety about dying may temporarily decrease, but you may be underlyingly *less* accepting of death and *more* anxious about it. Shelley Taylor has shown that Pollyannaish people sometimes are less anxious than realistic people.[4] But she fails to emphasize the underlying, covered-up anxiety of Pollyannaish individuals and fails to highlight the other disadvantages—such as increased defensiveness—to which their super-optimism typically leads. Optimism, as Martin Seligman has shown, can aid human happiness and function. But anti-realistic super-optimism has its own drawbacks. Realism, which lies between pessimism and Pollyannaism, is usually the better way to go.

Mabel was sure, when she first was afflicted with lethal liver cancer, that she had nothing to worry about because her soul was immortal and would never die, no matter what happened to her mortal body. As death approached, however, she realized that her immortal soul would most probably have a hard time enjoying her greatest pleasures—dancing, sex, and music. It just seemed too ethereal for all that kind of sensuality. So she made herself anxious about the likelihood of being unsensual for the rest of her "life." Fortunately, her roommate at the hospital where she was staying had used REBT to cope with her own serious health problems, taught Mabel some of the rational-emotive philosophy she had learned, and got her to read *How to Stubbornly Refuse to Make Yourself Miserable About Anything—Yes, Anything!*[5] Mabel decided that, whether or not her immortal soul went marching on forever, she'd better make the best possible use of her remaining life and stop worrying about what pleasures she would and would not enjoy in a potential hereafter.

Denial, Pollyannaism, and "Everything Will Happen for the Best"

Probably the worst form of Pollyannaism is the view taken in a popular song of the 1920's, "Everything Will Happen for the Best," and also taken in a number of other popular songs. The problem with this philosophy is that, except by the wildest stretch of imagination, it is obviously false—especially for anyone who is stricken with AIDS, cancer of the liver, a deadly brain aneurism, or some other insidious fatal ailment.

Of course, you could tell yourself, "Yes, I have fatal lung cancer, but I could also have AIDS as well. So isn't it great that I only have this one disease!"

Or you could say to yourself, "Just because I am dying so young and miserably, I am sure that the powers that be will feel that I have already suffered enough and will make sure that my next existence is exceptionally fair and beautiful."

One of our clients, Lois, often tried to think in this ultra-Pollyannaish way, when her only son, a drug addict, was diagnosed as being HIV positive. She insisted that his affliction would help him considerably, because it would finally force him to get some discipline and stop using heroin. Actually, the opposite occurred. Her son was so convinced that he would die very soon of AIDS—which notion his physicians contradicted to no avail—that he increased his use of heroin and died of an overdose a few months after his HIV diagnosis. At first Lois convinced herself that everything did happen for the best in this case, because her son avoided a long painful siege of AIDS by dying before it overcame him. But finally with some REBT help she acknowledged that her son's life had been generally bad and that it would have been much better without drugs and serious infection. Instead of *pretending* that her son's Adversities were really good, she finally accepted them as quite bad, but refused to depress or enrage herself about his demise.

Other everything-will-happen-for-the-best addicts often do not come to the kind of acceptance that Lois achieved. Instead, they almost convince themselves of the essential goodness of all things, but they usually let in the truth after a while, remain unaccepting of this truth, become disillusioned, come to view bad events as *worse* than what they actually are, and trade in their Pollyannaism for feelings of disgust and horror.

Everything-will-happen-for-the-best philosophies have a grain of sense in them that REBT calls reframing. Whenever bad things happen to you—or you make them happen to yourself—instead of only looking at their gruesome aspects and awfulizing about them, you can realistically look for the advantages that also go with the disadvantages. Thus, even impending death can help you think of what you can do to accomplish something you would really like to do in the remaining time you have left. Some say that mortality itself is a good thing, because it gives meaning to our lives, even before death is impending. Knowing that we only have a limited time on this earth may propel us to set priorities in life and force us to aggressively pursue goals we value while we can still do so.

Marlon, one of our clients, at first moaned almost all the time when he discovered that he was HIV positive. After six sessions of REBT he decided that it wasn't *awful* and *horrible* for him to be so badly afflicted. At the age of twenty-six he was already successful in the field of advertising and would have presumably had a long successful career ahead of him if he wasn't so badly afflicted, but with REBT as a new outlook, he saw his disease as very inconvenient and restricting but not a horror that *absolutely should not* exist. With this new attitude, he decided that advertising was all right but that what he really wanted to do in life was to write a play and get it produced. So he spent most of the next three years doing exactly that: writing a play about the evils of racial prejudice. He actually did get it produced; and even when he was finally stricken with AIDS, he was happy that his fatal disease at least had helped drive him to do what he most wanted to do before he died: Fight against prejudice in the way that he was most suited to do.

Reframing, which we shall discuss again under REBT techniques later in this book, also provides individuals headed toward death with a challenge—and quite a challenge!—to make themselves as happy as they can be in spite of their condition and to paradoxically enjoy the rest of life more successfully than they otherwise would if they were not so sorely stricken.

In contrast to those, like Elisabeth Kübler-Ross, who suggest that people facing death move through many emotional stages, we have observed that it is common for them to maintain a single emotional stage. Kübler-Ross, the best known of the stage advocates, proposed that dying people pass through five emotional stages during the course of their illness: denial, anger, bargaining, depression, and acceptance. According to this model people facing death first deny the very existence of their illness—to themselves and those close to them. When they can no longer deny its existence, they rage at its unfairness. The rage, having failed to change anything, then gives way to desperate bargaining with God, physicians, or other symbols of power. When the bargaining results in no saving deals, depression ensues. The stage that supplants the depression is acceptance. In this last stage dying people emotionally accept their coming demise with a benign placidity.

Kübler-Ross devised a convenient, but inaccurate, representation of the dying process. Dying is rarely as routine and symmetrical as she proposes. More often, as noted above, people tend to stay in one stage, which is based on their style of living before they were ill. For example, some people may stay self-pitying and hostile throughout the entire course of their illness. They believe that, "The world should understand what I am going through, so I don't owe anybody any courtesies."

Others may deny their illness throughout the entire process. Not only is there no compelling evidence that it is healthier to progress through the stages Dr. Kübler-Ross described, but there is evidence to the contrary.[6] People who refuse to accept the reality of their illness, and insist that they are not as sick as others say, tend to live longer than those who begin to "put their affairs in order."

In fact, there is a wealth of medical and psychological studies indicating that denial may aid survival. Cardiovascular surgeons have shown that people undergoing heart surgery do better when they deny the seriousness of their situation.[7] Similar results have been found in women suffering from breast cancer. The women who were in denial lived longer than women who examined and analyzed their illness. Women with primary operable breast cancer were evaluated for six to eight years after their surgery for cancer. The researchers found that those women who used denial as an emotional defense strategy were more likely to survive.[8]

Others have shown that denial serves to stabilize the ill person's relationships that could otherwise be threatened by knowledge of terminal illness. These authors suggest that the open acceptance of death does not serve to resolve anything; instead the acceptance of imminent death may serve to forestall social withdrawal by the patient and his or her social circle, as well as encouraging favorable attitudes to medical treatment. But it also has its disadvantages.[9]

We previously questioned the use of unrealistic and Pollyannaish attitudes to facing mortality. For denial carries with it certain risks, including those involving the changes and new forms that an illness can take. Each new adversity brought on by a fatal illness will tend to break through your or your loved one's denials, sometimes with grievous emotional consequences. However, denial can be useful under certain circumstances. If you tend to use it, also seek appropriate health care and knowledge about your illness. If you are taking advantage of all available treatments, and have made all appropriate preparations, some degree of optimism about your not dying may help you to keep fighting against your illness, perhaps prolong your life, and make yourself as happy as you can be under exceptionally difficult conditions. You thereby give greater value to your remaining days.

To be alive means that mortality and morbidity are our constant companions. But we do not have to obsess about them. If you are not ill, your best plans will include good nutrition, exercise, and avoiding deadly toxins. If you are seriously afflicted, persist at every good treatment—and then focus on the joys of still being alive.

Using Distraction Methods

You can use many kinds of distraction techniques to take your mind off the pain and anguish when you or your loved ones are afflicted with a fatal disease. REBT frequently recommends cognitive distraction methods, such as Yoga, meditation, Jacobson's progressive relaxation method, autogenic training, biofeedback, stomach breathing, and other diversions and distractions. All of these methods at least partly work because they divert your mind from your dysfunctional, awfulizing Beliefs and sometimes give you a chance to create new rational ones.[10]

Thus, if you are distinctly worrying about your or a loved one's impending death or are making yourself quite depressed about it, you can force yourself to think steadily of other things or to actively engage in some project that requires your steady attention, and in so doing you will become so occupied that—at least temporarily—you will not be able to think too much about death, nor awfulize about it. This is because your mind normally is only able to focus on one major thought at a time; so that if you really concentrate on relaxing your muscles, breathing slowly, doing Yoga exercises, meditating, or focusing on various other kinds of diversions, you simply have less energy and ability to focus on almost any kind of "horrors."

This is particularly true, as pointed out in *A New Guide to Rational Living,* if you acquire a vital absorbing interest on a long-range basis.[11] Suppose, for example, in spite of your having a fatal disease, you are determined to finish a novel you are writing, or are devoted to the cause of helping AIDS victims, or are absorbed in some other long-range project that allows you very little time for leisure. You may be so preoccupied with implementing this major goal that you hardly have time to worry about anything else, including your own or a close friend's fatal illness.

So by all means, if you can arrange this, get yourself a vital, absorbing, long-range interest even if you are not suffering from any disease. This kind of involvement will add to your steady enjoyment, give you something good to live for, and enhance whatever kind of life you have. It is usually the best antidote for obsessive rumination about almost anything, including fatal illness.

Will cognitive distraction by itself work to stop your anxiety or depression over impending death? Probably not. For nothing else in life is more important than life itself. So vitally absorbing yourself in big projects will usually help you cope better with approaching death, but will not drive it out of your mind completely. Dire thoughts about it will tend to return. So you had better learn to distract yourself, at times, from thoughts of dying—and also use some of the other coping philosophies that we shall describe in this book.

Particularly if you use the regular short-term cognitive

distraction and relaxation methods, you had better realize that they give temporary, palliative relief, that you have to keep repeating them many times (sometimes several times each day), and that they blank out your self-defeating Beliefs for a while but they do not often *change* them. If you strongly Believe that it's unfair that you are dying so young and that unfairness like this *absolutely should not* exist, meditation, Yoga, or biofeedback will shunt aside that Belief for a while but it will largely cover it up rather than remove it. Just below your level of consciousness, and still deeply engraved in your basic philosophy, your stout-hearted *refusal* to accept grim reality remains—and you'd better keep clearly seeing it (bringing it to consciousness) and vigorously Disputing it, until you really *dis*believe it. Otherwise, it will keep rearing its ugly head to smite you and depress you.

A great advantage of your using cognitive distraction effectively is knowing that you *do* have some control over your musturbatory and awfulizing thoughts. Once you see that you don't *have to* succumb to them, you will have more confidence about not only using distraction methods but also about using some of the more elegant methods of REBT that we describe in this book.

Maurice had prostate cancer and was told he only had a few months to live, so he kept using breathing exercises and Edmund Jacobson's progressive muscular relaxation techniques to distract himself from the panic he felt whenever he realized he was going to die soon. These methods worked, but only for an hour or so at a time. Learning REBT by telephone therapy sessions—because he was in no physical condition to come to our clinic—he still used these relaxation methods whenever he panicked. After relaxing, he then used the strong conviction that having a limited time to live was most unfortunate but was not *awful* and that he *could* stand it. He then was able to cut down his relaxing sessions from more than five times a day to a few times a week.

Relaxing techniques and other kinds of cognitive distraction, then, are quite useful and may be used at times by almost anyone who is upset about a fatal disease or any other serious life problem. You can use them if you are stricken with a serious ailment or if one of your close friends or relatives is afflicted. But try to employ them in addition to, and as an opportunity for, making what REBT calls a profound philosophical change. We shall go into this again.

Notes to Chapter 3

1. Ellis & Yeager, 1989.
2. Hoelter, 1979; Levy, Dupras, & Samson, 1985; Richman, 1980.
3. Bolt, 1977; Templer, Camppelletty, & Kaufman, 1990.
4. Taylor, 1990.
5. Ellis, 1988a.
6. Kim, Yoo & Park, 1989.
7. Janne, Reynaert, & Cassiers, 1990.
8. Dean & Surtees, 1989.
9. Beilin, 1981.
10. Benson, 1975; Ellis, 1983, 1984, 1988a; Goleman, 1993; Jacobsen, 1938; Lazarus, 1990.
11. Ellis & Harper, 1975.

4

What About Other Psychotherapies?

Psychoanalytic Therapies

Psychoanalytic and psychodynamic therapies try to give you insight into the origins of your emotional disturbances; to help you see how you are now continuing the dysfunctional feelings and actions that you presumably started to experience during your early life; to reveal your repressed, deeply unconscious thoughts and feelings; and to help you relate trustingly to your analyst so that he or she can enable you to have a corrective experience that will lead to a better present and future life.[1] Although you may possibly be helped by psychoanalysis it has its distinct disadvantages, especially if you are suffering from a fatal disease. Here are some reasons why psychoanalytic therapy may offer you an inelegant solution to your problems, and may even sidetrack you from working out the kind of more elegant solutions we recommend in this book.

Traditional psychoanalysis, and even shorter-term analytic procedures, normally takes a great deal of time—frequently from two to five years of weekly (or more than weekly) sessions. If you or one of your close relatives or friends is suffering from a terminal ailment, this kind of long-winded and overly complicated therapy is not likely to be very useful. Although it may give you interesting and important insights, there is no compelling evidence that they change you. Thus, if you discover that you now hate yourself because your mother and father demanded that you be perfect and severely put you down when you were not, this insight will hardly help you unless you also see that you, unfortunately *accepted* your parents' view of you, that you *still* agree with it, and that now you have to *change* your self-downing philosophy to one of self-acceptance. So *seeing* what presumably went wrong with you years ago will not eliminate the cognitive, emotive, and behavioral *work* you have to do today if you are to change yourself.

If REBT is correct—and we have much research evidence to show that it probably is—you originally became disturbed not because you had overly critical or demanding parents or teachers, but because you *chose* to react to them in a self-sabotaging manner.[2] It was not the Activating Events (A's) of your early life that upset you but mainly your own Beliefs (B's) *about* these A's. Thus, it was not your parents' telling you that you were imperfect and therefore worthless, it was your *agreeing* with them—"Yes, they're right, I *should* be perfect!"—that made you self-hating. And it wasn't your teachers giving you a hard time at school that made you overrebellious. It was your telling yourself, "They must not treat me this way! I'll fix them by deliberately not doing the horrible work they're giving me!" It was your philosophy (B), and not your teachers giving too much work to do (A), that largely led to your low frustration tolerance.

So psychoanalysis, under the guise of giving you insight into your past and its "causation" of your present disturbances, often gives you a cop-out and helps you falsely believe that unfortunate Activating Events (A's) originally produced your bad emotional Consequences (C's) instead of the greater truth—that *you* largely upset yourself as a child, and that you're *still* actively continuing this upsetness by *maintaining* your old dysfunctional Beliefs (B's).[3]

Thus, if instead of psychoanalytic insight into the "origin" of your disturbance, you merely tell an REBT practitioner that you hate yourself today, he or she can quickly help you see what you are telling yourself *right now* to create that hatred and can help you change your negative attitude toward yourself no matter *how* you originally acquired it.

Again, if your problem is your low frustration tolerance (LFT) about, let us say, carrying out the medical procedures that will help you with your ailments, a psychoanalyst would probably show you that your LFT harks back to your rebelling against your parents or against your early teachers who you thought made you work too hard. So you are now, says your analyst, rebelling against your physicians, who also make you do things you don't want to do and "work too hard." Perhaps so. But psychoanalysis doesn't quite explain why you originally became a rebel instead of a collaborator, or why you *continue* to hold a self-defeating "screw them!" philosophy today. It, again, doesn't help you to *change* this self-sabotaging philosophy and acquire one of high frustration tolerance.

REBT, as we shall show in detail later, encourages you and pushes you to keep working at changing your dysfunctional thoughts, feelings, and reactions. Psychoanalysis, on the contrary, provides you with so much irrelevant—and frequently misleading—insight about the past and its supposed contribution to your present disturbances that it often sidetracks you from making a real effort to work steadily to change your present disordered thinking, feeling, and behaving. Consequently, although it may help you review some interesting aspects of your life, it distracts you from what you'd better do *right now* to help yourself and to make the profound kind of philosophical-activity change that REBT and some of the other cognitive-behavior therapies help you achieve.

Finally, REBT and the related cognitive-behavior therapies encourage you to learn to use their methods on your own. There are no effective psychoanalytic self-help methods. Instead, psychoanalysis encourages dependency on the therapist to find your repressed and hidden "sources" of your problems. This arduous and prolonged therapy is almost always most inappropriate for someone facing a fatal illness.

Experiential Therapy

Many experiential and expressive therapies heavily emphasize—and commonly overemphasize—their clients' feelings and use techniques such as catharsis, abreaction, and rebirthing, to get people unusually in touch with their past and present feelings. Thus, Gestalt, primal, inner child, dianetics, co-counseling, past-life, and various other kinds of therapy use the Freudian hydraulic theory of emotion. This theory states that humans who bottle up and fail to fully express their feelings—such as anger and panic—rip up their bodies and their personalities and become very disturbed. Therefore, the solution to their problems is to explore and express their feelings, to let everything hang out, and thereby get release from their underlying pain and suffering.[4]

This theory has a little truth to it; because if you have strong underlying feelings—such as panic about socializing or rage against one of your so-called friends—and you do not *acknowledge* these feelings, it is unlikely that you would ever eliminate them. So you'd better acknowledge or be in touch with your self-defeating feelings, so that you can see what you are doing to create them and thereby find ways to reduce them.

The theory that violently expressing your unexpressed destructive feelings will help you to reduce or remove them is fallacious in several ways. If you fully keep expressing your hatred for a man, for example, and either openly fight that person or hit a pillow that represents his head, you may indeed feel very good about this expression of feeling—for you are probably telling yourself what a louse this individual is and what a noble person you are. But you are also, very often, repeating to yourself, "This man absolutely *should not* be the way he is! He *deserves* to be damned and punished for being that way! What a thorough louse he is!" How will this philosophy help you become *less* enraged? It won't. How will it help you become *more* enraged? Very easily!

Research has shown, moreover, that whether you express your rage at people and things *or* whether you feel it and hold it in, in *both* cases your feeling itself may lead to harmful pressure, increased heart attacks, and other physical problems.[5] Expressed rage, moreover, usually helps the people you are enraged at to return your "compliment," enrage themselves against you and your loved ones, and often cause feuds, wars, terrorism, and genocide. Not very good results! Forgiveness, on the other hand, tends to beget return forgiveness—and much better interpersonal and social relationships.

Similarly with self-pity. To acknowledge your own whining and self-pity is good—for you may then cope with it and change it to self-helping feelings of sorrow and disappointment about an unfortunate predicament you are in without *demanding* that you not be in this predicament. You can thereby work better at improving your bad situation.

If you keep expressing your self-pity loudly and wailingly—"Poor me! Woe is me! How can the world be so cruel to me, me, me!"—you will very likely *increase* your pain, do nothing to remove it, and focus only on your own miserable navel. How will that loudly and "honestly" expressed self-pity help you?

Most of the let's-get-it-all out "feeling" therapies have their distinct disadvantages, especially for people who want to face, accept, and overcome the real pains and disabilities that often accompany fatal diseases. Let's look at some of the main hazards of using these therapies.

They are frequently harrowing, as they lead you to dramatically relive and reexperience some of the most gruesome and grueling events of your life, along with the anguished feelings that originally accompanied these traumas. You certainly don't *need* this kind of drama if you or one of your friends is suffering from a fatal illness.

As noted above, using highly expressive techniques of therapy can easily help you to experience more, rather than fewer, destructive feelings of rage, self-pity, panic, and depression. Most of these therapies see emotions working like some kind of hydraulic system. They are said to get "pent up," "Bottled up," etc. The advocates of these therapies suggest that the way to get relief is to open the valves and let your harmful feelings out. Current research says otherwise. It shows that your emotions are created when you are exposed to some stimuli that provoke thought, and that to change harmful feelings you'd better modify your thoughts.[6]

Some let-your-feelings-hang-all-out therapists may convince you of early "traumas" or recent "disasters" that really did not exist or that were much less traumatic than you and your therapist make them out to be. Thus, in dwelling on the "horrors" of your life, you may make yourself falsely "sure" that you were a victim, during your early years, of incest, child abuse, and severe criticism by your parents and peers that did not actually occur or that was really much less severe than your present wild imagination makes it out to have "really" been.

Once again, then, any system of psychotherapy that helps you get in touch with your disturbed feelings and that encourages you to fully acknowledge them has its good points. Because unless you clearly see and admit these feelings and unless you realize what harm they often wreak, you are not likely to do much to change them. Enough, however, is enough! Tuning into your negative feelings is one thing, and obsessively-compulsively tuning them up, up, up, is quite another. Working to change them, as we try to do in REBT, to appropriate feelings—such as sorrow, regret, and disappointment about the unfortunate events of your life—is a much better way to go. We shall later show you some methods of achieving that kind of feeling.

Unconventional Therapies

There are hosts of new treatments to help people with terminal illnesses. These range from exploitive to excellent. For example, the self-help philosophy of Louise Hay gives comfort to some people, but has also helped to dishearten many others. She suggests that you can find emotional, and even physical relief, from fatal illness through stressing self-love. She also goes even further by suggesting that illnesses are actually caused by internalized hostility—the old Freudian theme of "anger turned inward against you."[7] This irrefutable and tautological idea may get you into trouble, because if you get better or feel better it is presumed the Louise Hays doctrine worked. If on the other hand, you get sicker, it is said to be because you are perversely insisting on hating yourself. Blame the victim! The dying person is dying because of his or her own anger. Since there is no evidence that self-hatred, anger, or personality problems actually cause cancer, AIDS, or other fatal illnesses, you had better not unrealistically believe that eliminating hostility will cure your or your loved ones' serious ailments.

Another unconventional therapy tells you to use imagery to come to terms with your past, or even to attack a disease like cancer cell by cell in your mind's eye. Advocates of this procedure believe that when you are ill you can direct your immune system to attack disease agents by imagining "good" cells annihilating your "bad" ones. Unfortunately there is no evidence that this is effective. This approach is a result of inverted logic. They assume that if destructive thoughts and feelings can impair your immune system—a theory that has some real evidence behind it—it follows that positive images can cure you. Would that this were really so!

Other "therapies" include magical versions of psychoanalysis. Thus, one advocate of music therapy for the dying contends that the expression of music will reveal unconscious conflicts more effectively than psychotherapy can.[8]

Another therapist suggests that the need for terminally ill clients and their families to express their feelings can be fulfilled through "art therapy."[9] In this approach, death symbols are created to reach a "level of reality" that cannot be achieved in any other way. One art therapist "finds" that his patients spontaneously recreate the universal symbols of death and rebirth, including Jung's archetypal symbol of the mandala and its variations of spirals, coiled snakes, and soul windows, and that they thereby achieve emotional and physical cures.

Most of the preceding therapies are variations of the psychoanalytic techniques we previously discussed. All tend to be dehumanizing because they suggest that dying people's feeling are not to be taken seriously—because they cannot *really* know what is bothering them. Only therapists, with their "deep" symbols and interpretations, can truly know.

Obviously people whose shortened life span necessitates genuine and immediate interaction had better not accept this "deep" psychodynamic therapy. People facing death require help in accepting their present situation. They'd better have encouragement to continue growing and perhaps even profit from this most difficult time in their lives. Each of them is going through a profoundly unique and personal experience. To reject their overt statements and interpretations of their experiences as mere symbols is to deny crucial aspects of these experiences.

Selecting a Form of Therapy

Therapies that teach unconditional acceptance of yourself and of others can help your state of mind, and also, frequently, your bodily health. If you reduce your unnecessary anxiety, rage, and depression, you will minimize emotional stress. There is, indeed, considerable evidence that severe distress can exacerbate and in some cases create disease. So reducing needless stress serves to promote health.

REBT and client-centered therapy are among the best

known of the humanistic therapies that stress unconditional acceptance of yourself and others. They show that all humans, including you, have failings, make mistakes—sometimes grave and hurtful ones—and often commit destructive acts. However, these defects and harmful actions never make *you* bad. Conversely, performing good acts and succeeding at important tasks do not make you a *good person.* Although responsible for your actions, you are not *defined* by them. If this were so, how would we define people who lead a life of crime, then give it up to become selfless charity workers? Are they "bad people" who became good? Are they "good people" who acted badly? How can we ever define or measure the total person when he or she, within one lifetime, does tens of thousands of good and bad deeds?

We propose, instead, that people never *are* good or bad. It is far better to say that they do good and bad things, sometimes they mainly choose to act badly—and at other times to *behave* well. Let us only rate their *actions*, but not their *being*, their *essence*, or their *personhood.*

You can apply these principles to yourself by avoiding classifying your worth as a human being. Avoid condemning yourself (your totality) for errors and mistakes. And abstain from damning other people (their personhood) for their failings. You can prove the usefulness of this kind of unconditional acceptance by looking at your own experience. Have you ever been helped by *damning* yourself? If you failed at a task and called yourself a *failure*, did it help you do better? Or did it blast your self-confidence and help you do worse? When you condemned others for doing hurtful, immoral, or bad things, who felt ripped up with rage, you or them? And if you expressed your rage, did the offenders respond with contrition and better behavior or did they mainly get angry back? With a little thought you can conclude that you will accomplish little by denouncing yourself or others. Criticize, if you will, some of your and their *performances*. But not your or their *self.*

In general, when considering any type of therapy, self-help or professional, try to hold to the same standard you would when seeking medical care. Answering the following questions would create a good basis for judging the merits of any therapy or procedure you may consider: Is it based on research or scientific evidence? Are its practitioners educated in the field they are professing? Can they cite some sources or basis for their theories and practices? If licenses are available for this treatment, do the practitioners hold them? Is any data kept on its effectiveness or outcome?

At a minimum, you preferably should assess mental health treatment with the same standards that you would evaluate medical care. You would probably not see a medical professional who does not hold a license or certification in his or her field. Nor would you accept a new drug or medical procedure if it has not been scientifically tested and validated. Why then would you not fully investigate psychotherapeutic care?

Notes to Chapter 4

1. Freud, 1965.
2. Beck, 1991; Ellis, 1979d; Engels & Diekstra, 1986; Lyons & Woods, 1991; McGovern & Silverman, 1984; Hollon & Beck, 1993; Meichenbaum, 1977.
3. Ellis, 1957, 1962, 1968, 1985c; Ellis & Dryden, 1987, 1990, 1991.
4. Freud, 1965; Perls, 1969.
5. Katz & Epstein, 1991; Lazarus, 1982; Royce, 1984.
6. DiGiuseppe, 1990.
7. Le Baron, 1989.
8. Forinash & Gonzalez, 1989.
9. Tate, 1989.

5

The Rational Emotive Behavioral Approach to Refusing to Disturb Yourself

Assuming that the various kinds of philosophies and therapies that we have been discussing have their good points and may help you if you are afflicted or if one of your close relatives or friends is stricken with a fatal ailment, what are some of the more effective and more elegant methods that you can use if this unfortunate Activating Event or Adversity occurs in your life? Naturally, we are going to favor REBT methods in this book. Because REBT is the pioneering cognitive-behavior therapy that I (AE) created in January, 1955, a decade before the methods of William Glasser, Aaron Beck, Maxie Maultsby, Donald Michenbaum, and other "cognitive" therapies were introduced. It also preceded George Kelly's personal construct therapy, which is in theory highly cognitive but employs no direct disputing methods in its practice. And it has pioneered the first popular therapy to emphasize cognitive *and* behavioral methods, while previous therapists, like Paul Dubois and Alfred Adler used a good deal of cognition but included no real behavior therapy.[1]

More importantly, REBT is one of the exceptionally few therapies that espouse what I have called the "elegant solution" to emotional problems and that shows people how to stubbornly refuse to upset themselves about anything

41

(yes, anything) even if the worst possible things happen to them. Thus, following my early versions of REBT, the other cognitive therapies show people that they exaggerate unfortunate events and therefore unrealistically "catastrophize," a term I invented in the 1950's. But REBT uniquely shows people that even when a real catastrophe occurs—when, say, an earthquake kills hundreds of people in your town, including several of your close relatives and friends—you can still make yourself feel exceptionally sad and grieving (which are appropriate, healthy negative emotions) rather than very angry and depressed (which are inappropriate, destructive emotions).[2]

How can you do this? By adopting an anti-awfulizing, anti-horribilizing REBT philosophy—as we shall show in the rest of this book. For REBT fully accepts the realistic view that many things that happen in your life are bad—meaning, against your interest and against the interest of the social group in which you choose to live. And some things are *very* bad—such as wars, terrorism, genocide, rape, child abuse, and AIDS.

Are you not, then, perfectly sane and truly in your right mind when you seriously depress, panic, and enrage yourself about these *very* bad, and sometimes frightfully inhumane, happenings? No, says REBT, you are not perfectly sane and rational when you incense yourself about or drive yourself to a near suicidal state about even such great evils.

Why not? For several good reasons.

First, let's consider your losing several dear friends or relatives and, as a result of this grievous loss, driving yourself to the depths of despair, even to the brink of suicide. Will your severe state of depression really make up for your loss? Will it bring back your loved ones? Will it help you console your other relatives and friends? Will it encourage you to build new relationships?

Sadly, no. On the contrary. Your depressed state will tend to immobilize you, take away your energy, disrupt your life, make you phobic about future relationships, and even help you to depress yourself about your depression. Perhaps your depression will help you temporarily withdraw from activity, harbor your forces, and set you up for a better future life. But most probably it won't—and will do you much more harm than good.

Or suppose that you suffer from a particularly traumatic event, such as being raped or nearly dying of a serious illness, and your suffering is so great that you panic, have nightmares, and obsess about this kind of trauma possibly happening again. Will your state of panic help you cope with the original trauma, ward off future ones, or learn good lessons and coping strategies? Most unlikely!

Finally, suppose that you witness wars, terrorism, rape, injustices, or other instances of inhumanity and you enrage yourself, become violently incensed about these evils. How will your intense feelings of rage help you to undo these atrocities, to help the victims, to prevent future crimes, and to make the world a less heinous place in which to live? They probably won't help; and, instead, your intense rage will most likely rip up your own gut, create grim psychosomatic reactions, interfere with your sane thinking and planning, and encourage you to perpetrate some violent and warlike, and perhaps unfair, incidents of your own.

Severe feelings of depression, panic, and rage, when provoked by traumatic and unjust events, may *sometimes* lead you (and other people) to good results. Rarely! However, what REBT calls appropriate or self-helping negative feelings—such as those of sorrow, regret, frustration, and annoyance—may serve you and the human race very well. For they motivate you—yes, *e*motions put you *in motion*—to deal with unfortunate and disastrous events, to cope with them, to try to improve them, and to plan for the future so that they may be prevented from occurring again. Thus, when a serious earthquake, hurricane, or volcano strikes, millions of us feel very sad and regretful and therefore galvanize ourselves and others to take part in relief work. So our deep feelings, including negative ones, are often healthy, constructive and happiness-enhancing. REBT, though it is highly cognative and philosophic, does not oppose or put down feelings as do some stoic philosophies. It highly endorses them—at least *some* of them!

That's the point. *Some* of our strong negative feelings are appropriate and self-helping, and some are not. If you think you may acquire AIDS or another fatal illness, by all means let yourself feel great caution, vigilance, and prudence; and if you or one of your intimates suffers from such an illness, by all means let yourself feel great concern, mindfulness, and watchfulness. But panic, terror, and horror, how will those feelings help? REBT clearly separates the first, appropriate set of these negative feelings from inappropriate, destructive ones like depression, horror, and rage.

Similarly, it puts intense sadness, sorrow, and grief—which may suitably stem from your or a friend's fatal ailment—into a different category from severe depression, despair, abject misery, and despondency. The former are distinctly negative feelings but they help you to deal with an alarming deadly situation—and perhaps correct and improve it. But the latter feelings are not only intensely negative but also are sabotaging and destructive. Quite a difference![3]

Tabitha at first made herself so depressed about her friend Joe's coming down with AIDS that she tried hard to suppress her feelings and made herself feel practically nothing when she was with Joe and when she thought about him and his sad state. But then she found herself neglecting to see him, not figuring out ways to help him, and acting indifferently to him when she did see him. Joe's other friends called her odd behavior to her attention and she acknowledged that she was hardly behaving in a friendly or helpful manner. She looked at her own behavior and was able to see that it warded off her feelings of intense pain but that her numbness also stopped her from helping Joe. One of Tabitha's friends, who knew REBT and often used it in his own life, showed her how to distinguish between making herself self-defeatingly depressed and horrified about Joe's condition and letting herself feel appropriate sorrow and regret. So she kept telling herself, many times and strongly, "It's really *very sad* that Joe is suffering the way that he is, but it's not *awful* and *horrible*, and I can bear to look at his suffering and sympathize with him without unduly upsetting myself about his condition." When she convinced herself of this kind of philosophy, her feeling for Joe and his painful situation returned, and she was able to think about ways of helping him and to carry out some of these plans when she visited him.

Is the REBT approach to negative feelings too controlling and therefore dangerous? That depends on how you use it. If you falsely believe that practically all negative feelings are useless and harmful, you may decide to use—or rather distort the use of—REBT so that you make yourself have practically none of them. Or if you think—wrongly, we would say—that all feelings, including very negative ones, are great and that you are a passionate, healthy person if you keep having more and more of them, you may use some of the principles of REBT to tell yourself the "right" things and indulge continually in a high state of negative emotions. You can—but we would hardly ever advise either of these procedures. If you give some thought to differentiating between your healthy and you unhealthy negative feelings—as mentioned above—you may sensibly select the kind of feelings that you think are most suitable when a fatal disease afflicts you or one of your close associates, and you can work at bringing on helpful rather than destructive feelings.

Not that you will ever make perfect choices. Sometimes you will want to feel sad and sorrowful, and you will actually feel panicked and dejected. So you won't perfectly feel the way you would prefer to feel. Not while you're human! But, as we shall continue to show in this book, knowing and working at REBT will give you a great deal of control over your negative, as well as your positive, feelings; and if you use that control wisely, especially about your or someone else's having a fatal disease, you may do yourself and your friends and relatives a lot of good.

So REBT says again: You do have choices. You can unthinkingly let yourself run away with unhealthy negative feelings (such as grandiosity). Or you can largely, though not entirely, create healthy negative and positive emotions. For REBT, along with Epictetus, Shakespeare, Bertrand Russell, and a host of other writers, says that you mainly, not entirely, feel the way you think.

Whether you are aware of it or not, you largely construct Beliefs (B's) about the unfortunate events (A's) that happen to you and you thereby tend to create feelings and actions (C's or Consequences) that quickly follow these B's. You often don't consciously and deliberately create your B's, because you tend to construct them automatically, habitually, and tacitly as soon as some unfortunate A occurs. So you don't willfully make yourself miserable as soon as you perceive one of these A's and view it as "bad" or "obnoxious."

No matter. If you acknowledge, as REBT teaches you to acknowledge, that your disturbed feelings and behaviors are largely self-created, and that they do not merely strike or overwhelm you as unpleasant A's occur, you can then practically always look for and figure out your A's, B's, and C's; and by significantly changing your B's, which is definitely in your power, you can change your self-defeating feelings and actions, minimize your disturbances, and lead a much happier and more productive life. How can you specifically do this? Keep reading!

Notes to Chapter 5

1. Adler, 1927, 1929; Beck, 1976, 1991; Dubois, 1907; Glasser, 1965; Kelly, 1955.
2. Ellis, 1962, 1965, 1971, 1973a, 1973b, 1988a; Ellis & Dryden, 1987, 1990, 1991.
3. Bernard, 1991, 1992; Bernard & Wolfe, 1993; Dryden & Hill, 1993; Ellis, 1962, 1965, 1988a, 1990a; Ellis & Abrahms, 1978; Ellis & Becker, 1982; Ellis & Harper, 1975; Walen, DiGiuseppe & Dryden, 1992; Yankura & Dryden, 1990.

6

Finding and Disputing Your Self-Defeating Irrational Beliefs

Rational Emotive Behavior Therapy (REBT) is a comprehensive form of psychotherapy that uses a large number of thinking (cognitive), feeling (emotive), and activity (behavioral) methods to alleviate emotional disturbances about unfortunate happenings that occur in human lives. Including impending death? Yes, including even that fatal occurrence.

The main theory of REBT, as mentioned earlier, is that people do not merely *get* disturbed. Rather, they largely, whether or not they realize it, *make themselves* needlessly neurotic. They do so by taking their healthy wishes (preferences) for approval, success, comfort, and physical fitness—all of which tend to encourage feelings of happiness and which they therefore legitimately and sanely pursue—and they add to these normal desires unrealistic and grandiose musts, shoulds, oughts, and demands.

Thus, if you have AIDS or some other fatal disease you often start very sensibly with, "I really hate being afflicted with this condition and feel that it is the worst thing that ever happened to me. How sad and obnoxious it is! I strongly wish that it would disappear and that I would somehow get better! I shall do everything in my power to fight it and keep it from getting worse. But if there's nothing I can do to stop this affliction, I'll still try to prolong my life and to enjoy whatever I can enjoy while I am still alive."

When you have a fatal ailment and think this way, you are clearly not feeling cheerful or happy. Why should you be under such poor conditions? But you do tend to feel appropriately sad, disappointed, regretful, frustrated, and annoyed.

Why are these negative, and sometimes quite strong, negative feelings appropriate and helpful? Because they motivate you to take your condition seriously, and to try to do whatever you can to treat it, to cope with the poor results it brings you and your loved ones, and to be as happy as you can be considering the limitations that it places on you. If you had no negative feelings about your affliction, you would hardly cope with it as well as you possibly could. Appropriate feelings *motivate* you to change unfortunate things that you can change and to accept those that you cannot change. So by all means let yourself *feel* very sad and frustrated if you are, or one of your associates is, fatally ill.

But watch it if you make yourself feel depressed or panicked. *Make* yourself feel? Yes, by adding to your healthy desires and wishes for good health these kinds of self-sabotaging demands and commands: "Because my disease is *so* bad, because it is imposing *such* handicapping and penalties, and because it is *thoroughly* unfair, it *absolutely should not, must not* exist! It's *completely awful* that it does! I *can't stand* it! My *entire existence* is worthless and the *whole world* is rotten and cannot provide me with any satisfaction *at all!*"

These highly destructive philosophies—which REBT calls unhealthy irrational Beliefs (iB's)—tend to create disturbed, neurotic feelings, especially those of panic, depression, and self-pity. And, as we noted before, people who have them frequently create secondary disturbances—that is, disturbances *about* disturbances—by inventing more demands. Such as, "I *must not* be panicked and depressed! These feelings are *terrible* and I *can't bear* them! What a weakling I am for experiencing them!"

The main point of REBT is: If you or your loved ones are fatally afflicted, even with a vile disease like AIDS, you'd better constructively feel very sorry and frustrated, but you do not *have* to bring on dysfunctional feelings of panic, depression, rage, and self-hatred. You can, using REBT, ward them off and get yourself to experience strong, but still appropriate, feelings of displeasure. And if you do slip into musturbatory thinking and do create dysfunctional feelings and behaviors, REBT can also show you what to think, feel, and do to reduce or eliminate them.

That is what we shall devote this chapter to: Presenting the common destructive irrational Beliefs (iB's) that people with fatal diseases create, and showing, if you suffer from such a disease or have a close friend or relative who does, how you can actively and persistently Dispute and minimize these iB's.

Disputing Your Absolutist Musts and Shoulds

If you are panicked, depressed, enraged, self-hating, or self-pitying about having (or someone else's having) a fatal disease, look for the absolutist rigid *shoulds* and *musts* with which you are largely creating your disturbed feeling. You may, right now, be unconscious or unaware of them. But if you keep asking yourself, "What are my musts, my demands on myself, on others, and on life conditions with which I am *making* myself—yes, *making myself*—disturbed?" you will quickly be able to find them. For example: "What are my *shoulds* and *musts* on myself now that I am depressed and guilty about having acquired AIDS?"

Answer: "I absolutely *should not, must not* have acquired this disease! I *should not* have been so careless, so stupid as to have let myself acquire it! I knew how risky some kinds of sex are at the time I got infected with the HIV virus, and I foolishly took a great risk, anyway. How could I behave so idiotically—as I *should* never have behaved!"

Once you discover your conscious or just-below-the-surface-of-consciousness *shoulds* and *musts,* actively Dispute (D) them and challenge them, using the same kind of scientific thinking you would use to Dispute and challenge any hypothesis that you have doubts about and want to question. Persist at Disputing until you arrive at an Effective New Philosophy (E) that uproots your *musts.* For example:

Disputing (D): "Where is the evidence that I absolutely *should not, must not* have acquired this disease?"

Effective New Philosophy (E): "There is no evidence. The facts are that I *did* acquire it. At the time I got this disease I *should* have got it because my actions, though stupid, were such that they *do* often lead to this ailment. Because I wrongly convinced myself, at the time I acted this way, that I was right in doing so, even though I *really* was wrong, I *should have* acted the way I did act on the basis of my supposedly "right' thinking. Too bad that I wrongly thought I was "right' at that time, but I *did* think so, and therefore really could hardly have acted otherwise. So I'm foolish for blaming myself *now* for what I mistakenly thought I was right about doing *then.*"

Disputing: "Why *should not* I have been so careless, so stupid as to have let myself acquire this fatal disease?"

Effective New Philosophy: "Again, I *should have* been so stupid at that time because that's the way I then *was.* Today I am wiser, I hope, and would not repeat this foolish, indulgent, risky sex act. But I *was not* wiser at the time I took this risk and therefore I *should have* been just as unwise as I actually was. How could I have then acted wisely, when I actually acted stupidly? In no way! How sad that I acted so unwisely—but I did! How can I now *accept* the fact that I obviously can't change what I stupidly did? By doing just that—*accepting without liking*—this grim reality. I can sensibly *dislike* the unwise way in which I acted but not senselessly *demand* that I *should not* have been so unwise and not damn *me,* my total *self,* for my unwise *behavior.*"

Disputing: "Did I really know how risky sex was at the time I got infected with the HIV virus and did I foolishly take a great risk, anyway? No, I *lightly* 'knew' it (because I knew that I *could* get infected with the HIV virus). But, because I wanted sex so badly at that time I *strongly* convinced myself, and therefore 'knew' that I *would not* get infected with the HIV virus. So my strong Belief, though wrong, won out over my weak Belief—as it should have won out over it at that time. My *delusion* of impunity was stronger than my *perception* of danger, and I unfortunately followed that delusion. So I really *didn't know* how risky it was at the time I got infected. In fact, I knew it was not risky, even though in *theory* I 'knew' *better.* So I followed my *false* "knowledge" and let myself get infected. Tough! but that's what I wrongly did."

Disputing: "How could I have behaved so idiotically?"

Effective New Philosophy: "Very easily! Although I generally act intelligently, I also, as a fallible human, am prone to behave foolishly and idiotically. That is my nature—to often act well *and* to often act badly. At the time I got infected, I mainly thought of the immediate sex gratification that I *must* have and, therefore, my powerful wish being father and mother to my thought, I *made myself* think idiotically and I foolishly *convinced myself* that taking a risk was not risky. Being a desire-driven and a need-driven human, I often *easily* make myself think and act idiotically in this manner. That's unfortunate, but I easily do! Quite frequently my behavior is foolish. So it is! If I accept this fact without damning myself, I can now make myself less foolish."

Disputing: "Prove that I never *should* have behaved as idiotically as I did behave."

Effective New Philosophy: "Again, I obviously *should have* behaved this idiotically because I actually *did* behave this way. As I noted before, whatever I idiotically (or nonidiotically) do, I *should* at that time do because *it is my nature* to act that way under those conditions on that occasion. I wish that it were *not* my nature to behave idiotically on many occasions under certain conditions. But it unquestionably *is.* Too damned bad! But, again, I'd better *accept* this reality without *liking* it. Some day I may possibly be a person who *doesn't* act that idiotically. But I wasn't that way when I contracted this fatal disease. I'm not perfect now, and it's unlikely that I ever will be!"

So, as we have just been showing, you can keep finding your absolutist *shoulds, oughts, musts,* and *demands,* can actively and persistently Dispute (D) and challenge them, and can arrive at an anti-musturbatory Effective New Philosophy (E) that will tend to make you feel healthfully sad, regretful, and frustrated about having (or having one of your close friends have) a fatal disease and that will help you stave off destructive feelings of depression, panic, self-hatred, rage, and self-pity.

One of the therapists we supervised had an unusual client, Ronnie, who wasn't guilty about her approaching death from serious breast cancer, because she realized that she had done nothing foolish to bring it on, even though some of her New Age friends insisted that her lack of spirituality had led to her disease. But she was a thoroughgoing nonbeliever, felt that death was a complete, painless nothingness, and therefore chose not to have any major operations or to resort to unpleasant chemotherapy treatments, which her oncologists said might prolong her life but would most likely stave off her death only by a year or two. At the age of thirty-five she was quite willing to take the next nine months, which her doctors gave her if she did not resort to radical surgical and chemical treatment, and live it as joyfully as she could.

Everything was going quite well for Ronnie, and she was actually enjoying her final months, when her lover of the last three years objected strenuously to her refusal to take radical treatment and suddenly broke off with her. Largely alone except for her mother who lived nearby, Ronnie made herself guilty by telling herself, "I *shouldn't* have refused surgery and chemotherapy, and thereby ruined my chances of being with Donald till the end. I'm really very lonely as a result of my stupid choice! I *shouldn't* have stubbornly held my ground and fought with him! I *should* have known he would leave, and leave me in the lurch! It would have been much better if I had undergone the treatment that my oncologist recommended, probably lived a year or two longer, and kept Donald around till the end. How senseless of me! What a stubborn idiot I am!"

Urged by her Rational-Emotive therapist to strongly keep Disputing this dysfunctional berating of her herself, Ronnie came up with this *Disputation:* "Why *should* I have not refused surgery and chemotherapy and thereby ruined my chances of being with Donald till the end?"

Effective New Philosophy: "I definitely should have done this, because I really believed, and still do, that living my final days without the great handicaps of suffering from surgery and chemotherapy is definitely better than living longer, perhaps, and finishing up with a quality of life that I definitely don't want to have. Yes, I seem to have ruined my chances of being with Donald till the end by my own decision, but do I really know that he would have stayed with me anyway and would have loved and supported me till the end? Maybe he was just looking for an excuse to leave and conveniently found this one. Anyway, even if I definitely lost him because of my 'strange choice,' as he put it, I am entitled to that choice, just as he is entitled not to want me to take it. It looks like we were just not born for each other in that respect."

Disputing: "Yes, I am lonely as a result of my own choice. But why was this choice really stupid? Where is it written that I *should not* have held my ground and *should not* have risked losing Donald?"

Effective New Philosophy: "My choice wasn't stupid or wrong, even though it may have got me bad results with Donald. For the most part, I find that it was intelligent and right for me. Not for him, of course, but for me. So I *should* have held my ground and fought with him: Because that is what I actually did and it is what I thought was the right thing to do at the time. So I should have done what I did, even though in some respects it turned out badly. But I could not have known, at the time I held my ground, that it definitely would turn out badly, so I did what I thought was right and unfortunately it had some bad results. That's what often happens when we do what we think is the right thing: We get some good and some bad results. Actually, even though I have lost Donald, I still think that I did the right thing and that, on the whole, I am better off than if I had let him influence me to do what I thought and still think was the wrong thing."

Disputing: "In what way *should* I have known that he would leave and leave me in the lurch?"

Effective New Philosophy: "In no way. I know it now but I could only have suspected it then. I really thought he would accept my decision and not leave me. But I was wrong. And I *should have* been wrong when I was wrong. Too bad, but hardly *awful!*"

Disputing: "How could I have known that it would have been much better if I had undergone the treatment that my oncologist recommended, probably lived a year or two longer, and kept Donald till the end?"

Effective New Philosophy: "I couldn't have *known* it then, but could have guessed at it. I still don't know, now, that it would have been better, though it's possible that it would have been. Anyway, I took the choices that I did, thinking them the best I could make at that time, and I now have to live with them. What good will it be if I put myself down for making them, even if I could now prove that they were the wrong choices? No good whatever!"

Disputing: "Was it really senseless of me to do what I did? Am I really a stubborn idiot for acting this way?"

Effective New Philosophy: "No, it made good sense to me when I did it, and it still mainly makes good sense. But even if I acted senselessly, that would only mean that I am a person who acted senselessly or idiotically at that time; and that would hardly make me a stubborn idiot. A stubborn idiot would practically always act senselessly and idiotically and that is hardly me! As a fallible human, I'll always act somewhat foolishly. Somewhat but not completely!"

When Ronnie did this Disputing and arrived at her Effective New Philosophies she lost her feelings of guilt and only felt appropriately sorry and disappointed that her choices had led to her breakup with Donald. Although lonely, she managed to lead a fairly happy and productive final eleven months of her life, and even helped her mother to accept her dying with appropriate feelings of intense grief but without dysfunctional feelings of depression and despair. So REBT Disputing of her own irrational Beliefs really worked for Ronnie. Or, rather, she worked well at doing the Disputing.

Once you (and other people) insist that you absolutely must do well, must be approved by significant others, and must not suffer discomfort, disease, and handicaps, you practically always create, and derive from these musts, a number of related and accompanying irrational Beliefs (iB's), such as awfulizing, I-can't-stand-it-itis, damning yourself and others, and allness and neverness. These iB's are corollaries of your grandiose demands, and frequently accompany them.

You'd better suspect, therefore, that along with your imperative musts, you also have related derivative irrational Beliefs. Look for them, and scientifically Dispute them along with your Disputations of your rigid shoulds and musts. Here are some of the main and most popular additional iB's that you can healthfully Dispute.

Disputing Your Awfulizing

Awfulizing: "Because I should not and must not have acquired a fatal disease, such as AIDS, cancer, or severe heart trouble, it's awful and terrible that I have acquired it!"

Disputing: "Why is it awful? What makes my affliction terrible?"

Effective New Philosophy: 1. "It's not awful and nothing

makes it terrible because: Awful means 100% bad or as bad as it could possibly be. But just about nothing is 100% bad, as it could always be even worse than it is. Thus although it may be 99% bad that I now have (or one of my close friends has) AIDS, I could also have cancer and heart trouble. Although I am now in great pain, I could have still more pain. Although I have little help with my condition, I could have even less help. So however badly off I now am, I could be worse off. Therefore, it is very bad but not awful."

2. "If I say that my fatal condition is awful and terrible I really mean that it is more than bad. But, of course, it cannot be 101% or 110% bad, even if it could be very bad or 99% bad. Many things in my life are very bad, and one or two, like this fatal disease, may be 99% bad. But that still does not equal awful or more than bad."

3. "When I call my ailment awful, I mean that it is badder than it should or ought be. But even if it is 99% bad that is exactly what it should and must be. For that is the way that it is! Anything, in fact, that is very bad right now should be exactly the way it indubitably is. And since its being awful really means that it must not be quite as bad as it indubitably is, nothing can really be awful, including my fatal ailment. It's only very, very bad!"

4. "If I see my affliction as bad or very bad, that view will motivate me to try to help it, to cope with it, and to still be capable of a reasonable degree of happiness in spite of it. But if I view it as awful, horrible, or terrible, or badder than it should be, I will tend to upset myself so severely that I will interfere with my coping with it adequately. So I'd better give up my awfulizing and just define my affliction as very bad but not terrible or horrible."

5. "If I define my condition as awful and terrible I will be able to see no good whatever in it. Actually, however, I can probably find at least a few good aspects of it—such as the challenge to be reasonably happy and productive in spite of it. So I think I'll choose not to define it as awful."

6. "I could probably justify my affliction as catastrophic,

because it is actually going to end my life and help upset some of the people who love me. So although most bad things that happen to me—like losing my job or failing an important test—are problems and misfortunes, they are hardly extremely serious, final problems, or catastrophes. But even if I view this disease as a catastrophe I don't have to awfulize about it—that is, I don't have to insist that it absolutely must not exist because it is so catastrophic and is totally bad and more than bad because it exists as it must not. Yes, maybe it is really catastrophic. But catastrophes, too, must exist when they actually do. Now how can I make it less catastrophic—and still have some enjoyment in spite of this catastrophe?"

Disputing Your I Can't-Stand-It-Itis

I-Can't-Stand-It-Itis: "Because my affliction is so bad, is incurable, and is final, as it must not be, I-can't-stand-it! I can't tolerate it! It's too much to bear!"

Disputing: "In what way can't I stand it? Where is the evidence that I cannot tolerate it? Why is it too much to bear?"

Effective New Philosophy: "I can't stand, tolerate, and bear it for several reasons:

1. "Usually, I can stand hassles and pains because I obviously won't die of them. This time, I will die of this fatal affliction, but I can still stand that grim reality. As a human, I have to stand dying sooner or later and this time it will merely be sooner. But even though it may be quite unfair that I will die before my normal time, and even though I may suffer from pain and trouble while I'm dying, I can still bear that. Not like it, of course, but gracefully accept it because it is inevitable and I can't change it.

2. "If I really couldn't stand dying before my normal time, I couldn't be happy at all while I'm dying. But this is false. I most probably can't be as happy as I would otherwise be. But I could find some way or ways to be happy during

this final stage of my life and I am determined to do so. Now let me see what things I can enjoy even though (or especially because) I have little time in which to enjoy them.

3. "Gracefully bearing my present unkind fate and the thought of my impending death is a great challenge that I can now take. Where many or most people would make themselves endlessly depressed and panicked about their approaching death, I am determined to think, feel, and act differently and to make myself appropriately sorry and regretful but not horrified and terrified."

Disputing Your Self-Downing and Feelings of Worthlessness

When you severely blame yourself for foolishly acquiring a fatal disease you can Dispute your irrational Beliefs (iB's) as follows:

Self-Downing and Feelings of Worthlessness: "Because I got myself into this grim condition, which I *absolutely should not* have done, my acts were incredibly wrong and stupid and I am therefore a stupid and pretty worthless person."

Disputing: "Did I entirely get myself into this condition or were there other factors involved in my being afflicted with it? And even if it could be shown that I largely got myself afflicted, by not taking sufficient care of my health or by taking foolish risks, how does that prove that I *absolutely should not* have done so and that I am therefore a stupid and worthless person?"

Effective New Philosophy: "No, I did not entirely get myself into this condition, because there were other factors involved. But even if it could be shown that I foolishly got myself afflicted when I could have chosen not to do so, that only makes me a *person who* acted stupidly this time (and at various other times). It never makes me a *total fool* or a *stupid person,* because these designations are false generalizations that ignore the fact that I often behave unfoolishly and wisely.

"Even if I usually or mostly acted foolishly I would still only be a *person who* frequently behaved that way, but I would never be a *worthless person*. Why? For several reasons:

1. "A worthless person would have no value to himself or herself and to all other humans. But obviously, no matter how badly I acted, *some* people, for whatever reasons, could easily claim that I have value or worth to *them*. My mother, for example!

2. "If I had *no* worth whatever to myself it would mean that I could find absolutely no pleasure or satisfaction at all in life, and that is an almost impossible state to achieve, because I could always arrange for *some* kind of enjoyment.

3. "I can only have zero worth to myself by *defining* myself as a worthless person. Thus, I could think, 'Because I do poorly at ping-pong I am no good' or 'Because I do fine at ping-pong but still do not do *well enough,* I am worthless.' But all such definitions of worthlessness (and of human worth, too) are only definitional and tautological and have no empirical or 'real' meaning. Thus, I can say, 'Because I do poorly at having sex, I am worthless!' and you (or anyone else) can say. 'Because you do poorly at having sex you are wholly and very worthwhile.' Which one of us, then, is right? Neither of us, for we both only measure my worth by our own special—and unprovable and unfalsifiable—definitions.

4. "If I call myself—or define myself as—worthless, what *good* does this evaluation of myself, my essence, or my being do me? No good! For if I see myself as thoroughly worthless, inadequate, or incompetent, I will seriously interfere, in all probability, with my efficiency, my pleasure, my relationships, my education, my career, and with practically all other aspects of my life; and I may even commit suicide. Hardly good results!

5. "Suppose that I not only foolishly got myself inflicted

with AIDS, cancer, or brain injury, but I am also one of those rare individuals who has so far failed in just about every other respect. Can I *then* not legitimately rate myself as worthless, as a no-goodnik? No. Because I am an ongoing *process,* not a finished *product;* and as long as I am still alive and kicking, I could always presumably *change* and do better in the *future.* In fact, a number of highly inept and villainous individuals—such as the famous Bird Man of Alcatraz—changed their bad ways toward the end of their lives and began to act remarkably well. Some of them changed mainly *because* they knew that they did not have much more time to live.

6. "What about a seriously mentally deficient or brain-injured person who, because of his or her great handicaps, can do practically nothing well and is even a burden to others or to the state? Is this person worthless? Shall we mercifully kill him or her? Of course not. Almost all such individuals could, with proper supervision, manage to have *some* kind of enjoyment—and they are entitled to live and to find (or to be helped to find) whatever pleasure is possible for them.

7. "If I say that I, you, or anyone has no worth or value, I strongly imply that we are so *essentially* rotten that we do not *deserve* any good things while we are alive—or even, perhaps, if there were an afterlife, that we don't *deserve* anything but eternal damnation and suffering. This concept of essence, undeservingness, and damnation is a most questionable idea, and has several important marks against it.

a. "Whether I, you, or any person has an essence, a spirit, a soul, or even an accurately definable self is distinctly debatable. We are all unique and have many traits that differ from those of other people but what our central core, personhood, or center *is* really defies description. Even our basic or central philosophy or value system is highly complex, changing, and often includes contradictory elements. Thus, we may be very pacifistic—*and* in favor of the death penalty for criminals. And we can consider ourselves to be very religious—*and* nationalistic *and* warlike. Moreover, today we may be mystical, tomorrow orthodoxly religious, and the next day atheistic. When we say that we *are* anything, as Alfred Korzybski pointed out in 1933, we had better use terms like *and/also* and *etcetera*. For we do not seem to have any unchangeable, immutable *essence.*[1]

b. "If I, you, or we have any conceivable kind of essence, spirit, core, or soul, how the devil can we rate, measure, or evaluate it? As I just noted, it has to be quite complex and changeable. And, if so, which are its *crucial* or *most important* aspects? Who can really say? I, for example, say I have a good essence or soul—and am therefore a good *person*—because I am kind to children, adults, and animals. But you may object that I have a bad essence or character because I chop down trees, or because I honor money too much, or because I am irreligious. Which of us, again, is right? Which one indeed!

c. "How can I (or anyone) prove that I am *deserving* or *undeserving* of life, happiness, or living in Heaven for eternity? Not very easily! Various individuals and groups can view me as deserving—or as *un*deserving!—because I hate dogs and children, or because I am a champion boxer, or because I play chess poorly. Now where are we? Nowhere! By the usual rules of everyday life, we tend to agree that I deserve good things (like high wages and A's in my school courses) when I at least try very hard to earn these things. But not everyone agrees with this—for some people may think that I deserve good things even if I don't make real efforts to earn them. Even if the rules of everyday life make some sense, do they really apply to *general* deservingness? Thus, if I study and practice music very long and very hard, most people may agree that I deserve to get an A in a music course. But do I *also* then deserve to lead a *generally* good life, to be happier than other people, and, if immortality truly exists, to merit everlasting bliss? Hardly. Nor, if I fail to study music and 'deservingly' fail my course, do I then deserve to roast in hell for eternity? So, the concept of deservingness may make sense in regard to my—and your—particular efforts in a limited area. But to validate it in regard to a generally good or bad life! Can I?

d. "The concepts of rating my (and anyone's) essence and deservingness often does immense harm and rarely does any good. For I will tend to only find myself a *good deserving person* when I have done many good deeds and practically no bad ones. Because, however, I (like others) am a very fallible human who will easily and often do bad and stupid acts, I will easily and often tend to find myself undeserving and worthless and that notion and the dismal feelings that go with it will usually make my days needlessly miserable. If I or one of my close friends were dying of a fatal disease, my life would naturally be bad enough. Why, with this unvalidatable and unfalsifiable concept of undeservingness, would I want to greatly add to my sad state?

8. "I may view myself as a damnable person because I have foolishly let myself contract a fatal disease like AIDS, have put others in jeopardy of catching it from me, and have caused those who love me great pain and trouble, particularly in regard to caring for me while I am very ill and dying. Why is my self-damnation for these reasons illegitimate and mistaken? Because:

"a. The concept and feeling of damnation is very similar to that of having a bad essence and being undeserving of joy on earth and in any presumed afterlife. Damnation is a concept that I cannot prove or disprove and that will do me (and anyone) little good and much harm. I am of course entitled to believe in damnation—along with Satan, evil demons, and eternal hellfire. But I'll be much better off if I refuse to believe in this kind of idea. Especially when I am dying!

"b. Damnation is a very hazy concept, because we have no evidence whatever that anyone in human history ever has been damned. We have considerable evidence that a great number of people *thought* that they were damned and therefore acted *as if* they were; and we have much more evidence that proves that people have damned themselves, and therefore literally tortured themselves and fairly often committed suicide. But all this evidence shows, and that very clearly, is that many humans devoutly want to believe in damnation—and in all likelihood invent it. You would think that somehow, out of the billions of people who presumably have been damned through eternity for their sins on earth, at least one of them would have somehow returned to earth and attested to his or her actual damnation. But not a single soul seems to have done so. Strange!

"c. The concept of damnation implies very strongly that some really cruel and evil force or God exists and that He or It simply refuses to accept the obvious reality that just about all humans are born and reared to be exceptionally fallible and that therefore there is no way in which they would not often grievously err and sin. If humans are created this way—and especially if some God or superhuman force created them to be the way they are—it seems most unlikely that such a force or God would then severely berate and damn them for their sins. This seems something like training a dog to retrieve birds, making sure that the dog is fallible and does not always retrieve them, and then damning the dog and punishing it severely whenever it fails to make a perfect retrieval. A sadistic child or adult might conceivably act that way—because, we would say, he or she has severe emotional problems—but it is difficult to imagine that a powerful God or Universal Force would be as disturbed and sadistic as such a aberrational person would be.

"d. Damnation and eternal punishment for sins are certainly included in many of our religions and our fables and myths. But these were obviously produced by humans, not by any kind of superhumans. Humans, therefore, clearly invent concepts of damnation, and we have a strong, probably biological, tendency to do so. But humans, too, invent all kinds of heavens and other elements of live-happily-ever-after, eternal bliss. Therefore, however strong our damning tendencies are, we can still fight them and uninvent them. And we'd better! So I'd better!"[2]

Disputing Your Allness and Neverness Beliefs

Beliefs in Allness and Neverness: "Because I behaved so foolishly and stupidly in not taking care of myself properly and in letting myself contract this fatal disease, I'll *always* keep doing stupid things like this and *never* be able to think intelligently and act sensibly!"

Disputing: "Did I really behave that foolishly in not taking care of myself properly and in letting myself contract this fatal disease? Even if I did, how does that prove that I'll *always* act this stupidly and *never* be able to think intelligently and act sensibly?"

Effective New Philosophy: "Maybe I really did act quite foolishly and stupidly in not taking care of myself but that was on the basis of my knowledge at that time. I *now* know how foolish my behavior was but did I really fully know it then? Most probably not, for if I had really known how foolish it was and what bad results it would bring, I doubt very much whether I would have done it.

"Granted, however, that I did, at least on the basis of my existing knowledge, act very foolishly, how does that prove that I am a completely foolish person who will *always* act stupidly in the present and future and can *never* possibly change? Of course it doesn't. Now that I know how idiotically I behaved, that very knowledge will help me change; and if I am able to behave so badly, I am also able to *refuse* to behave that badly. For almost anything that I can do I can also *refuse* to do again. *Always* and *never* are silly overgeneralizations. I practically never do all good or all bad things all of the time because I am just not that consistent and fixed in my behavior. I often do x but I also sometimes do y. I rarely do z but I sometimes do.

"*Always* and *never* imply very strongly that I am totally incapable of changing my ways. But I obviously went from correct to wrong behavior in contracting this disease, so there is no reason why I cannot change my actions again and go from wrong to right behavior.

"Seeing myself as *only* being able to *always* do the wrong thing and *never* to do the right thing will obviously harm me, keep me miserable, and actually keep me from changing—just because I *think* I can't change. So I'd better give up this self-defeating way of thinking and, instead, view myself as well able to change my disadvantageous ways. It may be quite hard for me to do so, but that doesn't mean that I can't."

Notes to Chapter 6

1. Bourland & Johnston, 1991; De Bono, 1991; Korzybski, 1933; Johnson, 1946.

2. Ellis, 1972c, 1973b, 1976c, 1977a, 1985b, 1988a, 1988b, 1991a, 1991b, 1992b, 1992f; Hartman, 1967; Hauck, 1992; Lazarus, 1977; Low, 1952; Mills, 1993; Tillich, 1953; Walen, DiGiuseppe & Dryden, 1992.

7

More Irrational Beliefs and How to Dispute Them

When I (AE) gave my first paper on Rational Emotive Behavior Therapy in 1956 in Chicago and when I authored the first edition of *A Guide to Rational Living* with Robert A. Harper in 1961, I listed ten major irrational Beliefs (iB's) that people use to needlessly disturb themselves. I kept adding to these ideas in various of my writings and was able to list about twenty-five self-defeating ideas that my clients commonly use to make themselves emotionally disturbed.

A little later on, in the early 1970's, I began to see that all the major irrational Beliefs that I had outlined, and that had been put into about thirty tests of dysfunctional beliefs and used in a number of research studies from the 1960's onward, could be subsumed under three major grandiose *shoulds* or *musts*: (1) "I must perform well and be approved by significant others or else I am a pretty rotten, undeserving person!" (2) "Other people absolutely must treat me kindly and fairly or they deserve to be severely damned and punished!" (3) "The economic, social, health, and other conditions under which I live must be exactly the way I want them to be and must never be very frustrating or uncomfortable, and if they are bad and against my interests, my life is rotten and the world is a miserable place and is so awful that I *can't stand* it and can hardly be happy at all!"

Since the time that I began to see that all the original irrational Beliefs that I had outlined could be put under one, two, or all three of these main headings, I have not been able to find a single new one that could not be fairly easily categorized in one or more of these three major categories. Moreover, as far as I can see, the twenty-five or so main dysfunctional beliefs that people upset themselves with, and the hundreds of other irrationalities that are not so common but that people often resort to all over the world, all seem to be a function of or are derived from these three major musts and commands.[1]

Let us illustrate. Suppose you are HIV positive or have AIDS and you ask a friend to go to the theater with you and she refuses to accept your invitation. You immediately tend to make the following irrational, and quite probably false, inferences and attributions: (1) (Personalizing): "She doesn't like me." (2) (Jumping to conclusions): "She knows that I have this serious disease, blames me for having it, and thinks that I am stupid and worthless." (3) (Self-downing): "She is right. I really should not have got myself into this terrible fix and I am no good for having behaved so idiotically!" (4) (Overgeneralizing): "I'll never be able to keep any of my old friends now that I've got this terrible disease and they know about it." (5) (Awfulizing and I-can't-stand-it-itis): "What's the use of going on like this? My life is not worth living at all."

Now all these negative self-statements about your friend, yourself, and the world are most probably exaggerated or entirely false. So why does a bright person like you illogically, unrealistically, and irrationally manufacture and believe in them?

REBT's answer is that underneath these questionable inferences and attributions you have some main musturbatory philosophies; and that, as long as you hold these musts, you will easily and often make such shaky inferences and attributions. Thus, you may well have all three of the grandiose commands that we listed above: (1) "I must perform well and be approved by all significant others," (2) "Other people must always treat me perfectly well," and (3) "The conditions under which I live always must be easy and comfortable." If you do have any or all of these, the questionable inferences that you just made would seem rather "obvious" and "true" and you will keep tending to make them.

For example, let us suppose that you have the first of these absolutist musts: "I must perform well and be approved by significant others." Because you did not perform that well (that is, you acquired the HIV virus or actually got AIDS) you can easily conclude, even though you're wrong about concluding, all five of the questionable inferences listed above; for they easily and naturally follow from your major must—that you absolutely must perform well and be approved by all significant others.

Then again, if you have the second of the three major neuroticizing commands, "Other people must always treat me perfectly well," and your friend whom you asked to the theater refuses to go, you can easily and often—though still wrongly—infer that she is a prejudiced person and that she is no damned good for being the way she is.

Finally, if you strongly hold the third of the major irrational musts that people commonly create—"The conditions under which I live always must be easy and comfortable!"—and actually your condition is far from being the way it supposedly must be, you can very easily and almost automatically, and still very falsely, conclude that you'll never be able to keep any of your old friends and that there is no use of your going on like this and trying to lead a life that has any happiness in it.

REBT, then, assumes that when you make highly negative inferences and attributions about yourself—about how bad things really are for you, how people are against you, and how you are no damned good as a person—they almost always stem from, and are "natural" derivatives of, your underlying absolutistic shoulds, oughts, and musts. If, on the other hand, you only *prefer* to do well, to be approved by others, and to have comfortable conditions of living, and never tell yourself that therefore you *need* these events to occur, you would have a hard time inventing the kind of devastating negative inferences that you often do invent when you strongly subscribe to your underlying, and crucial, musts and demands. Suppose you strongly believed, "I certainly *wish* that my friend would accept my invitation to the theater, but she doesn't *have to* do so; I don't *have to* behave as I would have liked to behave about acquiring my disease; and the conditions of my life *can be* arduous and uncomfortable even though I *wish* they were not that way," would you then make up the highly negative attributions about yourself, your friend, and the conditions of living that you invent when you turn this wish into an arrogant demand? No, says REBT, you most probably would not.

In any event, when you are emotionally disturbed about anything, especially a fatal disease that you or one of your close friends is afflicted with, you will most likely tend to create, first, the three major absolutist musts that we keep describing in this book; and you will also tend to derive from them, or believe along with them, a number of other self-defeating attributions and inferences. I (AE) originally pointed out most of these self-disturbing inferences in my early writings on REBT in the 1950's. Then, in the 1960's, Aaron Beck stressed and categorized them, and along with David Burns and other therapists, he has made them the core of what he calls cognitive therapy.[2] REBT agrees that all the misleading negative inferences that cognitive therapists stress and Dispute with their clients are indeed common among neurotic people. But it still holds that they tend to stem from these people's dogmatic musts. Cognitive therapists' followers dispute absolutist shoulds and musts but place them on the same level as the other negative attributions that they investigate and Dispute. REBT, however, puts absolutist shoulds and musts in the primary place and holds that the other dys-functional inferences and attributes largely follow from them. Therefore, REBT just about always looks for people's grandiose commands and demands first. Then it also looks for and Disputes and challenges their derivative inferences.[3]

REBT also holds that people's strong tendency to cre-ate both their musts and their self-defeating inferences is a biological as well as a socially learned tendency. Thus, our parents and our culture teach us rules of conduct, and tell us what is "right" and "wrong" behavior. They also add impera-tive demands to these rules. Thus, they tell us, especially when we are children, (1) "It is highly preferable if you per-form well and get along properly with other people," and (2) "Therefore you must do so." But by this second command, they usually intend merely to emphasize the first rule and to show us that we will get better results by following these rules than by rebelling against them. And that is true. In practically all societies, we will get better results if we follow social rules than if we fail to follow them.

When we ignore parental and cultural rules, we soon find that the musts that are attached to them are not literally true. For when we don't do what we supposedly *must* do and when we do what we supposedly *must not* do, we are rarely killed or excommunicated. Instead, we are mainly yelled at and perhaps moderately punished. Nonetheless, we often devoutly believe the musts that we are taught—and also make up quite a number of absolutist, rigid musts of our own. Such as: "I *must* be always loved and honored by my parents!" and "I *must* not only do well at school and at work but I also *must* do outstandingly well, or else I am no damned good!" So we seem to *naturally* be great mustur-baters and that is why we so easily accept the musts of oth-ers, even though they do not literally mean them.

Back to Disputing. As you Dispute your dogmatic, im-perative musts, and as you also Dispute your awfulizing, your I-can't-stand-it-itis, your self-deprecation, and your use of allness and neverness (all of which tend to stem from your

musts), you can also look for your other self-defeating inferences and attributions and Dispute them, too. Let us now
look at some of these destructive Beliefs that you may have,
as you would look for them if you were working with an
REBT or a cognitive therapist, who would help you find
them and sensibly challenge and question them.

Disputing Overgeneralizing

When you feel healthfully sad, sorry, and regretful
about your having a fatal disease (or having an afflicted close
friend), you tend to accurately generalize: "Some of my
friends may avoid me now that I have this disease." This is a
generalization and is probably true.

When you seriously upset yourself about having a disease, however, you may easily make a false generalization
that we discussed in the last chapter: "All my good friends,
now that they know I have this disease, will definitely aban-
don me and never visit me." So, as we have already noted,
you can look at this allness kind of overgeneralization and
can Dispute it and show yourself that you are exaggerating.

You may also tend to make other kinds of false generalizations that you can then actively and vigorously Dispute
and change. Let's look at some of these.

Overgeneralization: "Everyone is horrified about their
possibly getting a fatal illness themselves and therefore the
great majority of my friends will reject and neglect me now
that I have this disease and I will be left to suffer with it
alone, alone, alone!"

Disputing: "Is this really true? Will the great majority of
my friends reject and neglect me when they discover that I
have only a limited time to live? Will I be left to suffer alone,
alone, alone?"

Effective New Philosophy: "No, some of my friends will
probably reject and neglect me if they discover that I have a
limited time to live, but most of my good friends won't. If
this most unlikely possibility turns out to be true, I can al-

ways make an effort and find some other friends who know about my condition, who are definitely not turned off by it, and who will not reject me. Even if I discover that most people will reject me, which is probably untrue, I could well live without these kinds of people and would be much better off cultivating those who are not so prejudiced. If some of my friends actually boycott me because I have AIDS or terminal cancer, I never have to put myself down because of their rejection but can convince myself that this is sad and unfortunate that they may view me as a "bad person" but that I never have to agree with them about this. I am merely a person with a handicap. *That* is bad, but it never makes *me* bad."

Overgeneralization: "Because I have a fatal disease and am distinctly limited and handicapped, I can do practically nothing to become involved in important aspects of life and to make myself happy."

Disputing: "Even though I have a fatal disease and am distinctly handicapped, why can't I still do many things to make myself happy? Where is the evidence that I can do practically nothing to become involved in important aspects of life and to enjoy myself?"

Effective New Philosophy: "There is no evidence that I can do practically nothing to become involved in important aspects of life and to make myself happy. I may not have the time and energy to become as involved as I would like to be. But I can still find some good things to do within my limits of time and energy; and if I make a real effort to do this, I can most probably find a good deal of happiness."

Disputing Personalizing

If you or one of your close associates has an incurable, fatal disease and you choose to unduly upset yourself and make yourself miserable about this, you may often resort to personalizing. This means that, because you think that you *must* not be afflicted, you *should* not have allowed yourself to be afflicted, that you are a *no good person* for letting this state of affairs come about, you easily "find" things wrong with you, you are sure that others also find these "horrible" blunders and put you down as a person. This kind of personalizing is usually based on false premises and on misleading deductions from these premises.

You can therefore, especially if you feel pretty worthless, look for your illegitimate personalizing and use REBT to actively and vigorously Dispute it. For example:

Personalizing: "Just by looking at me and seeing how weak I am people can see that I have a debilitating fatal disease. They are pitying me and thinking I am a real weakling. I am sure that they see something seriously wrong with me and that they despise me for being in this miserable state."

Disputing: "Can people invariably see how weak I am just by looking at me? If they do notice that I am weak, do they always conclude that I have a debilitating fatal disease? Do practically all of them thoroughly pity me? Do those that do pity me really think that I am a real weakling? Do the people who guess that there is something wrong with me necessarily despise me for being in this miserable state? If some people do see my weak condition and do despise me for it, do I have to take them very seriously and agree with them that I am a despicable person?"

Effective New Philosophy: "Obviously, not all the people who look at me think I am weak and therefore a weak person. Most of them are hardly that interested in me to look that closely and to conclude anything bad about me. They have their own problems to think about! Even if they do notice my weak and debilitated state, do all of them profoundly pity me? I doubt it. But suppose they do—why is it so bad to have them pity me for my weakness? And do all those who pity me think I am a real weakling? What negative, hostile people they then would be! And why do I have to care that much if some of them do think that I am a weakling? Does their view of me actually make me a lowly person? Hardly! Whenever anybody thinks that I am a despicable person, because I have this fatal disease or for any other reason, I obviously do not have to agree with them. I can accept the fact that they have this prejudiced view and feel sorry about their having it, but I never have to take it too seriously."

Personalizing: "When people realize that I am as sick as I really am they will hate the fact that they have to help me and take care of me and they will hate to be with me at all. Even those that do stay around and help me will actually wish that I were dead and that they didn't have to bother with me. How *awful* that people who even help me will often underlyingly hate me and wish that I were dead!"

Disputing: "Will practically everyone who realizes that I am sick really hate the fact that they feel obliged to help me and therefore hate to be with me? Is it true that even those who do stay around and help me actually wish that I were dead and that they didn't have to bother with me at all? If some people who stay around actually do often underlyingly hate me and wish that I were dead, why is that *awful?*"

Effective New Philosophy: Perhaps a few people who realize that I am as sick as I really am will actually hate the fact that they feel obliged to help me and will therefore hate to be with me. But certainly all my friends and relatives will not feel this way. Some good Samaritans will even like the fact that I am so weak and dependent on them and will enjoy taking care of me. Will many or most people who do stay around and help me actually wish that I were dead and that they didn't have to bother with me at all? Most unlikely, though a few, again, may possibly feel that way. Even if some do, and some of the people who stay around and help me secretly wish that I were dead, that is sad and disappointing but it is hardly *awful.* They have a right to feel any way they actually do feel. If they do wish I were dead, I hope they have the good sense to be themselves and to somehow stay away from me. But if they don't, they don't. I can still live with that unpleasant reality, refuse to upset myself about it, and encourage such people, if I find out about them, to leave me alone and to go about their business."

Disputing Emotional Reasoning

People often have a tendency, which may be both biological and learned, to think crookedly and to invent "facts" when they have strong feelings about something. Thus, if you feel very angry at some individuals, you will tend to "see" them as plotting and scheming against you when they are doing nothing of the sort. Or if you love someone very much you will tend to ignore their foolish behaviors and "notice" that they have done something very well when they actually have done it imperfectly or badly.

If you or one of your close friends suffer from a fatal ailment, your thoughts will usually be so involved with its negative aspects that you will at times be so influenced by your feelings that you will resort to emotional reasoning. You may, for example, feel so terrified about being afflicted that you will see your condition as being much worse than it actually is. Or, conversely, you may realize that you will feel horrified if you are fully aware of your bad condition and you may therefore "see" it as much better than it actually is. Your strong feelings about your ailment, and about all kinds of things connected with it—such as your friends' and relatives' disturbance about it—may lead you to view some things in your life too seriously and other things too unseriously. Your wishful thinking may make you look at things too optimistically, but it may also make you look at many facts with undue pessimism, when they really are not that bad. Thus, you may so strongly demand that you be in perfect health that when you have a slight cold you will see it as raging pneumonia.

Watch out, then, for your biased emotional reasoning. It is often quire *un*reasonable! The more strongly you feel about something, you will often convince yourself that it is absolutely "true" or "false" when it is neither. Bigots, don't forget, who are 100 percent convinced of the truth or falseness of their ideas, often mislead themselves. Their very fervor blinds them to realities that may contradict ideas that they devoutly favor. Ironically, the stronger you are convinced about some aspect of a fatal disease, the more likely is your conviction to be false or misleading. Thus, if you powerfully believe that you will not suffer pain from your illness or if you just as powerfully believe that you will suffer excruciating pain, both these ideas are likely to be highly exaggerated. However, because your prejudiced ideas may influence your actual feelings, your strong belief that you will not suffer may actually lead you to feel less pain and your intense belief that you will suffer may actually lead you to feel more pain. So your powerful wishes and beliefs may sometimes—though not always—be father to your "actual" sensations and experiences.

Let us look at some common aspects of emotional reasoning that you may resort to when you have a fatal disease, to see how you can suspect them, look for them, and use REBT Disputing to minimize them.

Emotional Reasoning: "Because I very strongly feel that having this disease is horrible, that nothing could be worse than having it, that I can't stand it, and that it absolutely must go away, my convictions and feelings are true. It *is* awful and it absolutely *must* not continue to exist!"

Disputing: "How does my strong feeling about the horror of this disease prove that horror actually exists in the world and that my affliction truly *is* horrible? Because I greatly feel that nothing could be worse, that I can't stand it, and that this ailment absolutely must go away, what have my feelings got to do with the way things really are? If I strongly feel and believe that I am God Almighty and that I run the universe, or that I am the Devil Incarnate and that I make everything in the universe evil and rotten, do my feelings and beliefs actually prove that I am God or the Devil? Of course not. I am entitled to have any feelings and strong conviction that I have. But my beliefs and emotions, when especially strong, are mainly intense prejudices. The fact is that I truly have them. But my feelings do not prove any-thing about the state of the world or even about any 'noble' or 'satanic' part that I play in it."

Effective New Philosophy: "My strongly viewing that my disease is horrible and my consequent feeling that it is only prove that I do believe and feel this way. Certainly, I can le-gitimately feel that my ailment is very bad and I can strongly wish that it would disappear. But my strong feeling that I can't stand it, that nothing could be worse than my having it, and that it must go away does not make any of these things true. It only leads to increased misery on my part and it hardly helps me in any way. So I'd better accept my feelings, see that they do me much more harm than good, and work hard to change them. Because I feel them today does not mean that I must continue to feel them. As REBT shows, I mainly create my feelings, including these, and therefore I have the ability to change them and to bring on other, more useful feelings. Now let me see what I can do to effect this kind of change."

Emotional Reasoning: "Because I feel very strongly that people, including my best friends, hate me for being in this very bad state and for having to be careful and take care of me much more than they otherwise would have to do, I know that this is true and that they actually do hate me."

Disputing: "How does my strong feeling that people, including some of my best friends, hate me for being in this bad state and for having to be careful—and to take care of me much more than they otherwise would have to—prove that this is actually true? Even if, in some cases, the facts are that it really is true, and that some of my best friends now do hate me, why can't I accept this reality without defining it as *awful* and *terrible* and without making myself increasingly miserable about it?"

Effective New Philosophy: "My strong feeling that peo-ple, including some of my best friends, hate me for being in this bad state only proves that I have this feeling and that it sometimes conforms to the facts and sometimes doesn't.

Some of my friends may hate me some of the time for having this affliction but it is highly unlikely that they all hate me all of the time. Those that do, of course do. And that is most unfortunate but it is not *awful* and *terrible,* because it could even be worse than it is and it *should* be just as bad as it is. If I really find that some of my best friends hate me for being in this condition, I will try to talk to them and help them change their feelings; but it's not absolutely necessary that I get them to change, and I can lead a reasonably happy life even if their unfortunate attitude persists."

Catastrophizing or Exaggerating Bad Conditions

I (AE) invented the term catastrophizing shortly after I began to do REBT in 1955. For I soon saw that practically all my neurotic clients often took relatively small hassles, difficulties, and misfortunes and built them up into supposedly major catastrophes. This seems to be the human trait and perhaps has some evolutionary value. Tens of thousands of years ago, when primitive men and women lived in dangerous jungle conditions, they may have had to take a slight danger—such as tripping over a fallen tree or encountering a dog in the woods—and build it up into an enormous risk to be confronted. In doing so, they would of course make themselves much more vigilant and anxious than they really had to be; but they would also preserve their lives in situations where these slight dangers might occasionally lead to life-threatening ones.

Be that as it may, humans still often catastrophize about bad and not-so-bad events and thereby make themselves more tense than they really have to be. They may occasionally still save their lives by being overly vigilant. But they often lead miserable existences, and sometimes create psychosomatic reactions, such as ulcers and heart trouble, that may ultimately actually kill them!

As we might expect, people with AIDS and other fatal

diseases easily catastrophize about their illness—which really is quite serious—and about numerous other things. Thus, they often tend to see slight rejections by other people as gross insults, to view mild physical pains as indications that they will die shortly, and to see the health precautions that they had better take as enormous impositions and deprivations.

If you or one of your close friends is suffering from a fatal disease, be suspicious of your catastrophizing and your awfulizing about the catastrophes that you may invent. You may commonly tell yourself, for example, "My friend, Sam, has AIDS and that means he will continually be in agony and I must spend practically all my whole life taking care of him." Then you may awfulize about this catastrophizing: "This is terrible! I absolutely must not be put in this situation! I can't avoid devoting my whole life to taking care of Sam; and if that occurs, I couldn't bear it at all, would be miserable all the time, and might just as well kill myself!"

As we have noted previously, you can stop your awfulizing about this imagined catastrophe by showing yourself that even if it did occur it would be most inconvenient but hardly *awful* or *more than* inconvenient. But you can also go back to your catastrophizing and undo it, as in the following examples:

Catastrophizing: "My friend, Sam, has AIDS and that means that he will continually be in agony and that I must spend practically my whole life taking care of him."

Disputing: "Will Sam continually be in agony just because he has AIDS? Even if this turns out to be the case, must I spend practically my whole life taking care of him?"

Effective New Philosophy: "No, it is highly unlikely that Sam will continually be in agony because he has AIDS. At times he may be, but most people with AIDS do not experience agony all the time and when they do experience acute pain they can often resort to sedation that will alleviate most of their agony. If Sam is in great pain, I don't have to spend all of my life taking care of him. I can choose to be around him and care for him when he seems to be suffering most. I may well at times choose to do this. But I still have my own life to live, and I have other people to think about, too. So I will give Sam just as much time and care as I can manage but I am not obligated to spend all my time with him. While he is dying, I expect to have a very hard time. But I can bear that and not turn my whole life into a nothingness."

Catastrophizing: "Now that I am suffering with this fatal disease, I have to think about it all the time, there is nothing I can possibly do to help myself, and I have to be utterly miserable until the day I die."

Disputing: "I certainly will give a good deal of thought to this fatal disease and coping with its ravages. But why do I *have to* think about it all the time? Is there really *nothing* I can do to help myself? Must I be utterly miserable until the day I die?"

Effective New Philosophy: "I obviously don't have to think of my fatal illness all the time, though I shall certainly keep it in mind and see what I can do to cope with it. There are doubtless many things I can do to help myself, even though I won't be completely cured of this ailment. Now let me see what some of these helpful things are. I clearly don't *have to* be utterly miserable until the day I die. I can distract myself in various ways from obsessing about my disease and work against awfulizing about it. I can also very definitely look for and find some constructive and enjoyable things to do even though I am limited. Now let me give some real thought and effort to doing these things."

Ignoring and Discounting Positive Aspects of Life

When we live a normal existence, with many good and bad aspects to our lives, we frequently tend to focus mainly on the latter and not on the former aspects. This, especially in the early days of human existence, may have been and may still be life-preserving, because if we mainly focus on harmful things, we may be better able to ward off dangerous happenings. Pleasant things that happen to us, on the other hand, may easily be glossed over, because it was nice that they occurred but if they do not happen we will hardly be annihilated and will merely live somewhat less happy existences.

Focusing on the negative and ignoring or discounting the positive aspects of your life, however, has decided disadvantages. You then tend to predict that bad things will keep occurring and that good ones will not. You actually may look avidly for the bad occurrences and "find" them when they hardly exist and you may develop a pessimistic outlook, as Martin Seligman has shown, that seriously interferes with your joyous living and may lead to psychosomatic and other ills. If you are biologically prone to ulcers or heart trouble, you may bring on these ailments by worrying too much. And even if you have healthy propensities, your grim outlook may interfere with the restorative powers of your immune system and make you more liable to serious illnesses than you would otherwise be.

This may be particularly true if you (or your friends) have immune system deficiencies, such as those involved with cancer, HIV infection, or AIDS. By indulging in a pessimistic outlook, and thereby making yourself prone to severe depression, you may increase the ravages of any serious disease you may have.

When you take a pessimistic attitude and focus mainly on the bad aspects of your life, you often do what we mentioned previously: You catastrophize and make the negative things that happen much worse than they actually are; and you wrongly conclude that these things will always happen. These negative attitudes, as we have shown, can really harm you. You may also ignore your good traits and benefits, and when these are called to your attention, you discount them, make them seem insignificant, and predict that they will not last.

One of our clients, Mike, had two lovers who had died of AIDS, and several acquaintances, both male and female, who either had AIDS or HIV infections. So he kept think-ing—in fact, obsessing—about these grim realities and was absolutely sure that any other lover that he took would de-velop AIDS and that his relatives would be stricken with fatal cancer or heart conditions.

When it was pointed out to Mike that although he was in his early fifties none of his close relatives had already died, including his mother and father and his nine uncles and aunts, and that all his existing relatives had unusually healthy lives, he objected that his four grandparents had only lived to their eighties and that there was still an excel-lent chance that his parents and his uncles and aunts would suffer from long, debilitating diseases. When it was also brought to his attention that his two lovers who had died of AIDS had really not suffered that much while dying, he im-mediately objected that he had heard about several other people who had suffered greatly before they died. When his friends and his therapist showed him that so far, in spite of his promiscuous sex life, he had not contracted any sexually transmitted disease, and that he had also been in fine health just about all his life, he insisted that this was pure luck and that just because he had been lucky so far he was sure to be stricken soon with some deadly ailment.

No matter what evidence was shown to Mike about many of the highly fortunate aspects of his and his relatives' lives, he ignored or discounted it; and even after he had sev-eral months of regular Rational Emotive Behavior Therapy he refused to modify his pessimistic outlook and to accept the fortunate aspects of his existence. The authors of this book conferred with each other about what could be done to convince Mike to change his depression-creating attitude and to realize that although the world was hardly a bed of roses, it definitely could be seen with better-colored glasses than he used. So we devised a set of strong rational coping statements (which we will describe in more detail in our next chapter) and induced him to forcefully say them to himself at least five times a day.

He did even better than we suggested with this agreed-upon homework assignment. For the next month he said the strong rational self-statements to himself at least ten times a day, until he began to change his one-sided negative attitude. Some of the main powerful coping statements that he kept using during this month were:

"My life really has a good many unpleasantries and hassles, *but* it also has provided me with, and still does give me, a great many satisfactions and pleasures!"

"I certainly have screwed up many times in the past and I still have a strong tendency to do so, *but* I have also done very well at times and have done some helpful things for other people. So I *can*, yes I definitely *can*, often figure out what to do to help myself and to help others."

"I don't care *how* rotten the world is and *how* badly it may treat me and my friends. Nonetheless, it *does* have many good things in it, and it *does* include many happy events and happenings. I am utterly determined to look at *all* its sides, the good *and* the bad, until I see it the way it really is and not merely focus on its bad sides."

When he kept strongly repeating, and thinking about, these two-sided self-statements, Mike was able to considerably change his views of himself, of others, and of the world, and to acquire a realistic idea of his life. Surprisingly, he soon began to see that in many ways he was more fortunate than most of the other people he intimately knew and that he had better keep focusing on the enjoyable things in his existence and not cavalierly edit them out.

If you keep discounting the positive aspects of life and keep obsessively-compulsively focusing on its negative aspects, you can Dispute and help keep Disputing this negative tendency as follows:

Ignoring and Discounting Positive Aspects of Life: "Yes, not everything that happens to me is bad or horrible. But let's face it: Even the good things that happen are not that good and the bad things easily outweigh and overwhelm them. Yes, I sometimes think and act well. But look at the times I behave idiotically and self-sabotagingly! I should keep my eye on those times! I must stop behaving those foolish ways! And look at the many bad things that keep happening to my close friends! They obviously shouldn't be happening that way, and because they do keep occurring, the world is a rotten place! Why can't these bad things be eliminated and much better things keep happening? I *can't stand* these awful aspects of life and *must* keep dwelling and dwelling on them if I am to do anything about coping with and changing them!"

Disputing: "Isn't the good that happens to me really that good? Do all the bad things that happen easily outweigh the good? Must I mainly focus on the times I behave idiotically and self-sabotagingly? It would be better if I stopped acting in self-sabotaging ways but do I really have to *completely* stop doing so? Why mustn't bad things keep happening to my close friends? If they do keep happening, does that truly mean that the world is a completely rotten place? I don't *like* these bad aspects of life but can I really not *stand* them? Do I *have to* keep endlessly dwelling on them if I am to do anything about coping with them and changing them?"

Effective New Philosophy: "Yes, the good things that happen to me often really are that good and if I stopped discounting them I would often be able to enjoy them. The bad things in my life sometimes outweigh the good, but they hardly always do so. The more I focus on them and exaggeratedly think and complain about them, I will *make them* outweigh the good things! Of course I don't have to keep obsessing about bad things and thereby make them worse than they are. So I'd better concentrate on doing something about them or think of some of the good things in my life, instead of compulsively dwelling on these bad things. I don't have to completely stop acting in self-sabotaging ways and it is not my nature to completely do this. But I can often stop myself from doing so if I really work against my self-sabotaging instead of putting myself down for engaging in it. The more I call myself a worm for behaving self-defeatingly, the more I will convince myself that I have to keep acting that way and the more self-destructive I still make myself.

Bad things, obviously, must at times keep happening to my close friends; and I'd better accept that unfortunate reality instead of thinking that I can magically change it. The world surely has many rotten things in it but that never makes it a totally rotten place. Although I'll never like the bad aspects of my and my friends' existence, I can definitely stand them; and the better I stand them the better I can cope with them and perhaps help change them. No, I'd better not keep dwelling on them except insofar as I can possibly do something to make them better. So I can try to constructively think about these bad things without compulsively ruminating about and foolishly insisting that they are so bad that therefore they absolutely should not, must not, exist."

Notes to Chapter 7

1. Ellis, 1973b, 1977a, 1988a, 1990a, 1990b, 1990d, 1991f, 1991g, 1991h, 1992a, 1992d, 1991c, 1991f, 1993a, 1993b; Ellis, Abrams & Dengelegi, 1992; Ellis & Harper, 1975; Ellis & Velten, 1992.

2. Beck, 1976; Burns, 1980

3. Ellis, 1988a; Ellis & Dryden, 1987.

8

Additional Disputing
of Dysfunctional Beliefs

The self-defeating, irrational Beliefs (iB's) that you can take over from others or manufacture yourself when you or one of your close friends has a fatal disease are practically endless, because people, including you, are talented in devising such destructive ideas. Let us, in this chapter, consider a few more of the very common iB's, so that you can see whether you have some of them and, if so, what you can do to Dispute them and to arrive at a New Effective Philosophy.

Disputing Pollyannaism and Sweeping Bad Things Under The Rug

Some people would horrify themselves so much if they acknowledged the really bad things in their life that they ignore them, deny that they really exist, and sometimes view them Pollyannaishly. This kind of head-in-the-sand attitude, as Shelley Taylor has pointed out, has some advantages. For if you are stricken with a bad fate and honestly face this fact you may dwell on it, worry excessively and depress yourself about it, imagine that it is even worse than it is, and make yourself so frantic that you can hardly do anything to improve it or cope with it. So Pollyannaism is not completely bad or unproductive.[1]

It is, however, dangerous, as we have shown in Chapter 3. For everything will not happen for the best in your life—especially when you or one of your close associates has a fatal disease. And by unrealistically assuming that everything will turn out fine you will not do what you otherwise could do to help rid yourself of your underlying feelings of terror and horror. Instead, they will likely rise again, along with your basic Beliefs that really bad things *absolutely must* not happen to you and that it is *completely awful* when and if they do. You may even feel terrified and horrified without realizing where your feelings came from.

Pollyannaism about your or a close associate's fatal illness therefore has its great disadvantages. Try to give it up, and instead adopt a realistic but not awfulizing attitude about serious conditions. Let us now show you how you can Dispute any Pollyannaism attitudes that you may hold.

Pollyannaism: "This fatal disease is really not so bad. There's a good chance that they'll find a cure for it soon and that I will be completely over it. Even if it continues, I can easily do all the things that I did before I acquired it and can be just as happy as I previously was. So who cares that I am afflicted?"

Disputing: "Is it true that my fatal disease is really not so bad? Is there really a good chance that they'll find a cure for it soon and that I will be completely over it? If it continues, can I easily do all the things I did before I acquired it? And can I be just as happy as I previously was? Should I really not care that I am afflicted? Is it true that it doesn't matter at all?"

Effective New Philosophy: "No, it isn't true that my fatal disease is not so bad. It is bad. And it's almost as bad as it possibly could be—because it is almost sure to be fatal. But it could even be worse—I could be in more pain than I now feel. And it's not *awful* and *terrible* just because it's bad. There probably is damned little chance that they'll find a cure for it soon so that I'll get completely over it. I'd better not get my hopes up unrealistically and assume that they will find a magical cure. If the disease does continue, as I'd better expect that it will, I will not be able to do all the things that I did before I was stricken. No, but at the same time I will be able to do many of the things I enjoy. I'm certainly going to try to do as many as I can. I may never be *as* happy as I previously was. But I still, if I look for them, can find a number of real pleasures. Yes, I really do care that I am afflicted. It does matter. So I definitely care and, because I care, I'll do everything I can to live as long as I can with this ailment and to improve my condition.

Damning and Raging Against Other People

We previously noted that although you may rightly (self-helpfully) criticize and even damn some of the things that you do, it is wrong (self-defeating) to damn your entire self, your being, your essence. You, like all humans, do many wrong, stupid, and sometimes immoral things. But you are a *person who* does those things, and not a *rotten, stupid, evil, damnable person.* You'd better believe that you deserve to be alive and to enjoy yourself just because you exist, because you are human, and not because you have to do anything special to prove that you are worthy of life and enjoyment.

This also goes for other people—whether they are close to you or not. None of them are damnable, though they all do wrong, foolish, and sometimes criminal acts. For they, like you, are fallible humans. None of them, even when mentally deficient or severely disturbed, are subhuman. Some of them may be worthless to you, because they frustrate or harm you. When you find these kinds of people you may choose to avoid or refuse to have close relationships with them. You are even entitled to stay away from your relatives, or some of your previously close friends, if you find their companionship undesirable.

How about hating others? Is that also okay? When people keep acting badly or unfairly should you rightly hate them and try to punish them for their "sins"? No, according to REBT you'd better not. You can certainly hate what they do—or, sometimes, what they don't do. You can strongly prefer them to act well and, in your eyes, they act badly. Because you are entitled to have preferences and dislikes, it would be amazing if you did not sometimes hate what some people do and hate their sins of omission.

When, however, you hate *them* for their "bad" *acts* (acts that you view as "bad" because they are against your own wishes, goals and choices) you are evaluating them *as a whole* for some of their *behaviors*. Even when, for example, John acts badly to you on many occasions—steals from you or lies to you much of the time—he may act well to most other people, he may be very accomplished in some ways, and may have a good many friends who enjoy being with him. How, then, can you accurately label him as a *bad person* or a *rotten individual*? As we have noted previously, your view of him as a whole is a false generalization; and it really describes only a portion, and perhaps a very small portion, of his total thoughts, acts, and feelings. So you are unfair to John in some important respects when you detest, loathe, and feel angry at him, his personhood, rather than when you detest some of the things that he does.

Anger, rage, and fury, moreover, almost always get you, yourself, into various kinds of trouble. They stir up your gut and often give you poor psychosomatic consequences. They preoccupy you, ironically, with people whom you hate and would like to stay away from. They consume vast amounts of your time and energy and keep you from other productive and enjoyable pursuits. They often lead to return rage, punishment, fights, and vindictiveness from the people at whom you angrily act.

Anger, rage, and fury stem from the second great *must* that you concoct when people, according to your view, treat you or others badly. To enrage yourself at them, you usually start off sanely enough with, "They did the wrong thing and

I wish she or he had acted differently—fairly and justly, as people had better act."

This *preference* for others behaving nicely and fairly is, of course, okay. For why should you not strongly *wish* that they acted well? But if you really hold to it, this wish would only lead to your feeling highly displeased with others' poor behavior but not really incensed at and blatantly condemning them for it.

When you make yourself angry, you add to your wish this demand: "Because I would like other people to act fairly and justly, and because I am pretty sure that I, they, and others would be better off if they did act that way, they *absolutely should not* behave in an unfair and nasty manner; and because they are behaving the horrible way that they *utterly ought not* behave, they are really *rotten people!* I *can't stand* them, and I *have to* do something to make them stop and to punish them severely if they don't!"

Severe anger and rage, in other words, go along with your godlike demand that when people are (in your eyes) wrong they *absolutely must not* be the way that they indubitably are and that they *should be* denounced, forcefully made to stop, and damned by all good people at all times. Your intense feelings of rage can be tracked down to your irrational, unrealistic demands on others and you can definietly Dispute and refute these commands if you use REBT.[2]

It is important that you Dispute your damning of others, especially if you have a serious illness, because rage may help make you even sicker and perhaps help deteriorate your immune system. Moreover, the ravages of disease already place you under undue stress, and your rage will tend to increase this stress and will help turn off people who could help you cope with your ailment. Thus, you may tend to turn off friends and health professionals who might be most helpful.

How, specifically, can you Dispute your feelings of intense anger and the irrational Beliefs with which you usually create them? Here are some examples:

Damning and Raging Against Others: "Now that I am so sorely beset with the ravages of this horrible disease, people *absolutely should* recognize what an unusually bad condition I am in and they *must* be exceptionally considerate of me and never unduly treat me badly. They should always go out of their way to help me in whatever manner they can. Life is already so utterly unfair to me that they must never do anything to add to its unfairness. When they do know about my bad condition and they still treat me very shabbily they are horribly rotten individuals and they deserve to be severely damned and punished. If I can possibly get back at them I will do so if it's the last thing I do! Even if I do myself in while punishing them, it's definitely worth it for I will then have the great satisfaction of seeing them writhe and scream!"

Disputing: "Where is it written that people *absolutely should* recognize my very bad condition and that they *must* be exceptionally considerate of me and never treat me badly? Who says that they always *must* go out of their way to help me? Just because life is already so utterly unfair to me, how does this prove that people *absolutely should* never do anything to add to its unfairness? Even if they do know about my condition and still treat me shabbily, how does that make them horribly rotten individuals who deserve to be severely damned and punished? Will it really do me any good to spend my limited time and energy getting back at them? If I act vindictively will my satisfaction in seeing them writhe and scream really be worth it?"

Effective New Philosophy: "It's not written anywhere, except in my silly head, that people absolutely should recognize my bad condition and that they must be exceptionally considerate of me. I would very much like them to go out of their way to help me, but there is obviously no reason why they have to do this. Just because life is extremely unfair to me hardly proves that people should absolutely never do anything to add to its unfairness. When people treat me shabbily they are *acting* wrongly, but they are not *horrible people* who deserve to be damned and severely punished. Even if I could really get back at them I would take so much time and energy doing so, that it will do me much more harm than good to occupy myself in this vindictive way. I may get a little pleasure if I punish them, by seeing them writhe and scream, but that will hardly be worth it and will distract me from getting more satisfactory kinds of pleasure."

Disputing Irrational Beliefs That Change Is Impossible

Perhaps the worst form of neurosis is the staunch Belief, "Because I have tried to change my disturbed thoughts, feelings, and actions and I haven't been able to change them yet, I am sure that I can't change. So what's the use of even trying to do so?"

This irrational Belief is particularly pernicious, because it tends to end all progress in changing yourself and especially ends your efforts to keep working to make such progress. If you strongly believe that there is no way in which you can possibly change your neurotic behavior, you will almost certainly create a self-fulfilling propensity—and then, when you actually block your changing, you can "truthfully" tell yourself, "See! I knew it all along. I knew I can never change, and have to stay this miserable way that I am. Now that I have tried for quite a while and still haven't changed, that proves that my prediction was correct!" It proves, of course, not that your prediction was correct at the time you made it but that, subsequently, you have really worked your butt off to make it correct as of now. And it does not prove, as you most probably believe that it does, that therefore never, in any kind of foreseeable future, can you reverse this self-sabotaging prediction and then make it incorrect.

The profound view that you have really tried to change and because you have not done so yet there is no possibility that you can ever change, now or in the future, is stultifying and false, particularly because you probably never did try that hard to change. For while you were "trying," say, to modify your irrational Beliefs and your dysfunctional feelings and behavior, you were probably only half-trying and were continually interrupting your efforts with the views, "It's too hard to keep going on like this when I have to make such a difficult change," and "Obviously, the more I try and the more I see that I do not rapidly and completely change, this proves that it is impossible for me to do so, so I might as well quit trying."

Usually, when you try to change a habit—such as the habit of smoking or drinking too much—you very much want to get the result of changing it but you really don't want to go through the pain that you will almost necessarily feel as you go through the process of change. However, because you often would be ashamed to stop your self-modifying efforts without a good excuse to do so, your view that you can't change no matter how hard you keep trying serves as a good excuse to stop changing instead of trying even harder to change.

Because the highly irrational Belief that you can't change is so likely to result in a self-fulfilling prophecy and to "prove" that your Belief is "accurate," you had better work hard and persistently to uproot it whenever you find that you are sneaking it into your thinking. Whenever you feel exceptionally discouraged and depressed, and when you are stopping your previous effort to change, suspect that you have this iB, try to concretely see what form it takes, and then actively and forcefully keep Disputing it. Here, for example, are some examples that may help you do this.

Irrational Belief That You Can't Change: "I've really tried very hard to use REBT to change my irrational thinking and my disturbed feelings but I have hardly succeeded at all. Even when I do temporarily change them, I soon find that I have sunk back again and sometimes believe and feel them stronger than ever. It's pretty clear, therefore, that I really can't change my neurotic behavior. It could be, in my case, that my disturbed feelings just aren't connected with my thoughts and that they come about by themselves and can't be changed by modifying my thinking. Or it could be that my thoughts are the real culprit but that I've held them so strongly and persistently since my early childhood that I'll just never be able to change them. I know that if I forcibly change some of my actions—such as my avoiding taking my medication—and make myself do what I am afraid to do, that my irrational thinking will also significantly change. But that's much easier said than done! There's no way in which I can make myself change these phobic actions or inactions and make myself do the things that I feel so terrified of doing. So there's really no way out. I guess I'll just have to stay the way I am and somehow get by with my crazy thinking, feeling, and behaving."

Disputing: "Have I really tried that hard, and kept trying, to change my irrational thinking and my disturbed feelings? Because I easily sink back to these self-defeating emotions and behaviors, does that prove that I can't ever change them? Is it really true that my disturbed feelings aren't connected with my thoughts and that they just came about by themselves and cannot be changed by modifying my thinking? Or is it true that, even though my thoughts are mainly the real culprit, I've held them so persistently and strongly since my early childhood that I'll just never be able to change them? Can I prove that there's no way in which I can modify my phobic actions or inactions, make myself do the things that I am terrified of doing, and thereby significantly change my irrational thoughts that go with these phobias? Do I truly have no way to change but must stay the way I am and somehow get by with my crazy thinking, feeling, and acting?"

Effective New Philosophy: "Well, I have to some extent tried to change my irrational thinking and my disturbed behavior, but I can't honestly say that I've tried and kept trying that hard. Even though I easily keep sinking back to my self-defeating emotions and actions this only proves that it's quite difficult for me to change my neurotic behaviors but it hardly proves I can never change them. It is possible that some of my disturbed feelings are not connected with my thoughts but that they just spontaneously overwhelm me and therefore cannot be changed by modifying my thinking. But it is highly unlikely that they are all of this 'spontaneous' nature and much more likely that at least some of them are importantly connected with my thinking.

"Thinking and feeling normally are interrelated. So even if I spontaneously turned up with disturbed feelings I would then find it almost impossible not to think about those feelings, and thereby probably exacerbate them. Pure feelings may never exist; but if they do they would last for only a few seconds, and then I would think about having them. So I'd better face the fact that to some extent my disturbances go along with and are somewhat created by my thinking; and therefore I'd better keep working to see exactly how this is so and to change my thinking as well as my feeling. Although I may find it very difficult to modify my irrational thinking and may also find it very hard to force myself to act against my phobic reactions and to help change my irrational thinking that goes with these actions, I again will only find it difficult, but hardly impossible, to do this. My terror about acting against my phobias will tend to deter me from doing so, but no matter how terrified I feel about taking my medication, or doing other frightening acts, I can still force myself very uncomfortably to do them in spite of my terror. I'll never be able to comfortably get over some of my phobias. But I can still make myself do so uncomfortably, and I will hardly die in the course of my bringing on this discomfort. If I keep making myself uncomfortable, by working against my disturbed thoughts, feelings, and actions, I in all probability will find a way out, a way—or several ways—to change them."

Disputing Phonyism About Changing Oneself

As Maxie Maultsby, Jr. and a number of other psychotherapists have pointed out, once you begin to change your ways and to think, feel, and act radically differently than you have been doing for a long time, you often make yourself feel "strange" and very uncomfortable about your "new you," and tend to think it is false and that you'd better disown it and go back to your old comfortable rut.[3] Thus, you may tell yourself, "Now that I'm getting myself to take more risks of failing at important tasks and at being rejected by people whose approval I used to think I absolutely must have, this isn't really me. I'm probably being dishonest and merely acting as if I don't care that much about succeeding and about being disapproved, when, if I were honest about this, I would admit that I really do care much more than I am admitting I do. You know, I think that I'm really a phony! And that's really bad, to pretend and to be a phony like this!"

To think that you are a phony while you are changing yourself, that your changes are really a sad pretense, and that if people realized how phony you are they would hate you and deservedly boycott you is, as you can well imagine, one of the worst blocks to changing and keeping yourself changed. Joanie, for example, hated her mother-in-law, who was dying of lung cancer, and who, at the insistence of Joanie's husband, Don, had come to live with the couple in what was predicted to be the last few months of her life. But Joanie came for several sessions of REBT and learned that her hatred of her mother-in-law did not exactly stem from this woman's nasty behavior to Joanie during the last twelve years but that, rather, it stemmed from Joanie's convincing herself that her husband's mother, Sarah, had *no right* to treat her that way, that she *absolutely must not* do so, and that she was *a horrible person* for acting the way she did for those twelve years.

Joanie, after a few REBT sessions, understood this, and saw that she could change her grandiose demands that her mother-in-law must be exactly the way that Joanie thought she should be, and she started giving up these demands and changing them into realistic preferences. To her amazement, her great hostility toward her mother-in-law vanished, she forgave her almost completely, and she began to feel sympathy for Sarah's plight, and to feel even some degree of love for her—especially when she remembered that Sarah had done a fine job of rearing Don and helping him become an unusually kind and loving husband and father.

Practically all Joanie's close friends, who had heard her complain for years about Sarah, were skeptical about her new sympathy for her mother-in-law and Joanie began to doubt the sincerity of her feelings and to think, "Maybe I'm just *pretending* that I love her. Maybe I'm just a phony. My God—suppose I am? Wouldn't that be awful! My God—just a phony!"

Going back to her REBT, however, Joanie, was able to conclude: "No, I don't think my new feeling for Sarah is phony. She *isn't* no good, though some of her *habits* are pretty bad. And me, too. If my thoughts and feelings are at times phony—which they could of course be—they don't *make me* a phony person. Just a person *with* some pretense. So let me look at my feelings more closely, to see how false they sometimes may be."

Using REBT in this manner, Joanie decided that her new feelings for Sarah were usually genuine, only occasionally put on, and that she was hardly a *phony person*.

Suppose that you (or one of your friends) has a fatal disease and has destructive, irrational Beliefs relating to phonyism. Finding these Beliefs is not very difficult, because the person who has them feels like a phony and is obviously telling himself or herself something to create that feeling. So these iB's can normally easily be found; and they can then be Disputed along the following lines.

Irrational Phonyism Beliefs: "In spite of my having a fatal disease I am really not having a very rough time of living and being fairly happy. I can accept the fact that my life will be shorter than it otherwise would be but that's not awful and I can still get along reasonably well until my actual demise. And I can still show the people who love me that I am doing all right and can help them avoid endless pain and horror over the fact that I will not be around too long. However, maybe I am just putting all of this on. Maybe I am kidding myself and others and only pretending that I accept my condition when I really am terribly upset about it underneath and am just denying that I am. If so, I am really a phony and I'd better face the fact that I am and not pretend that I'm not. What a mess! Here I am claiming that I am accepting my unkind fate when I really am not accepting it at all. And I am greatly misleading many of the people who are really concerned about me. How hypocritical! How rotten of me! Pretending like this, and turning myself into a phony is surely one of the worst things I can do. It really is most dishonest and shameful! Why don't I just let everyone know what a phony I am? That at least would be honest and would get me out of this terrible fix I am putting myself in. Then I shall die as myself, an honest person!"

Disputing: "Where is the evidence that I am only pretending to accept my fatal illness and that I am dishonestly putting on a good face about it to those who care for me? How do I know, in spite of my seeming acceptance of my unkind fate, that I am really denying it underneath and am truly very upset about it when I am pretending that I am not upset? Even if I am pretending and even if I am denying my true feelings about my illness, how does this make me a complete phony? Why is it shameful if I am really being dishonest in this fashion? Even if I am acting somewhat dishonestly and falsely, do I have to confess this to everyone I know? Will that kind of superhonesty do any good for them, for me, or for anyone? In order to be myself, do I have to be 100% honest to myself and to others all of the time?"

New Effective Philosophy: "I don't see any real evidence that I am only pretending to accept my fatal illness and that I am dishonestly putting on a good face about it to those who care for me. As far as I can tell I do really accept it—though not 100% of the time and not always completely. Perhaps I really am more upset about it than I care to consciously face and perhaps I am at times in something of a state of denial—though I don't think I am most of the time.

But even if I am at times pretending to be much less upset than I really underlyingly am, that doesn't make me a complete phony, but only a person who sometimes acts in a phony way and sometimes really faces grim reality. If I do at times act dishonestly in regard to my fatal illness, that has it disadvantages and its limitations but it is not shameful and it does not make me a bad person. It merely proves that I am still a fallible human who sometimes behaves less well than I would like to behave. But it hardly proves that I absolutely must never behave badly and that I am a shameful, worthless person when I do behave that way. If I do think that I am acting somewhat dishonestly in regard to my acceptance of my fatal illness, or in any other respect, I obviously don't have to confess this to everyone I know. I may tell a few close friends about my dishonesty but it would probably do much more harm than good if I routinely told all of them about it. It would be good if I could be 100% honest to myself and to others all of the time, but this is a utopian concept and it would be impractical to always under all conditions live up to it. So if I do think that I am acting falsely about my illness or anything else I will confront myself about this and try to face things more honestly. But I will not necessarily go to the other extreme and make myself be compulsively honest. I will work on it and do my best to give up my phony attitudes and behaviors, and while I am doing this I shall try to wisely decide just how much I'd better confess them to others with whom I have been somewhat dishonest. Honesty is usually the best policy, but not in all circumstances!"

Notes to Chapter 8

1. Taylor, 1990.
2. Baldon & Ellis, 1993; DiGiuseppe, 1990; Dryden, 1984, 1990; Dryden & Gordon, 1991; Dryden & Yankura, 1992; Ellis, 1977a, 1985c, 1988a, 1992f; Ellis & DiMattia, 1991; Epictetus, 1890; Epstein, 1993; Hauck, 1974, 1992; Rogers, 1961; Vernon, 1989; Walen, DiGiuseppe & Dryden, 1992; Wolfe, 1992; Young, 1974.
3. Maultsby, 1984.

9

Other Cognitive or Thinking Ways of Coping with Fatal Illness

As we have mentioned several times in this book, Rational Emotive Behavior Therapy (REBT) is an integrative form of psychotherapy that uses a large number of cognitive, emotional, and behavioral methods to help people overcome their disturbances about unfortunate Activating Events (A's) in their lives. Yes, including their, or their close friends', being afflicted with a fatal disease.

We have been reviewing some of the main irrational Beliefs (iB's) that people subscribe to when they consciously or unconsciously upset themselves and have been demonstrating how you (and your afflicted friends) can look for, find, and Dispute these dysfunctional Beliefs. We shall now describe a number of other cognitive, philosophic, or thinking methods that are commonly used in REBT to change disturbed thoughts and feelings. When you are disturbed about practically anything you can use these therapeutic methods. Though they are not guaranteed to help, literally thousands of people, in the course of hundreds of research studies, have benefited by using them.[1]

Rational Coping Self-Statements

When you think irrationally and unduly upset yourself about the unfortunate Activating Events (A's) of your life, you can find your irrational Beliefs (iB's) and actively Dispute (D) them until you reduce or surrender them. When you do so, you arrive at an Effective New Philosophy (E) that enables you to think more self-helpingly and to improve your dysfunctional feelings and actions. You can write down your E's or record them and use them as rational coping self-statements, which you can repeat to yourself many times until you really start to believe them and to act on them. Suppose, for example, one of your relatives has AIDS and you view this as "absolutely horrible," are convinced that a terrible condition like this should never exist, and believe that you can't stand thinking about this awful situation. Using REBT you look at your irrational Beliefs (iB's) and actively dispute them:

Why is it absolutely horrible that my relative has AIDS? Where is the evidence that a terrible condition like this should never exist? Is it really true that I can't stand even thinking about this awful situation?

You think about the answers to these disputes and you come up with some *Effective New Philosophies (E's)*. You put these E's into simple positive statements and write them down as follows:

"My relative's having AIDS is bad and unfortunate. But it is not 'horrible' because it is not *totally bad*, not as bad as it possibly *could* be, and is certainly not *more than* 100% bad."

"A very bad condition like AIDS should exist because it does exist, and my relative has to have it when he actually has it. This is exceptionally harmful, but deplorable things like this do exist. How rough! But whatever shall be shall be! I'll never *like* thinking about this grim situation but I definitely can stand doing so. If I keep facing it and thinking about it I may be able to help my relative cope with it and think of things that would help other AIDS victims. Let me do, not stew!"

Once you write down these Effective New Philosophies and firmly keep repeating them to yourself you will find that you are often able to improve, and restate them in a catchy, succinct way that will help you, and possibly other people, to cope with this and other tragic situations. For examples:

"AIDS is a really rotten condition but it can be accepted and coped with."

"Whatever exists should, right now, exist—no matter *how* bad it is."

"I cannot change many brutal situations but I can cope with them!"

"I always *can* stand what I don't like—if I strongly *believe* that I can stand it!"

If you will create coping statements like these, actually think them through (rather than unthinkingly parrot them), and keep repeating them to yourself and noting how helpful they are, you will find that you start to really believe them. Second, you will dwell much less on the "terrible" Activating Events that you encounter. Third, you will start automatically using them when you meet up with "horrible" adversities. Fourth, you will start to feel self-helpingly about "awful" A's—that is, feel sorry, sad, and displeased and only rarely feel panicked, depressed about them. Fifth, you will tend to do what you can do to change these A's and may figure out some improvements that you could not previously come up with because you were so horrified about them. Sixth, you will be able to help others who experience "horrible" Activating Events and to teach them to use their own rational coping self-statements.

So try this REBT method. As new bad situations arise, figure out a list of rational coping statements that seem to work, write them down, and keep using them several times a day, until you really believe and act on them.

General coping self-statements have been used for many years—by philosophers, by writers, by members of self-help groups (such as Alcoholics Anonymous, Rational Recovery, and Recovery Inc.), and by REBT therapists and their clients. These general statements apply to a great many potentially "horrible" situations and can be used to make yourself healthfully sorry but not desperately miserable about them. REBT writings, such as those of Albert Ellis, Paul Hauck, Howard Young, Windy Dryden, Jack Gordon, Jack Trimpey, Kishor Phadke, Janet Wolfe, Ann Vernon, and Bill Borcherdt include a good number of these statements.[2] Here, for example, are a few of them:

A hassle is not a horror.

Masturbation is good and delicious but musturbation is evil and pernicious.

Anything that's worth doing is worth doing badly—yes, badly.

Shouldhood leads to shithood.

I always have a right to be wrong.

Let me rate people's doings but not the doers.

Give me the courage to change what I can change, to accept what I cannot change, and the wisdom to know the difference.

When I think I have to be perfect I am behaving like an almost perfect ass.

People will act the way they want and not the way I want them to act.

When I demand that things always must go well for me, I am pretending that I am God.

I do not need what I want but only think that I do.

My life has been filled with terrible misfortunes—most of which never happened.

Whining very rarely leads to winning.

No one can insult me without my permission.

Genuis is nine-tenths perspiration and one-tenth inspiration.

The perfect time to do something important is immediately.

Short-range hedonism is antihedonism.

Only I can make myself enraged.

I had better try to *be* myself instead of trying to *prove* myself.

I *can* stand what I don't like.

Frustration will rarely kill me.

Win an argument, lose a friend.

Loneliness is usually being alone plus feelings of shithood.

Being a good or a bad person is a matter of definition.

Tyrants are fallible, screwed-up people who behave very badly, but are not really bad, horrible people.

Accept the sinner but not the sin.

No matter how many alcoholic relatives you have, liquor rarely jumps out of the bottle and pours itself down your throat.

Self-correction is light years removed from self-condemnation.

God helps those who help themselves.

REBT is simple but it's often not easy!

How funny it is to claim that you can change other people and that you cannot possibly change yourself!

When you or any of your close friends or relatives are

afflicted with a fatal disease you can create a good many rational coping self-statements. Here are a few suggestions:

Even fatal diseases are not absolute horrors—unless you view them as such.

A serious disease makes life less enjoyable—but not totally unenjoyable.

Whining about my (or my friend's) fatal ailment will not make it any better.

I'll never like having AIDS or any other fatal illness but I can make myself gracefully lump it.

I don't have to obsessively worry about my (or my friend's) fatal illness but I can constructively think about what I can do to help deal with it and improve it.

Just because I have this incurable ailment is why I'd better figure out how to have some real enjoyments while I am still capable of having them.

People have the right to be inconsiderate of me, no matter how much I am suffering. In fact, many of them are talented at being inconsiderate!

Just because I am suffering from a serious ailment does not mean that other people must recognize this and be nicer to me. They still behave the way they do and never have to act the way I would like them to act.

When others neglect me and leave me alone I can still refuse to make myself utterly lonely and miserable and can find things that I can enjoy by myself.

The world should be quite unfair to me, as it is right now, because that's the way it frequently is. Injustice is in many ways the human condition.

If I demand that life be better than it now is, it is most unlikely that the universe will listen.

If people hate me because I have a fatal illness, they have a real emotional problem.

People who run away from me mainly because I have a serious illness are not the best kind of people to have in my life.

There are times when I really don't like being around or taking care of my friends who have serious illnesses but it won't kill me to help them and I can sometimes get real satisfactions from doing so.

Whining about my illness will not get me a winning life.

I never have to make myself feel guilty just because I am in good health and some of my friends are suffering from serious diseases.

Even if I foolishly did things to contract my fatal illness, I am never a rotten, undeserving person. My acts were stupid but I still deserve to be as happy as I can possibly make myself for the remaining days of my life.

Just because I am seriously afflicted, I'd better try harder than most people to have a reasonably happy existence and had better not complain that it is horrible that I have to try so hard.

Yes, I may have acted badly and put myself in my present state but I still deserve to have others help me and devote some time to me, even when I cannot equally serve them.

Referenting

People mainly become addicted—or addict themselves—to bad habits, including obsessing about the grim aspects of their lives, because they focus upon, and hence keep referenting, the advantages of indulging in these habits and refuse to focus upon—or referent—their disadvantages.

Suppose, for example, that you "know" full well that smoking is very dangerous to your health, and that it also annoys and alienates other people. Yet you still keep smoking like a fiend. What's going on in your head every time you lift a cigarette to your mouth?

We can easily guess that you are, at that time, thinking about the pleasures of smoking: the good taste of the cigarette, the relaxation you get while smoking, the time out you are taking from other onerous pursuits, etc. And we can be pretty sure that you are not focusing on the pains that go with smoking: the money you are spending, the valuable time you are wasting, the turning off of some of your friends and partners, the ravages of emphysema and lung cancer, the risk of cardiac problems, etc.

So your "smoking habit" is largely your habit of concentrating on the gains rather than the pains of indulging in cigarettes. If you really kept thinking, practically all the time, of the great disadvantages of smoking, you would probably smoke much less. In fact, when you do stop smoking and go through painful withdrawal symptoms, you manage to bear the pain by making yourself think, think, think about the "agonies" rather than the "delights" of smoking; and if you do that forcefully enough, you will be able to cut out cigarettes.[3]

Referenting, of course, can be done in a false or misleading manner. Thus, you can make yourself keep thinking about the disadvantages of smoking, but can insist that they are slight, that they apply to other people but not to you, and that they even include advantages (for example, "The more money I spend on cigarettes, the less I'll spend on booze, so smoking will keep me sober"). Only if you do honest referenting of the pains of indulging in a bad habit will you be likely to help yourself.

In regard to fatal diseases like AIDS or cancer, you can use referenting to ward them off in the first place. Thus, you can make a list of the great dangers of these diseases and, every time you are foolishly risking acquiring one, you can look at this list to help you stop taking such risks. If, for example, you strongly keep in mind the enormous problems of having AIDS, you can make sure that you routinely use condoms when you have sex, stop being the receptor in anal intercourse, avoid taking drugs, etc. The more you referent these dangers, and keep going over them in your head, the fewer risks you will tend to take about acquiring AIDS, lung cancer, and other potentially fatal diseases.

Suppose you already have an HIV infection or AIDS, or suppose one of your close friends has it? Can you then use referenting to good advantage? Definitely, yes—especially to helping take good care of yourself and your friend medically. Thus, you list the great disadvantages of your (or his or her) neglecting physical symptoms, shunning proper medical attention, eating improperly, getting insufficient rest, and working too hard. Again, the more you read this list and focus on the hazards of neglecting your health, the more you are likely to take care of it.

The same with your emotional attitudes. If you keep worrying obsessively about your physical condition, depressing yourself about your limitations, enraging yourself about how your friends neglect you, and pitying yourself for your sad condition, indulging in such inappropriate feelings will sabotage your coping with your illness and may help deplete your immune system so that your disease may intensify. But if you acknowledge that destructive emotions do not just automatically overwhelm you but that *you* largely bring them on you can then referent thoughts that will help you change these feelings.

For example, you can first make a list of the dangers of your needlessly upsetting yourself about your ailment (or about anything else)—a list that shows how your upsetness will tend to make your physical problems worse, will sap your time and energies, will interfere with your taking care of yourself medically, will turn off potentially helpful friends, etc. That list will probably encourage you to give real consideration, and perhaps use REBT, to tackle and overcome your emotional difficulties.

A second list that you can make could be a list of the irrational Beliefs (iB's) that you commonly use to upset yourself with—iB's like, "I'm no damned good for having got myself into this terrible fix!" and "Life under this dreadful condition will deprive me of all joy and make me incessantly miserable!" Review this list to remind yourself of the self-defeating ideas you are telling yourself. You can also have a third list, as we showed in the preceding section of this chapter, that includes several rational coping self-statements that you can use to combat your dysfunctional Beliefs.

Because you can referent both negative and positive items, you can make still another list of the specific things that you can do to help yourself with your physical condition and with the other aspects of your life. You can even make a list of possible pleasures and involvements that you can resort to, such as the list in the Appendix to *A Guide to Personal Happiness* by Albert Ellis and Irving Becker.[4]

If you really put your mind to it you can referent many bad consequences of your self-sabotaging thoughts, feelings, and actions, so that by steadily going over these (sometimes several times a day) you will keep them solidly in mind and decrease the irrationalities. You can also referent a number of different thoughts and actions that keep reminding you of things to do to ameliorate your condition and to lead a happier existence in spite of your limitations.

In sum, don't let your mind "naturally" focus on the "good" things about your harmful behaviors; and don't let it "naturally" dwell on self-sabotaging thoughts. Make lists of some of the destructive and the beneficial things that you do. Keep referring to these lists until you sink them into your consciousness and start acting self-helpfully instead of self-defeatingly. Keep referenting in these useful ways.

Cognitive or Thinking Homework

REBT firmly encourages homework, because people not only think crookedly, feel disturbed, and act poorly when they upset themselves about almost anything, but they also do so repetitively, *keep practicing* disturbed homework. Therefore, although they quickly see how they are upsetting themselves and may begin to change, they have to keep practicing, over and over again, new thoughts, feelings, and behaviors. Homework is the very essence of their changing and remaining changed.

REBT encourages you how to do several kinds of cognitive homework. Let us now describe some of them.

Monitoring Irrational Beliefs and Their Disputation

One of the common cognitive homework assignments we suggest to our clients during their first session is, "Whenever you feel emotionally disturbed or are acting against your best interests, assume that you have (or are imagining having) some unfortunate Activating Event (A) that precedes your disturbed feeling or behavior (that is, your Consequence, at point C) and assume that you have both rational and irrational Beliefs (iB's) about your Activating Event and that it is your musturbatory (irrational) rather than your preferential (rational) Beliefs at point B that largely create your disturbed Consequence. If you assume that your disturbance includes these ABC's, you will usually be able to quickly find your irrational Beliefs (iB's) and then go on to Dispute them at point D."

If you start doing this kind of cognitive homework, you can either do it in your head or you can write down the ABC's of your upsetness; thereby you may clearly see what you are thinking and feeling, and start to change your iB's. Thus, if you feel distinctly depressed because a couple of your friends have recently come down with AIDS, you can review the ABC's of your depression as follows:

Activating Event (A): "I now see that two of my close friends have been afflicted with AIDS."

Rational Beliefs (rB's): "I don't like this news. I wish that my friends were not afflicted. How unfortunate! Let me see what I can do to help them."

Irrational Belief (iB's): "My friends never should have been afflicted! How *awful*! I can't bear it! What a rotten world this is, where so many people are now getting AIDS and no cure for it is in sight. Human existence is much worse than it *should* be!"

Consequences (C's): Feelings of depression and hopelessness. A tendency to cop out and avoid seeing your afflicted friends.

You then keep going over these ABC's of your depression in your head and perhaps write them down or put them on your computer. Every time you think about your afflicted friends and feel depressed you review these ABC's, to make sure that you really understand what is going on and clearly see how you are creating irrational Beliefs (iB's) and how you are disturbing yourself with them.

You then try to actively Dispute (at point D) your iB's by yourself, with some of your other friends, with a self-help group, with a therapist, or with a therapy group; and you keep doing this kind of Disputing (as we have shown you how to do in Chapters 6, 7, and 8, until you are able to come up with, and to solidly convince yourself, of Effective New Philosophies (at point E) that help make you feel appropriately sad, sorry, and displeased with what is happening to your friends with AIDS but not to feel seriously depressed. You can keep going through this kind of cognitive homework, in your head, on paper, on a blackboard, on a computer, or in other suitable ways, until you devise an Effective New Philosophy and really are inclined to believe it.

Using REBT Self-Help Forms

Several REBT practitioners have devised cognitive homework forms that you can keep using to go through the ABCDE's involved in your disturbed feelings and behaviors. These forms usually outline the ABCDE's; allow suitable spaces for you to fill in your own Activating Events, rational and irrational Beliefs, emotional and behavioral Conseuences; show suitable ways of Disputing your iB's; and encourage Effective New Philosophies when you do scientific Disputing. The one used at the Institute for Rational-Emotive Therapy in New York is the regular RET Self-Help Form, shown in Figure 1. Another popular form is that devised by one of the main supervisors of REBT and the writer and editor of many books on Rational Emotive Behavior Therapy, Dr. Windy Dryden, who has been appointed the first full professor of Counseling in Great Britain.

Psychoeducational Methods

When I (AE) first created and started to use REBT in January, 1955, I was still influenced by the psychoanalytic therapy that I had been previously using. So I mainly did individual psychotherapy and only occasionally worked with groups or with several family members at the same time. I also rarely used psychoeducational materials with my clients.

Soon after I started to do REBT, however, I realized that its main principles and practices were so clear-cut that they could be taught in books and pamphlets as well as sessions with my clients. So I began to write articles and books for the public (as well as for the profession) and published my first book on REBT, *How to Live With a Neurotic* in 1957.[5] I encouraged my clients to read this book, as well as several of my articles, and found that many of them received great help from this material. In fact, some of them learned to understand and to use REBT better from the written material than they did from my face-to-face sessions with them!

RET SELF-HELP FORM

Institute for Rational-Emotive Therapy
45 East 65th Street, New York, NY 10021
(212) 535-0822

(A) ACTIVATING EVENTS, thoughts, or feelings that happened just before I felt emotionally disturbed or acted self-defeatingly:

(C) CONSEQUENCE OR CONDITION—disturbed feeling or self-defeating behavior—that I produced and would like to change:

(B) BELIEFS—Irrational BELIEFS (IBs) leading to my CONSEQUENCE (emotional disturbance or self-defeating behavior). Circle all that apply to these ACTIVATING EVENTS (A).	(D) DISPUTES for each circled Irrational BELIEF (iB). Examples: *"Why MUST I do very well?" "Where is it written that I am a BAD PERSON?" "Where is the evidence that I MUST be approved or accepted?"*	(E) EFFECTIVE RATIONAL BELIEFS (RBs) to replace my Irrational BELIEFS (iBs). Examples: "I'd PREFER to do very well *but I don't* HAVE TO." "I am a PERSON WHO acted badly, *not* a BAD PERSON." *"There is no evidence* that I HAVE TO be approved, though I would LIKE to be."
1. I MUST do well or very well!		
2. I am a BAD OR WORTHLESS PERSON when I act weakly or stupidly.		
3. I MUST be approved or accepted by people I find important!		
4. I NEED to be loved by someone who matters to me a lot!		
5. I am a BAD, UNLOVABLE PERSON if I get rejected.		
6. People MUST treat me fairly and give me what I NEED!		

(OVER)

7. People MUST live up to my expectations or it is TERRIBLE!		
8. People who act immorally are undeserving, ROTTEN PEOPLE!		
9. I CAN'T STAND really bad things or very difficult people!		
10. My life MUST have few major hassles or troubles.		
11. It's AWFUL or HORRIBLE when major things don't go my way!		
12. I CAN'T STAND IT when life is really unfair!		
13. I NEED a good deal of immediate gratification and HAVE to feel miserable when I don't get it!		
Additional Irrational Beliefs:		

(F) FEELINGS and BEHAVIORS I experience after arriving at my EFFECTIVE RATIONAL BELIEFS: _____

I WILL WORK HARD TO REPEAT MY EFFECTIVE RATIONAL BELIEFS FORCEFULLY TO MYSELF ON MANY OCCASIONS SO THAT I CAN MAKE MYSELF LESS DISTURBED NOW AND ACT LESS SELF-DEFEATINGLY IN THE FUTURE.

One client, for instance, told me, "I really didn't understand some of the things you were telling me about upsetting myself when my boss kept screaming at me, and was
sure that he was upsetting me by his terrible criticism. But
when I read *How to Live With a Neurotic* I could see right
away that he was wrong in screaming but that I was foolishly
taking his criticism too seriously and really *upsetting myself*
by what I told myself. I saw that his words could not make
me angry and self-hating unless I did something with them
in my own head, and therefore used them in a self-disturbing fashion." A good many of my other early REBT clients
gave similar reports; and many of them also said that when
they gave REBT educational materials to their family members or their business associates, these people also often
benefited considerably by reading this material, even though
most of them had had no therapy experience.

I found that the same thing happened with my public
talks and with my radio and TV appearances. Not only did
my clients benefit from them but other members of my audience told me that they used some of the REBT practices
that I had spoken about and helped overcome their disturbances. After I gave a talk on "How to Improve Your Sex and
Love Relationships" to an audience of a thousand people at
Cooper Union Auditorium in New York and broadcast over a
New York radio station, twenty-one people called or wrote to
say that they now felt less anxious and were doing better at
meeting and relating to heterosexual or gay partners.

When the Institute for Rational-Emotive Therapy
opened its building in New York in April, 1965, I instituted a
series of talks, workshops, and other public presentations on
REBT that made the Institute into one of the main pioneer
growth centers in the world—which it still is to this day. I especially started my regular Friday Night Workshops, where
at 8:30 PM every Friday I give live demonstrations of REBT
with members of the audience who volunteer to come up to
the platform with me and bring up a real emotional or behavioral problem. So for about forty-five minutes first I, and

later a number of other people in the audience, talk to the volunteers and show them how to use REBT in solving their problems. I make a cassette recording of the public demonstration and give the cassette to each volunteer to take home for repeated listening.

A study that I have been doing of the results of these workshop sessions on Friday evenings shows that most of the participants are distinctly helped by the public airing of their problems and that a good many of them keep using REBT principles long after their workshop presentation has ended. What I find even more fascinating is that literally hundreds of the audience members over the years have come up to me after the workshop and said something like, "You know, Dr. Ellis, I've come to your Friday Night Workshop several times; and although I have not had the courage yet to come up to the platform and present one of my emotional problems to you and the audience, I find that most of the volunteers who do present have troubles very similar to some of my own. So by listening as you show them how to use REBT, and by doing the same kind of thinking and action that you urge them to do, I have considerably helped myself and I want to thank you for the help you have given me in this way. I intend to keep coming and to get some of my friends to come with me, for we find your workshops exceptionally useful."

Because REBT educational material can be very effective, the Institute's clinic recommends to its clients that they read REBT self-help pamphlets and books, attend talks and workshops, and listen to the audiovisual material that the Institute produces and distributes. I have received thousands of letters from people all over the world stating that they have received considerable help from REBT self-help written and audiovisual materials.

That is why we have written this book: To present some of the most popular REBT self-help teachings, so that you can understand and use them on your own or together with some regular REBT therapy sessions. We have included in the References a list of starred items that you may find particularly useful to read, listen to, or view. You can send for the latest free catalogue of the Institute for Rational-Emotive Therapy, 45 East 65th Street, New York, NY 10021-6593, (212) 535-0822, FAX (212) 249-3582. This catalogue includes materials and current presentations on REBT in New York and gives the addresses of the main REBT institutes throughout the world.

The more REBT self-help materials you use, the better you may learn the main REBT principles and practices and become more adept at using them. If you have relatives, friends, and associates who have their own emotional problems, you may find that they, too, can be considerably helped by reading and listening to REBT materials.

Correcting Your Self-Disturbing Language

As Benjamin Whorf, Alfred Korzybski, and other students of language have pointed out, when humans use language, they tend to put their disturbed thinking into the conventions of this language, and then their language itself helps them to think more destructively. Korzybski founded general semantics by realizing in the 1920's and 1930's that improper use of the English (and other) languages tends to render us unsane though not insane; and that if we would consistently use language accurately we would avoid much of our personal and social unsanity. Following some of his ideas, REBT has always encouraged people to watch their ways of talking to themselves and to others and thus to cut down on their irrational and self-defeating thinking.[6]

Suppose, for example, that you poorly take care of your physical condition when you are stricken with a serious disease. You can accurately tell yourself, "I am failing in this important respect and I'd better acknowledge this and arrange to stop failing." You thereby assess your performance and help yourself improve it.

But suppose you then add, "Because I am failing in this

important respect I am a rotten failure! That proves that I'm worthless. Because I'm so imcompetent and worthless, I'll never be able to do better!" If you speak to yourself in this inaccurate manner, you will not only feel sorry and disappointed about your failing, and push yourself to correct it, but you will also feel depressed and self-hating and will discourage yourself from changing. In this instance, not only your thinking is self-defeating but the very language that you use helps you to think badly. For it includes inaccurate terms like "I am a rotten failure," "I'm incompetent and worthless," and "I'll never be able to do better."

Why are these terms inaccurate and misleading? Because they are false generalizations which the English language, and practically all other modern languages, "naturally" include. Thus, your phrase, "I am a rotten failure," strongly implies, "Because I failed this time, I am basically inadequate and I will always be doomed to fail at all important tasks." Your term, "I'm incompetent and worthless," is an even worse generalization, because it implies that you *cannot* do well in any respect and that you therefore deserve only pain and no pleasure for the rest of your life. Your term, "I'll never be able to do better," is another false generalization, because no matter how poorly you have been doing there is a good chance, if you keep trying to do well, that you eventually will do better. It is even probable that you will later do well most of the time at this project and at other important tasks that you undertake.

Why does the English language (and practically all other languages) include these kinds of self-sabotaging, false generalizations? No one knows why exactly, but the REBT answer is that virtually all humans, especially when they are children, tend to think in these inaccurate ways, and that therefore their languages, which are designed to reflect the ways they think, include terms that encourage false generalizing. If people always thought straightly, in accordance with what is going on (WIGO) in their world, they would probably not incorporate unrealistic generalizations into their languages and would make themselves conform better to reality.

David Bourland, following Korzybski and general semantics, has attempted to modify the English language and has invented what he calls E-prime, a form of English that eliminates all forms of the verb, "to be," and thereby minimizes the *is of identity* and the *is of predication* that Korzybski opposed. The *is of identity* arises when you identify yourself with some of your behavior and tell yourself, "Because I have done badly in this respect, I am a bad person." The *is of predication* arises when you say things like "The rose is red." Actually, both these is's are inaccurate, because you are a *person who acted badly this time*, but certainly not one who will act thoroughly badly all the time; and the rose has what we call redness right now but tomorrow it may fade and become gray, black, or what-not.

How can you use general semantics to help make yourself less emotionally disturbed? Well, you can correct your inaccurate language and make it more precise. By doing so you will not completely think accurately all the time and eliminate your emotional problems. But you can help yourself by using the REBT method of tending to your language, observing its inaccuracies, and making it more accurate.

Thus, when you note that you are telling yourself, "I performed badly at this important task, and that makes me a bad person," you can change this to, "I performed badly at this important task and that is unfortunate, so I'd better try to correct my ways. But I am merely a *person who* acted badly this time and I refuse to wrongly label myself as a *bad person*, a *worthless individual*, or a *rotten human*."

More specifically, in regard to disturbances you may feel when you or one of your close friends has a fatal disease, you may look at some of your inaccurate language and correct it as follows:

Inaccurate Self-Statement: "When I don't take care of my health, as I *absolutely should do*, I am an idiot!"

More Accurate Self-Statement: "When I don't take care

of my health, as I preferably should do, I am acting idiotically but am a reasonably sensible person with a good amount of intelligence who can see this error and work at acting much less idiotically."

Inaccurate Self-Statement: "People who do not treat me considerately when I am suffering so much from this ailment make me very angry. They are really very rotten individuals!"

More Accurate Self-Statement: "People who do not treat me considerately when I am suffering so much from this ailment are acting much worse than I would like to see them act and may be *behaving* badly but are not *rotten people*. I choose to anger myself about them."

Inaccurate Self-Statement: "My friend's fatal illness is no good and therefore *should not* exist."

More Accurate Self-Statement: "My friend's fatal illness has many poor aspects but cannot be said to be totally no good, because it also maybe has some neutral or good aspects, and there is no way of proving that in all respects it will be no good for all time to come. It *preferably* shouldn't exist, because it does more harm than good and he and I would be better off if it didn't exist. But it should exist right now because it obviously does exist and there is no way of curing it at this time."

Inaccurate Self-Statement: "It makes me very angry when I see that the government is neglectful and is not doing half as much as it could do about fighting and preventing AIDS and about doing much more research so that we can find a cure for it as soon as possible!"

More Accurate Self-Statement: "I choose to make myself very angry when I see the government is neglectful and is not doing half as much as it could do about fighting and preventing AIDS and about doing much more research so that we can find a cure for it as soon as possible. I am demanding, instead of strongly wanting, the government to act better in this respect; and I can choose to keep my wishes that it do so, while giving up my demands, so that I then make myself displeased and disappointed about the govern-

ment's actions without enraging myself about its wrong behavior. I can then try more effectively to get the government
to change."

Inaccurate Self-Statement: "Because my having AIDS
and some of my close friends having it is so painful and so
debilitating, we absolutely *must* find a cure for it quickly and
I *need* this cure to be found soon."

More Accurate Self-Statement: "Because my having
AIDS and some of my close friends having it is so painful
and so debilitating, it would be highly *preferable* if we found
a cure for it quickly, but there is no *necessity* that we find it.
I very much *want* that result to occur but there is no way in
which I absolutely *need* it! Now let me do my best to aid the
search for a cure."

Using REBT with Other People

As many religious groups have discovered over the centuries, and as several leading educators—such as John
Dewey—have pointed out, once you begin to teach something to other people, you tend to learn it better yourself
and to practice some of the teachings that you may be
preaching. This especially is true of REBT. As we have discovered over our many years of showing people how to use
it, when they attempt to employ it with themselves and then
they actively try to teach it to others, not only do they often
succeed in doing so and thereby benefit their pupils but they
themselves often learn to apply REBT better to their own
problems.[7]

I (MA) had a member of my AIDS self-help group who
at first seemed to understand the principles of REBT very
well; but when he became enraged at some of his acquaintances having promiscuous sex with others and not telling
these others that they were HIV or AIDS infected, he insisted that these people, with their very unethical behavior,
made him furious and that he was legitimately damning
them. I and his group were not able to get him to see that he

was needlessly angering himself and that he could stop doing so, and thereby help himself emotionally and physically. But when he started teaching REBT to one of his relatives who continually upset herself about things that went wrong in her life and about the way in which people were behaving unfairly to her, he soon began to see how he was unduly enraging himself against unethical people. He realized that although they were wrong, his rage was useless, so he made himself much less infuriated at them while still solidly deploring their actions.

You can similarly practice teaching the main principles of REBT with emotionally disturbed people and thereby learn the principles better yourself. How do you know whether your friends are good candidates for this teaching? By observing their self-defeating feelings and behaviors.

For example, you may see that some of them are panicked, or terrified about their jobs, their relationships, or almost anything else. Or, after they have failed and got rejected in important affairs, they may be severely depressed. Or they may not seem to be too disturbed emotionally but remain seriously addicted to nicotine, alcohol, drugs, or health-destroying foods.

You can easily find people with these and other disturbances. When you observe them, do tentative ABC's on them in your head. When, for example, one of your friends is depressed after she has had a career setback, you can say to yourself: "At point C, she is obviously depressed. At point A, her main Activating Event is losing her good job and not finding another one. Now what irrational Beliefs is she most probably telling herself at point B? Very likely, 'I *should* have done better at my last job and *should not* have let myself lose it. I also *must* have better interviews to get myself another good job. Because I *should have* done better on my last job, and because I now *must* have better interviews, I am an *incompetent person* who will *never* be able to have a career. How awful!' If she is saying things like this to herself and is depressing herself by strongly believing them, I may be able to show her this, to teach her how to use REBT Disputing to give up her irrational Beliefs, and to help her overcome her depression. Now why don't I see if I can do this?"

If you think this way and try to show others how to use REBT in their lives, you have nothing to lose. For you may help your friends and take pleasure in doing so. But whether or not you succeed with them, you will be teaching yourself the same kind of Disputing of irrational Beliefs that you are trying to teach them and you will benefit even when they do not listen and learn. So go to it. Teach yourself the methods of REBT that we explain in this book. Strongly and persistently use them on yourself. But also try to teach them to others—to help them, and to impress REBT methods more deeply into your own head and heart.

Using Cognitive Distraction

As we noted before, the human mind has difficulty focusing fully on two things at the same time. You can, for example, do a somewhat mechanical or automatic task, like driving a car while at the same time listening to the radio, composing a song, or thinking about a business deal. But just try to compose a song while planning a business deal! Try figuring out two different business deals at the same time!

When you create worrisome thoughts, such as, "I must do perfectly well at this job" or when you angrily think, "That so-called friend of mine is ignoring me and treating me very badly and he *absolutely must not act* like that, the bastard!" you can usually manage to distract yourself, think intently about something quite different, and at least temporarily stop feeling panicked, depressed, furious, self-hating, or self-pitying. You can use many distractions but some of them work better than others and have been widely adopted by people over the years.

Suppose, for example, that you feel panicked because you have just discovered that one of your sex partners, who you were sure was free of all sex diseases, now has AIDS and could have transmitted the HIV virus to you. So you are ter-rified about this possibility and keep obsessively thinking about your getting AIDS and suffering immensely from it. You try to think of other things, especially because you don't know yet whether you actually were infected by this partner. But no matter how you try to distract yourself, you keep re-membering the times when you did have unprotected sex and you keep imagining all kinds of terrible things happen-ing to you and your loved ones.

What to do? Force yourself to concentrate steadily on something else, until your distracting thoughts drive away your panic-stricken images and beliefs, calm you down, and enable you to resume the regular business of your life.

One way to do this is to try various forms of meditation, such as saying a word, sentence, or mantra over and over to yourself, so that you can think of nothing else but the mantra and so drive out your worrisome thoughts. Or you can do a series of Yoga exercises, which require that you concentrate on the movement of your body and focus so steadily on that movement that you can think about little else. Or you can use Edmund Jacobson's famous progressive relaxation tech-nique, in the course of which you focus on relaxing the dif-ferent muscles of your body, starting at your toes and finishing up with your head muscles, so that you concentrate so fully on this procedure that you have no time or energy to go back to thinking about your worries.[8]

You have endless possibilities of distraction techniques to help turn away your disturbance-creating thoughts and feelings. Thus, you can resort to TV or other entertainment. You can write, paint, or compose. You can engage in various kinds of sports or physical exercises. You can throw yourself into a hobby. You can socialize with other people. Etcetera. All these activities will at times work because you will be thinking only of the distracting activity itself and not on how *awful* something is, how you *can't stand it*, how you are *no good* for failing or being rejected, and not on other "horri-ble" activating experiences.

Yes, all of these techniques of cognitive distraction work—temporarily! However, they rarely actually change your disturbances creating thoughts and feelings but mainly cover them up and push them under the surface of your consciousness, always prone to return to awareness and to panic and depress you again.

Edward, for example, thought incessantly about his poor relationship with Sidney. He kept expecting Sidney to find him out almost any day now, see how inadequate he really was, and leave him for a much more adequate lover. He especially worried when Sidney did not come home at his usual hour and might have conceivably had sex with another man. Edward had never heard of REBT but he did know something about cognitive distraction, so he learned how to meditate and got so good at it that he gave some workshops on it.

Every single day, Edward spent at least one full hour, sometimes two, meditating; and after each session he felt fine, experienced renewed energy, and went back refreshed to his work as an artist. Unfortunately, he still was obsessively jealous about Sidney, and as he got older and began to lose his youthful appearance, he became even more insecure and almost drove Sidney away because he kept falsely accusing him of being interested in other men. Only when Edward read *A New Guide to Rational Living* and went to some REBT workshops on jealousy and possessiveness did he overcome most of his insecurity and cement a better relationship with Sidney. Meditation worked temporarily, but only REBT Disputing of his irrational Belief that he *absolutely had to* have Sidney's exclusive love worked permanently.

So by all means use meditation, Yoga, Jacobson's progressive relaxation technique, biofeedback, stomach breathing, or any of the cognitive distraction methods that work for you. But don't use them alone. Employ them to calm yourself when you feel quite emotionally upset. Then, when you feel calmer, use some of the REBT active-directive Disputing methods to construct a truly Effective New Philosophy about unfortunate Activating Events that you make "terrifying."

This is what Edward did. He kept using meditation to temporarily interfere with his obsessive-compulsive jealousy over his relationship with Sidney. But when he was no longer exceptionally upset he went back to strongly Disputing his irrational Beliefs (iB's) that he *must have an absolute guarantee* that his lover would not leave him for another man and that he must *always*, under all conditions, remain so physically attractive that Sidney would not even think of leaving. Once he began to make inroads against these iB's, he was rarely afflicted with intense jealousy and when a bout of it returned, he resumed his forceful Disputing and was again fairly free of his obsession. He still retained some rational jealousy, as REBT calls it, because he preferred that Sidney never break up with him; but he no longer absolutely *needed* this relationship in order to have a good life.[9]

The kind of distraction that works best to help people get over their extreme feelings of anxiety and depression is what is referred to in *A New Guide to Rational Living* as a vital, absorbing interest.[10] When you have such an interest, you pick some big and usually long-range project—like raising a family, building a business, or writing fine novels—and for a long time you really commit yourself to that project.

Actually, you can have two or more such absorptions, though one big one will do. Thus, you can be devoted, for a period of thirty or forty years, to developing a business or a profession; and, at the same time, you can also try to be an outstanding poet. Sometimes your two or more vital absorbing interests can be integrally connected. Thus, the authors of this book both are devoted to building successful psychological institutes but they are also devoted to developing the principles and practices of REBT and to training others to use them.

Vital absorbing interests are great therapy because they absorb so much of your time and energy that you have little left to get overconcerned with the usual hassles of life. Moreover, when you are devoted to some long-range project or cause you tend to have such an enjoyable, flow-involving existence that the rest of your troubles, which may still exist, fade into insignificance. Moreover, vital absorbing interests often include a constructive kind of philosophy that easily outweighs the destructive, irrational philosophies with which you otherwise may occupy yourself. If, for example, you push yourself to build a happy family or you keep working for a cause such as ecological improvement of the world, you tend to become so involved with healthy, creative, happiness-producing goals that many of the petty and destructive goals that you might otherwise have (such as damning yourself for being imperfect), fall out of the picture, being overcome by your healthy attitudes and actions.

Sally hated her ex-husband and all his close relatives, because he had been a drug user and had acquired and given her AIDS. She thought that his entire family had raised him to be an irresponsible, drug-taking person (because many of them were druggies and problem drinkers themselves) and she kept ranting and raving against him and against them to her friends, to her children, and to anyone who would hear her complaints. She made some progress in giving up her vitrolic tirades when she joined one of our Rational Emotive Behavior Therapy groups. But she also helped herself enormously when she became very busily involved with a gay rights coalition that was working to help educate the public about AIDS and its prevention. She devoted so much time and energy to this group and its work, and made so many close friends in the process, that she was no longer obsessed with the villainies of her ex-husband and his relatives; and she was able to accept the REBT message that their *acts* may well have been heinous but that *they* were not horrible people who deserved eternal damnation.

Using Positive Imagery and Affirmations

As we showed previously, the use of positive coping self-statements often replaces highly negative, disturbance-creating statements and therefore can be successfully used to combat irrational and especially unrealistic Beliefs. Thus, if you keep telling yourself, "I can't at all cope with this fatal disease that I have!" you will make sure that you do not cope with it and you will bring on depression. But you can use positive thinking, instead, and persistently and strongly tell yourself, "Even though this fatal disease is the worst thing that ever happened to me, I *can*, yes I definitely *can*, cope with it and still lead a relatively happy existence." Then you will be able to cope much better and overcome your deep feelings of depression.

Although some philosophers and religionists invented positive thinking centuries ago, and some of it is incorporated in books like the Bible, the main modern originator of it was Emile Coué, a French dentist, who realized that when people are emotionally disturbed they often devoutly believe in very negative thinking, and that under hypnosis they listen to the hypnotist's more positive thinking, adopt it, and thereby significantly improve. Hippolyte Bernheim, a French hypnotist a few decades before Coué, also realized that hypnotism, when it works, mainly consists of positive suggestion and that its therapeutic effect lies in the subject's taking the hypnotist's suggestion and making it her own.[11]

Coué, however, went beyond Bernheim and clearly saw that when we are disturbed about something, we frequently suggest to ourselves—autosuggest—all kinds of negative, and frequently false Beliefs. Therefore we can change this and use our powers of positive autosuggestion, or what Norman Vincent Peale, a half century later, called the power of positive thinking.[12] Coué really was years in advance of his time, because he also saw that we often tend to upset ourselves with negative imagery and that, instead, we can replace this with positive imagery, and thereby unupset ourselves and accomplish things that our negative imagery blocks. So Coué's followers, with or without realizing that he was the father of positive imagery, have advocated the use of positive affirmations, including confident self-statements and self-images.

You can use both positive images and self-statements successfully because they are a form of behavioral rehearsal. Thus, if you practice imagery and keep visualizing yourself successfully hitting a tennis ball correctly, your imagery practice may serve as well as actual practice, and you may improve your game. But, if you negatively keep seeing yourself hit the tennis ball badly, you will ruin your game. Positive visualization helps, while negative imagery sabotages your goals.

Both positive imagery and self-statements, however, can easily cover up your negative philosophy about the horror of doing poorly. Thus, you may think that you must be good at tennis and that you are no damned good if you play badly. Using positive thinking, you keep telling yourself, "I really can play tennis pretty well! I am sure that I can!" and using positive visualization you keep imagining yourself winning and winning. You may consequently improve your tennis game.

But you still have not given up your grandiose demand that you *absolutely must* play well or else you are a lousy player and an inadequate person. When, therefore, you fall back again and you don't play tennis too well—which at times is inevitable—you will tend to think, "Oh, hell! I played badly again—as I absolutely must not! How awful! What an incompetent individual I am!"

So even when they work, positive thinking and visualization usually cover up, rather than remove, your underlying demandingness. You still believe that you *completely have* to do well and you will only conditionally accept yourself *when* you succeed. You will be far from achieving the unconditional self-acceptance that REBT tries to help you achieve—that is, fully accepting yourself *whether or not* you perform well and *whether or not* significant people approve of you.

So if you use positive imaging, do so while also acquiring an Effective New Philosophy that prevents you from damning yourself, other people, and the world even when things go wrong. Suppose, for example, that you have a severe illness, and you keep seeing yourself as unable to cope with it and unable to follow the advice of your physicians to take proper care of yourself. You can keep imagining situations where you definitely are able to cope with your condition, and where you are following the regimen your physicians have advocated. As you keep visualizing and believing yourself able to cope with your illness you will tend to cope better.

However, it would be wise for you to also keep probing your underlying negative attitudes and to keep actively Disputing them. Thus, if you find that you are once again feeling discouraged at your seeming inability to handle some aspects of your illness, you can look for your sabotaging thoughts, for example, "What's the use? This illness is much too much for me and I really can't handle it very well!" You can replace this with an *Effective New Philosophy* such as, "This illness really is very hard to handle well but there's no reason why it must be easier and why I cannot handle it pretty well."

Also, when your positive thinking and visualizations are not working too well and you fall back to some degree of despair you can eliminate your possible secondary symptoms— that is, your disturbance about becoming disturbed again—and can construct more helpful philosophies, such as, "Yes, my positive thinking and imaging aren't working that well, but they don't have to. I am allowed, as a fallible human, to fall back at times to upsetting myself again. Now let me see what irrational Beliefs I fell back to and how I can vigorously Dispute them."

Positive thinking and positive visualization, then, can be successfully used in REBT as long as you also use the other

more elegant methods of finding and Disputing your disturbance-creating ideas and working at healthfully changing
them.

Notes to Chapter 9

1. Beck, 1991; Ellis, 1979d; Engels & Diekstra, 1986; Lyons
& Woods, 1991; McGovern & Silverman, 1984; Meichenbaum, 1977;
Seligman, 1991; Silverman, McCarthy & McGovern, 1992.

2. Borcherdt, 1993; Dryden, 1990; Dryden & Jordan, 1991;
Ellis 1973b, 1988a, 1992a, 1992f; Miller, 1986; Nottingham, 1992;
Phadke, 1982; Trimpey, 1989; Vernon, 1989; Wolfe, 1992; Young,
1974.

3. Danysh, 1974; Ellis, 1976b, 1978, 1979a, 1980a, 1985c,
1988a.

4. Ellis & Becker, 1982.

5. Ellis, 1957.

6. Bourland & Johnston, 1991; Danysh, 1974; De Bono,
1991; FitzMaurice, 1991; Hayakawa, 1965; Johnson, 1946; Korzybski,
1933.

7. Ellis, 1965, 1985c; Ellis, Abrams & Dengelegi, 1992; Ellis
& Velten, 1992.

8. Benson, 1975; Ellis, 1983, 1984; Goleman, 1993; Jacobson,
1938.

9. Ellis, 1985d.

10. Ellis & Harper, 1975.

11. Coué, 1923.

12. Peale, 1952.

10

More Cognitive Methods of Reducing Disturbance

In working with REBT since its creation in 1955 we have discovered so many cognitive or thinking methods of dealing with emotional disturbance that it would take more space than we have available in this book to describe all of them. Here, however, are several more that we often find especially useful when employed with people who have, or who have close friends who are afflicted with, a fatal illness.

Modeling Methods

Albert Bandura and other psychologists have shown that children and adults can often learn better ways of coping with their emotional problems by finding examples of emotional health and copying some of the thinking, emoting, and behaving of these models.[1] Thus, when you are panicked about an impending "disaster" and you encounter people who are facing the same "horror" but are dealing with it calmly and less anxiously, you can take on their anti-awfulizing manner and deal with the situation more sensibly.

Question: How can you find some good models to help you when you unnecessarily disturb yourself? Answer: They do exist, but you may have some difficulty in finding them!

Most people, like yourself, are fairly easily disturbable. They are both born and raised to take many things too seriously, and to demand that bad conditions must not exist. Possibly, as we have suggested previously, we inherit this awfulizing tendency from primitive times. Then it may have been necessary, if our ancestors were to survive, for them to be aware of possible dangers and so panicky at the thought of them that they became preoccupied with warding them off.

No matter. The origin of our tendencies to seriously upset ourselves about both minor and serious things isn't that important. The fact is that most of us definitely seem to have it—and to indulge in it. Therefore, for you to find a few people who have less of this tendency may not be easy. But they are findable, if you keep looking for them. You can always find some friends, relatives, teachers, therapists, and other individuals who take things with more equanimity than you do.

In the psychotherapy groups that we regularly conduct, there are almost always at least one or two members of the group who use REBT teachings remarkably well and who serve as good models for the other members of the group. But the reverse is also true. In one of our groups Ronald kept complaining about his boss and all the people he worked with, until some of the other group members were turned off and sometimes angrily reacted to him. They were shown, however, that it was good that he was a group member, because he set such a bad example for the other members that they could see how self-defeating he was. Thus they saw that they could behave differently from Ronald if they wished to feel less disturbed, and that his bad modeling could be used to their advantage.

Then, fortunately, Kristen joined the group. She had severe life problems, including a husband who was dying of cancer, a very critical mother who lived with her, and a mother-in-law who drank herself into a stupor every night and denied that she had a drinking problem. Kristen used

REBT so well, to overcome her rage and depression about her family situation, that the other group members began to model themselves after her, to use REBT better themselves, and to keep pointing out to Ronald that he was foolishly whining about relatively small issues when Kristen was accepting her serious problems with a minimum of whimpering and rage.

So find, if you can, some good models and mold your behavior after some of theirs. You can find some of them in autobiographies and biographies of unusual people, such as Christy Brown, the author of *Down All These Years* and the hero of the semi-documentary film, *My Left Foot*.[2] Brown, who was born with an extremely spastic condition, taught himself to type with his big toes on an electric typewriter and to paint with his left foot; and despite his great handicaps he lived a reasonably happy life.

If you have a serious disease, then, try to find a few people with similar handicaps who bear up well and refuse to make themselves miserable about their unusual disadvantages. Look for people like Warren Johnson, who wrote *So Desperate the Fight*, a splendid book that tells how this previously physically fit man, a professor of physical education, developed one of the worst and most painful diseases, scleroderma. Using REBT, which he had fortunately used on himself and taught to others before he was afflicted, Warren for the next ten years of his life kept himself unanxious, undepressed, happy, and an excellent husband and father.[3] If you model yourself after someone like this, you can marvelously serve yourself, and others, even if you are stricken with a fatal ailment.

Problem-Solving Methods

REBT is a comprehensive and integrative system of psychotherapy that mainly deals with what we call the B-C connection but that also looks at the other aspects of the ABC's of human disturbance and tries to solve them as well.

The B-C connection means you see that your disturbances (C's) largely follow from your Beliefs (B's) about Activating Events (A's) and not merely from A's alone. However, you had better see that A's and C's are also importantly connected, because you would rarely act self-defeatingly, at point C, unless something unfortunate happened, or seemed about to happen, at point A. So the events and conditions (A's) of your life importantly affect you and significantly contribute to your emotional and behavioral problems (C's).

According to REBT, however, your B-C connection is usually even more important, because you rarely feel and act destructively unless you hold irrational Beliefs at point B. Irrational B's do not inevitably lead to unhealthy C's, but they very frequently do. However, the unfortunate Activating Events or Adversities (A's) you experience are important in their own right, because even when you do not needlessly upset yourself about them they still lead to considerable pain, trouble, and unhappiness. When, therefore, you are beset at point A with poverty, injustice, ethnic or other discrimination, physical handicaps, neurological problems, serious diseases, or other misfortunes, you not only want to ward off neurotic feelings (C's) but also to do good problem-solving so that you can do everything possible to eliminate these bad conditions (A's).

REBT, therefore, includes a good deal of practical problem-solving. When you are afflicted by serious Adversities—such as one of your close friends having a fatal disease—you first want to use REBT to ward off destructive emotional Consequences (C's), such as panic, depression, and rage. Let us suppose that, in one way or another, you are succeeding in doing this and you mainly feel sad, regretful, annoyed, and frustrated about your and your friend's Adversity (A).

Now what? Now you go back to this unfortunate A and look for ways of improving or eradicating it. If your close friend has a fatal disease, you obviously are not going to eradicate it. No way, assuming that it had been diagnosed properly. But you still can often help afflicted people get good medical attention, take excellent care of themselves, live in more comfortable surroundings, have suitable companionship, get involved in satisfying activities, and lead better lives.

How, specifically, can you figure out ways to help a person with a fatal disease, including yourself if you are the victim, have less pain and more gain? Naturally, you'd better not be utopian for it is unlikely that you'll be able to help a dying person lead a perfectly happy existence. No, but you can work out some practical, helpful solutions. How? By using some problem-solving methods like the following.[4]

Analyze the Situations and Problems to Be Solved

Look at the specific difficulties of the problems to be solved. Try to find the worst aspect of what is going wrong and the conditions that are leading to these aspects. Discover, for example, that your friend's condition is bad because of poor medical care, because of noncompliance with physician's instructions, because of poor nutrition, because of rigid rules that block dealing with the illness, etc. Discover what main elements help create the poor situation, which of them are changeable, and which are not.

Consider Possible Solutions to the Problems

Think about the best possible solutions to the problems you or your friend with a fatal disease faces. There rarely is only one solution, so consider a number of them. Look at the advantages and the disadvantages of each solution. Think about the usual and conventional solutions first. But also think about some unconventional and unusual solutions. Sometimes you only have a choice between one solution or another and may have to make an either/or decision. But usually, if you remain flexible, you will find several possibile solutions to choose among; and you may end up with an and/also rather than an either/or solution.

One of our clients who had terminal cancer at first thought that she had to pick one oncologist who was highly recommended or pick another who was equally recommended. She decided to pick the first one but also to work with an internist who was a good friend of the second one and who kept conferring with this second one about her physical problems. She was therefore able to use the services of both oncologists at the same time, although only the first one was officially her physician. She found that flexibility, in selecting solutions, really counts.

Check Your Chosen Solutions to See How They Work

Solutions are only effective when they actually work to solve your problem. No matter how much faith you have that a chosen path will work, don't let your faith serve as "proof" that it will. Look at the results of each pathway that you choose. Because you are so involved in the choosing, try to get other observers to also check the results with you. Find as much information as you can on how your chosen path worked out in other cases. But mainly try to discover how it works for you.

Rosalie found that when she tried to help her friend Marianne resort to radiation treatment for an inoperable malignant tumor, Marianne wouldn't agree even though several physicians had recommended this kind of treatment. So Rosalie gave up trying for that solution and, to her own surprise, was able to talk Marianne into accepting chemotherapy that did work.

Look for Better and New Solutions

When we think of a "good" solution for a problem and it seems to be working, we frequently accept it too easily and refuse to seek out a still better solution. Several psychological experiments have shown that when intelligent teen-agers are given a problem to solve and it has one elegant solution, one lesser solution, and one low-level solution the majority of the youngsters pick the last of these three possibilities while only fifteen percent or fewer pick the most elegant of the three solutions. Why? Because the worst of the three possible solutions is the easiest and quickest for the subjects to try and therefore when they arrive at it they refuse to look for a still better answer to the problem.

Don't indulge in low frustration tolerance in this respect. When you have found a tentative solution for a difficulty, use it tentatively, check on it to see how it works, and then continue to look—undesperately!—for better answers. You don't, of course, *have to* arrive at the perfect solution because that rarely exists. But better answers often are possible. So work against your low frustration tolerance to try to find them and to test them out.

Assume That a Good Solution Is Possible and Even Probable

Good solutions for problems are sometimes not possible, especially when you or one of your close associates has a fatal illness. The best solution is to recover from the illness completely; but this cannot be done. Other solutions—such as the dying person's leading a pretty happy existence until the end comes—often can be achieved.

Thomas Alva Edison assumed he probably would find a filament that would not quickly burn out when he was inventing the electric bulb; and although he had 799 failures, he refused to discourage himself and finally found one that worked. You don't require the profound patience of an Edison to solve difficult problems but you'd better not have great impatience! If at once you don't succeed, try, yes try, again.

Trudy tried many times to induce her husband, Mark, to accept a kidney transplant. Their son, Trent, was a willing donor, but Mark refused to agree to it because he was thoroughly opposed to bringing possible harm to Trent. She finally said to Mark, "I've tried to convince you a hundred times because Trent, I, and all your doctors think that it would by far be the best thing for you to do. This is my last and final try, and if you still resist, we'll all think you are acting very foolishly but that you have the right to your decision. Now let me go over, once more, the reasons why we all think it would be best for you to have this transplant." Even before she finished her arguments, Mark agreed to go through with the operation, did have it, and everything turned out fine for him and Trent. Trudy later confessed to one of her friends that if this hundredth time had not succeeded, she would have undesperately kept trying until she finally did succeed in persuading Mark. For she strongly believed and felt that it was possible, and even probable, that she would eventually succeed, so she was determined to keep trying.

Use All the Resources You Can Find

Whenever you want to solve a difficult practical problem, about a fatal disease or almost anything else, look at all possible resources you can find and don't hesitate to make full use of them. Resources can first be found among people. You can discover useful information, problem-solving techniques, and actual help from your friends, relatives, business associates, and even casual acquaintances. If you do not have sufficient information yourself, do not hesitate to ask other knowledgeable people for it. Also, written and recorded materials comprise some of the best gatherable. So if you are in doubt about how to solve a problem, talk to others about possible solutions, and go to libraries and bookstores to find the materials in which these solutions are often written and recorded.

Search your environment to discover other resources that you can use. In any normal-size city you can find stores, schools, lectures, workshops, community agencies, clinics, hospitals, psychotherapy centers, and other environmental resources that may provide help.

Phillip, for example, lived a thousand miles away from his aging parents. But when his mother was in the process of dying from a cancerous skin condition, he was constantly on the phone and was able to get her proper medical attention, home attendants, charitable funds, meals on wheels, and a number of other helpful services that his aged father was in no condition to arrange. After his mother's death, Phillip honored his father's request not to be placed in a nursing home and arranged for him to keep living alone by again calling several community and religious services that helped his father live comfortably at home for another five years. Finally, again mainly by phone, Phillip arranged for his father to enter an unusually good nursing home, where he spent the rest of his life.

Again: When practical problems arise from your own fatal illness or that of your close relatives or friends, don't hesitate to look up, check out, and take advantage of people resources and community resources that are often available. You can find problem-solving to be most intriguing and enjoyable, and can successfully distract yourself from any disturbed feelings you may experience. But you are not alone, and you can seek out and find cooperative people and agencies that will ease your burden and help you come up with better solutions.

Expect Some Failures When You Problem-Solve

No matter how bright or energetic you are, you will often fail to come up with great solutions when you or your friends have a terminal illness. Expect this, and avoid creating a secondary symptom about your failure. As we keep noting, when you make yourself panicked or depressed about anything you can easily upset yourself about your upsetness: Make yourself very panicked about your panic or depressed about your depression. You then have two serious emotional problems for the price of one!

Similarly with your failures to solve practical issues. You can do your best to help someone who is suffering from a fatal disease, distinctly fail to help him or her, and then neurotically tell yourself, "I *should* have succeeded, and there's no good excuse for my not doing so! I could have done more and gone to greater lengths to help this sorely afflicted person and I failed to do so. How awful! I'm really a rotton, incompetent person!"

If you damn yourself in this manner for not being helpful either to yourself or others, use REBT again to look for your irrational Beliefs (iB's)—your absolutist shoulds and musts, your awfulizing, and your self-deprecation. Forcefully Dispute these iB's until you change them back into preferences and end up with Effective New Philosophies. Such as, "Yes, I didn't do as well as I might have done to solve this important problem, and I'd better admit this. But there's no reason why I *have to* always do as well as I possibly can do. It's unfortunate that I didn't do that well in this instance, but it's not *horrible* or *awful*. I am a *person who* did badly this time but that doesn't make me a *rotton, incompetent person*—just a fallible human who can try to do better next time I am faced with trying to solve an important problem."

Reframing

When we are disturbed about anything, particularly about a fatal disease, we tend to view it in a highly negative way and to ignore its positive or neutral aspects. Because we dislike it so much, and often tell ourselves that it *absolutely should not and must not exist*, we tend to see it as more negative than it actually is, and we even may add to it dismal aspects that hardly exist. Thus, if you are going for an interview for a job that you really want and you think that you must get, you will negatively interpret some neutral or slightly bad aspects of the interview, and even some of its favorable aspects. You may wrongly perceive that the interviewer's firm tone means she is hostile to you, and that her telling you she will get back to you later means that she has really rejected you.

Again, when you think you have to win a partner's love you may notably frame her words and actions in a very negative light. If she refuses to date you, you may feel sure that she is totally rejecting you when she actually may not be available on the day you suggested. If she kisses you lightly, points out one of your failings, or forgets an appointment with you, you often conclude that surely proves that she no longer loves you—when, of course, there may be other reasons why she is behaving in these ways. Sometimes she may even try to be lovingly helpful—as when she goes over an error with you and tries to help you correct it—and you still may conclude that she is being overly critical, that she does not care for you, or even that she thoroughly hates you.

Particularly if you have a fatal disease and are blaming yourself for having acquired it—as when you have lung cancer and you are damning yourself for continuing to smoke for a number of years—you will tend to project your own negative view of yourself onto others and to insist that they loathe you as much as you disrespect yourself. If you put yourself down, your best bet is to take your self-damning conclusions as hypotheses rather than facts, and to question, challenge, and Dispute them just as you would do with your other unrealistic and neurotic Beliefs.

You can say to yourself, for instance, "Granting that Domena has looked at me oddly, does this really mean that she is very critical of what I am doing? Even if that is so, does that prove that she no longer loves me? Even if she no longer loves me, does that prove that I am worthless?" If you are skeptical of your negative conclusions and keep questioning them, in this manner, you may soon change them.

Another way of changing your disturbed views is to reframe them, and to make a real effort to see many "bad" or "awful" things in a neutral or a favorable light. You don't have to go to the other extremes and be Pollyannaish—as we have warned against in Chapter 8—but you can use realism and optimism to do effective reframing. Suppose, for example, you have been ill and one of your friends has promised to see you and has not done so. Your first reaction may be, "He really doesn't give a fig about me, is only pretending that he will be helpful, and actually feels selfishly neglectful disrespect. How can he behave so hypocritically? That lousy rotter!"

On second thought, however, you can reframe your conclusions as follows: (1) "He is somewhat irresponsible and treats some of his other friends just as badly as he treats me." (2) "He sees that I am too dependent on him and other people and wants me to work at being more independent and taking better care of myself." (3) "He has his own problems to take care of and it is good that he is tending to them. He will probably be more considerate of me after he deals with them." (4) "I really don't need him to help me, though that would be nice if he did. I can take the time that I would have spent with him to do other things that I really enjoy!" (5) "It's too bad that he doesn't want to be with me but it's good that I have discovered this. I can find other people who really do want to be with me and in that way lead an even better existence than if he grudgingly forced himself to be with me."

In ways like these you can realistically reframe unfortunate occurrences and see them in a less horrifying, or sometimes even in a fairly good, light. Remember Shakespeare again: "There's nothing either good or bad but thinking makes it so." So watch, and work to change, your thinking when you are faced with "terrible" happenings.[5]

You can also use bad events and your gruesome reactions to them as a real challenge and can deliberately "take advantage" of them to practice making yourself unneurotic. If a close friend or relative comes down with AIDS, terminal cancer, serious cardiac trouble, or some other "awful" ailment, you can say to yourself, "Look, this is really grim and I'm not going to stick my head in the sand and claim that it is not. I hate the fact that Nancy is so sorely afflicted and that I cannot prevent her from dying. But this adversity is a real challenge for me not to unduly upset myself, even though I shall sorely miss her and be very sad when she is gone. Now what can I do to accept this challenge?" With this kind of attitude, you can make yourself accept, without liking, this dismal situation. Then you can do your best to help your friend, contribute to research efforts to cure fatal diseases, lead a support group of afflicted people, volunteer to help other people with terminal illnesses.

You can accept the challenge of using REBT to refuse to make yourself miserable about your friend's sad condition. You can try to show her how to use it with her own problems. You can try to help other people who are seriously panicked about diseases (or anything else) look at their self-disturbing attitudes, change them, and make themselves feel genuinely sad and disappointed but not horrified about the unfortunate conditions. You can turn it into a real challenge, when grim things happen to you and to others, to refrain from unduly upsetting yourself and to try to help others do so, too. Yes, a real challenge![6]

Notes to Chapter 10

1. Bandura, 1986.
2. Brown, 1985.
3. Johnson, 1981.
4. Meichenbaum, 1977; Spivack & Shure, 1977.
5. Ellis, 1988a.
6. Ellis, 1988a.

11

Emotive Methods of Coping with Fatal Illness

The theory of REBT holds that thinking, feeling, and behaving are rarely, if ever, separate processes, even though they sometimes seem to be. When you think about something—such as how to do well at your job—you normally evaluate how important this thing is to you (that is, slightly, moderately, or very important) and in the very process of evaluating it you create feelings about it.

Thus, if you evaluate your job as being very important, you tend to wish strongly that you will succeed at it, and you feel satisfied, content, or happy when you think you are succeeding and feel dissatisfied, discontented, and unhappy when you think you are failing at it. If, moreover, you evaluate your job as very important and also evaluate your performance of it (and other people's view of your performance) as good, you will tend to keep working at the job, try to improve it, and try to continue your "good" work and to change or discontinue your "bad" work. So your thinking about this job and evaluating how important it is and how well you are doing at it—and remember that evaluating is a form of thinking—leads to your having feelings about it and to your performing or avoiding it.

Because thinking, feeling, and behaving are interrelated

and integrated, you can affect and change any one of these processes by working at changing the other two. As REBT shows, if you want to change your emotions and your behavior, you can usually do so by changing some of your thoughts. Specifically, if you want to change your disturbed emotions (such as rage and depression) and your dysfunctional actions (such as procrastination and compulsive activities) you can find your self-defeating, musturbatory Beliefs that go with them and change these into self-helping, preferential thoughts.

That is good to know. But you can also usefully realize that you can change your self-absorbing thoughts (such as being obsessed with murder or suicide) by changing your feelings and your behaviors. Thus, if you bring yourself to love instead of to hate certain people, you will not obsess about murdering them; and if you keep engaging in some highly enjoyable pastimes, such as listening to music or skiing, you will not obsess about killing yourself.

REBT goes one step further in regard to feelings and holds that your strong emotions usually are encouraged by your having "hot" cognitions or "hot" thoughts, and your minimal emotions are instigated by "cold" thoughts. If you tell yourself, for example, "This is a book I am reading and it is about coping with fatal diseases and is two hundred pages long," this descriptive or cold thought will probably not lead to your feeling very much about this book.

If you tell yourself, "I really like the contents of this book and believe they will help me considerably," you will warmly evaluate the book, and will probably feel happy while you are reading it. But if you tell yourself, "This is one of the worst books I have ever read, is a waste of my time and money, and absolutely should not have ever been written!" your hot evaluation of it will most probably lead you to feel angry and depressed about the book.

Strong and hot evaluations, therefore, lead you to have powerful (good or bad) feelings about people and things; and while you hold such thoughts, and are powerfully convinced of them, you will have a difficult time changing the powerful feelings that go with them. Moreover, says REBT, when you look at your strong evaluations of something and when you only namby-pambily or lightly challenge and Dispute them, you will not be able to modify them very much and the feelings to which they lead will also not appreciably change.

Suppose you really hate reading the present book and you keep intensely convincing yourself, "This damned book is terrible! It is one of the worst ever written! The authors and the publisher shouldn't have been so stupid as to produce it, and no bookstore ever should be allowed to sell it!" With these strong Beliefs, you will almost certainly not only dislike the book but will also feel very angry about it, its authors, its publisher, and the bookstores that sell it.

Suppose, now, you realize that your rage about the book is self-defeating, and you wish to change it so that you only feel displeased but not horrified or furious about it. You then can Dispute your irrational Beliefs (iB's) about it and create mild objections to it along these lines: "Well, it really is a pretty bad book, but lots of other poor books like it exist, and I don't have to read them or this one. I wish the authors and publisher hadn't bothered to write and publish it, but I guess they have a right to do so and probably won't do too much harm by bringing it out. Maybe I'd just better ignore it and go about my business."

Now this new evaluation of the book, its authors, and the publisher seems much more sensible and rational than your previous one, and will probably temporarily remove some of your rage and depression. But, alas, while holding this new view, you may also, at the very same time, keep *strongly* holding your previous view, because you have now only *mildly* contradicted it. So although at times you may merely moderately dislike the book, at other times you will tend to return to powerfully telling yourself, "Who cares if other bad books like this one exist? This one really is *awful*! Yes, I don't have to read it but it still is an extremely rotten book and I am sure it will do a lot of harm. Its goddamned authors and publishers *should* have had enough sense to recognize this and *should* never, never have brought it out. They really have *no right* to publish this kind of trash and *they should all drop dead!*"

If, then, you mildly conclude, now that you have given the matter some thought, that the present book is not very good but that it still has a right to be published and sold, and at the same time you strongly hold that it is an awful volume, that it will do much more harm than good, and that its authors and publishers have no right to foist it on an innocent public, you will most likely still feel basically enraged and depressed about the book and its creators.

REBT assumes, therefore, that when you have intense irrational Beliefs (iB's) that lead to mildly neurotic feelings, and when you mildly Dispute these iB's, you may temporarily make yourself feel appropriately sorry and disappointed rather than unhealthfully horrified and depressed. But you will not fully surrender your underlying musturbatory philosophy and disturbed feelings, and they will soon return and keep undermining your healthy emotions.

Therefore, you had better use several of the kinds of Disputing and other cognitive techniques that we have been describing in the last few chapters of this book. But you had also better do more than this and had better strongly, vigorously, vehemently, and powerfully Dispute your irrational Beliefs, until you effectively (though not necessarily completely) change them for a convincing Effective New Philosophy that you not only believe but definitely feel and actively follow.

To this end, REBT has devised a number of emotive and dramatic methods that you can use to Dispute and minimize your irrational, musturbatory thinking; and it has borrowed a number of emotive methods from other forms of therapy.[1] In this chapter, we shall describe several of the emotive methods that REBT commonly uses and show you how to apply them to problems related to fatal illnesses.

Unconditional Self-Acceptance

Unconditional self-acceptance is not exactly an original concept of REBT, as it is at times endorsed in the Bible— "Let us accept the sinner but not the sin"—and in the writings of several ancient Asian and Greek-Roman philosophers. Carl Rogers vigorously espoused it. But, ironically, he thought that it can only be achieved by another person's, such as a therapist's, accepting you, and when it is thus achieved it clearly becomes conditional rather than unconditional acceptance.[2]

Unconditional self-acceptance means that you fully and completely accept yourself without any qualifying conditions—such as your accomplishing something, being of service to others, or doing great in science, art, or music. All these achievements are fine, because they will often bring you satisfactions. So your goals in life can very well include success, approval, comfort, and good health. Don't denigrate any of these pursuits.

You can have valid preferences for performing important tasks well and being loved by significant others. Few people lack these values, and practically all of us benefit from attaining them. Our problem, however, is that virtually all of us tend to elevate our strong preferences and desires into absolute necessities; and when we fail to achieve any of these "necessities" we then define our self or essence as "undeserving" or "worthless." We consequently suffer from what is variously called feelings of inadequacy, low self-esteem, lack of identity, and worthlessness.

This—if we look at it from, say, a Martian standpoint— is very odd. For we would expect that practically all of us would have a strong sense of personal worth, because we are all unique individuals; and although we are born and reared to be social creatures, and have much in common with each other, we can only have our own thoughts and feelings, and we never really merge with others (although in some odd states, such as that of being madly in love, we may delude ourselves that we do).

All of us, moreover, "deserve" to have life and to survive for a number of years simply because we were, without our ever asking to come into the world, born. Once we are born, we obviously exist; and we seem to have the right to continue to exist, for a while though not forever, and to be as safe, sound, and happy as we can be during the course of our existence.

Along with deserving life, we also seem to "deserve" relative freedom from pain and some experiences of enjoyment. For if we were constantly in pain or we never had any kind of pleasure, we would probably find the effort of continuing life unrewarding and would welcome death.

If our lives have any "worth" or "value," therefore, they seem to have it because (1) we are alive, (2) we can somehow manage to stay alive for a while, (3) we are not in too much pain, and (4) we have the reasonably good expectation of experiencing some amount of pleasure. Because the great majority of humans fulfill these conditions, it would appear that practically all of us are intrinsically worthy, good, or valuable, at least to ourselves, and that we deserve to keep living and to seek out personal enjoyment, as long as we do not seriously harm the other humans with whom we normally live. We are intrinsically, by virtue of our aliveness, valuable.

This, alas, is not the concept of self-worth that we are usually raised with and choose to accept. Almost all of us are taught, by our parents and our culture, that we should only accept ourselves, and think of ourselves as deserving creatures, when we properly fulfill certain kinds of conditions, especially success and lovability. Even when we are occasionally taught, or figure out a system of philosophy like REBT, and "know" that we have the right to exist and enjoy ourselves unconditionally, we have enormous difficulty in accepting this concept. Instead, we almost always wind up by damning ourselves and considering ourselves quite unworthy of living and enjoying because we find ourselves lacking in certain skills or achievements. We usually convince ourselves, instead, that we *have to be* successful and that we *must be* loved in order to feel self-worth.

Whenever people are shown that it is highly desirable to perform important tasks well and to win the approval of significant others, they tend to raise their desires into absolutist commands and demands and then to denigrate not only many of their performances but their entire self, being, or essence when they do not live up to these demands. Specifically, they adopt the self-defeating philosophy, "I *have to* perform important tasks well and I *definitely must* win the approval of significant others or else I, my totality, my personhood, my identity is no good, and therefore I do not really deserve to live and to enjoy myself."

People, then, almost always *define* themselves as "good" and "worthy" when they fulfill certain desirable conditions and *define* themselves as "bad" and "unworthy" when they fail to fulfill these conditions. Why do they do this? Probably because tens of thousands of years ago, in jungle and cave days, this kind of conditional self-acceptance enabled them to survive and to carry on the human race. The command, "I *absolutely must* perform important tasks well and *must be* approved by other members of my clan!" may well have aided survival in ancient days. Today, under quite different conditions, when it is still desirable but not necessary for us to perform important tasks well, and when it is still importnt but hardly obligatory that we be approved by significant other people, we still often place these absolutionist demands on ourselves.

The main result of these demands? Our neurotic feelings and behaviors. For if we keep telling ourselves that we *absolutely must* perform well and be lovable in order to accept ourselves, and if we are fallible humans who frequently perform poorly and are not approved by many others, we will almost universally conclude that we are worthless. Even when we do well and are approved, we realize that this state of affairs may well not continue tomorrow and the next day. So we often make ourselves anxious and depressed. This will not work! The solution, as we have been indicating, is to accept yourself *un*conditionally, without any qualifying musturbatory demands. Then you will not put yourself down when you behave poorly, and when you behave well you will not panic yourself about your not doing just as well the next time.

REBT offers you two main methods of unconditional self-acceptance. The first is somewhat inelegant, but if you consistently apply it, you will find that it works. Just keep convincing yourself, "I will accept myself as a worthwhile individual just because I exist, just because I am alive, just because I am human—*whether or not* I perform important things well and *whether or not* significant people approve of me. Why will I accept myself in this unconditional manner? Simply because I *choose* to do so and because I know it will work much better than if I damn myself or if I accept myself conditionally. Do I need any other reason for accepting myself? No, none whatever. Again, I merely *choose* to do so."

This form of unconditionally accepting yourself is safe. For until you die you will always be alive and human— therefore, by your own definition, acceptable and worthwhile. So you leave no out for nonacceptance. As long as you *choose* unconditional acceptance, you can obviously keep choosing it.

This is what serious neurotics do with self-damning. They have no good reason for hating themselves and considering themselves undeserving. They just *choose* to do so. And no matter how anyone tries to show them that they are good and deserving, they simply keep asserting, "No, you're wrong. I just am no good, and you'll never convince me that I really am any good when I know that I am no good." Then, of course, you cannot convince them. They are really "no good" *by definition*; and they allow no one to contradict this definition. By the same token, then, you can *define* yourself as "good" and if you stick to this definition you obviously cannot define yourself as "bad."

So this inelegant solution works, pragmatically. You can't prove that you really *are* "good"—or *are* "bad." But if you insist that you are "good" you will get some good—meaning happiness-producing—results. Philosophically, however, this solution to the problem of human "worth" is somewhat shaky. Because some people can come along and say, "Well, you keep saying that you're good, defining yourself that way, but we insist that you are really bad, no matter what you say. First of all, you do *some* bad things—and, to us, that obviously proves that you are a bad person. But even if you never did any bad things—which is highly unlikely!—we still say that just because you're human you are bad. In fact, all humans are obviously bad—including you."

Now, of course, these objectors cannot prove that their view is true or valid, but you can't prove that it is false or invalid. You are both maintaining different—in fact, radically different—*definitions* of your "badness" and your "goodness." Why is their definition any worse—or better—than yours?

You may answer, "Well, these people's definition of human worth won't work to make me (or anyone) happy; and my definition will work." But they can answer, "We don't care whether it works or not. We still say you are bad rather than good; and if you are bad, you obviously don't deserve any happiness. So it doesn't matter whether our definition works."

Now which one of you is right? Neither is. Because you are both entitled to any of your views. You, for example, may hold to the Christian religion and the objectors may be Hindus or atheists. Even if you could prove—which you will have a hard time doing—that your religion will lead to more happiness and productivity than will theirs, they are still entitled (at least in a free country) to hold their opinions.

Definitions of your global "goodness" and "badness" are really theological views, and cannot very well be proven or disproven, though it is possible that their results may be shown to lead to greater or lesser human happiness. So they are philosophically inelegant.

What then? Well, you can use the second, more elegant, REBT solution to defining your "goodness" or "badness." You can convince yourself, "I am neither good nor bad, as a total person, because I am just a *person who* does good and bad deeds. I will try to do more good than bad acts, because they will help me live and enjoy myself, and will also tend to help other people. Once I (and others) *decide* to keep living and to try to be happy, I can discover whether my deeds and performances aid or sabotage these goals and can call self- and socially-destructive acts "bad." But I shall do my very best to *only* measure my acts, deeds, performances, thoughts, feelings, and behaviors as "good" or "bad," so that I can repeat the "good" ones and correct the "bad" ones. I shall keep trying to refrain from giving myself, my being, my essence, my self, or my personhood *any* rating or measurement whatever. I shall not falsely generalize in this manner. Then I shall not have any *global* or *total* measurement, no rating of my "self," but only a practical, nondefinitional measure of the "goodness" of the things I do and do not do."

Now this nonrating of your *self*, while you still keep rating your *acts* and *deeds*, is not exactly perfect and unarguable. For it implies that you are worthy, as a human, of having the goals of living and of enjoying yourself; and we might say that kind of worthiness" is itself definitional and unprovable. So this more "elegant" definition of your goodness is itself somewhat definitional and can theoretically be argued with. But it seems clearer and nicer, in that it makes fewer assumptions than the "inelegant" definition that we described above. In one way, it includes no measure of yourself or being, even though it clearly does measure what you do and do not do. So in REBT we tend to prefer it.[3]

Anyway, you can use both these answers to the problem of *unconditional* self-acceptance; or you can combine them in some way. You can also use other fairly safe definitions: such as the Christian concept of Grace. You can believe, for example, that a man called Jesus of Nazareth existed, that He was the Son of God; that He allowed himself to be crucified to save you; and that therefore, if you believe in Him and in God, He will give you Grace and will unconditionally accept you, even though you do a number of bad acts and deeds. If you believe this theory of your always being able to have Grace, you come *close* to unconditionally accepting yourself—but, as you can see, you are making a few additional assumptions that you can't prove, and are therefore getting into what REBT would call an inelegant solution to the problem of your "worth." But it is a fairly decent solution; and you can use it, or some similar solutions, as long as they include your never damning yourself for *anything* you do and your *always* accepting yourself (but not your bad deeds) under *all* conditions and at *all* times.

If you have real trouble accepting yourself unconditionally—or, for that matter if you have trouble successfully using any of the other methods described in this book—we would recommend that you have at least a few sessions, either in person or by phone, with a trained REBT therapist, who will be able to help you in this respect. To find such a therapist in your vicinity, or one that you can reach by phone, call the Institute for Rational-Emotive Therapy, 45 East 65th Street, New York, NY 10021-6593, (212) 535-0822. FAX (212) 249-3582.

Rational-Emotive Imagery (REI)

Rational-emotive imagery (REI) was created by Maxie C. Maultsby, Jr., a rational psychiatrist, in 1971, and is a combination of the cognitive method of Disputing your irrational Beliefs (iB's) and replacing them with rational coping self-statements and an emotive method of helping you get in touch with and change your disturbed feelings. The particular form of REI that REBT uses is heavily emotive as well as cognitive and behavioral.[4] You can perform it as follows:

Instead of imagining positive things that can happen, imagine some very negative things—such as your suffering from a fatal disease and getting little sympathy and help from your relatives and friends, even though they say that they will do everything in their power to help you. Let yourself vividly—very vividly and forcefully—imagine this event actually occurring, and let yourself feel whatever you negatively feel about when you visualize it. Usually, you will feel quite panicked, depressed, or enraged. Or perhaps all three! Anyway, let your feelings well up and get in touch with them and feel, really feel them. Don't do anything, at first, to suppress or get rid of them. Feel them, feel them, feel them. Don't tell yourself what to feel—that you must, for example, feel extremely depressed or enraged. Just feel what you honestly feel.

Once you begin to feel disturbed as you vividly keep imagining this bad event happening, keep imagining and feeling negatively about it for a few minutes. Let yourself feel exceptionally upset. If depressed, implode that feeling and feel as depressed as you can be. If enraged, again let yourself feel greatly enraged.

Now, when you are really experiencing a disturbed feeling, decide to feel a different negative feeling, one that is quite negative but still healthy. If you feel very depressed, for example, do your best, instead, to feel *appropriately* sorry and disappointed instead of *unhealthfully* depressed. If you feel panicked, do your best to make yourself feel, instead, highly concerned and vigilant but *not* panicked. If you feel enraged, try to feel, instead, appropriately and self-helpingly displeased at what your relatives and friends are failing to do for you, but *not* horrified and enraged at them for behaving badly.

Once you pick an appropriate, self-helping, but still negative feeling to substitute for the inappropriate and self-sabotaging feeling that you are experiencing while imagining some really bad things happening to you, work at making yourself actually feel this healthy way and hold that feeling for a minute or two. Work at it, work at it, work at it; and you will almost always succeed because, according to REBT theory, it was not the imagined Activating Event (A) that actually made you feel very upset, it was your musturbatory, irrational Beliefs (iB's) about this event. Therefore, because you created these B's and your disturbed feelings (C's) that go with them, you can always uncreate and change them. Try it—and you will see!

What's the secret of your working on your self-destructive C's and changing them to self-helping ones? As you have already probably guessed, you can change your feelings by changing your irrational Beliefs (iB's) to rational Beliefs (rB's). Thus, you can strongly say to yourself, when you are imagining your friends and relatives promising to help you with your illness but rarely doing so, "I would really LIKE them to back up their promises and help me as they said they would, but they never HAVE to do so. I think that they are really behaving badly, but they, as fallible humans, have a right to be wrong. I WISH they wouldn't behave this way! But they are doing so, and I CAN STAND IT!"

Every time you disturb yourself by imagining one of the worst things actually happening, you can replace it with a substitute healthy, though still strong, negative feeling. How? By creating a rational coping self-statement that produces the substitute feeling. If you go over this new coping statement very strongly several times in your head, you can change your inappropriate to appropriate feelings. Moreover, you can usually do so within a few minutes, if you really work at this.

We recommend that you do rational-emotive imagery (REI) about the same disturbed feeling once a day for twenty or thirty days. If you do, you will usually find that after ten or twenty repetitions, as soon as you imagine, once again, the bad Activating Event (A) actually occurring, you will start experiencing self-helping rather than unhealthy negative feelings. That's because after a while you start to thoroughly *believe* your rational coping self-statements, so that they become a consistent part of your "personality."

If you have trouble doing rational-emotive imagery at least once a day, you can use reinforcement principles, which we explain in more detail in Chapter 12 on Behavioral Methods. Thus, you can allow yourself to do something you really enjoy—such as eating a good meal, or socializing with your friends—only after you have done REI and actually changed your feelings. You can also use penalties to make sure that if you have failed to do REI to change your inappropriate to appropriate negative feelings at least once on a given day, you will then force yourself to do something you consider very unpleasant and therefore often avoid doing—such as cleaning your apartment, scrubbing your toilet, talking to boring people, or engaging in some other unpleasant task.

Should you also, when you use REI and bring on some disturbed feelings, try instead to make yourself feel happy instead of miserable? Usually not, because that also would be inappropriate. Thus, if you imagine your friends not caring for you as they said they would and you bring on strong feelings of rage, you could actually keep the same image and make yourself feel calm, indifferent, or even happy about their poor behavior. But that would be inappropriate, and would not help you try to do something about their behavior and perhaps unangrily confront them about it. So try to change your destructive feelings, when you use REI, to still negative but much more constructive ones—such as, again, disappointment, sorrow, regret, frustration, irritation, annoyance, and determination to try to do something about the negative Activating Events that you are vividly imagining.

You can do REI, as we have just demonstrated, by vividly imagining bad things that could easily occur but that may not ever actually happen. But you can also do it *in vivo*, when such things are actually happening. Dora, for example, often depressed herself badly when her migraine headaches became exceptionally painful and knocked her out for a day or two. She didn't want to use REI to imagine her headaches occurring in advance, because if she at first made herself feel depressed while doing this kind of visualization, she might actually help bring on a migraine attack. But whenever a migraine attack did occur she at first allowed herself to feel very depressed about it. Yet, even in the midst of her attack, she was able to change her depressed feeling to one of real sorrow and disappointment instead of depression; and after practicing this change of feelings several times, she found that she automatically began to feel sorry and disappointed, but rarely depressed, when she had a severe migraine attack.

The changed feeling that you use in the course of REI can also be used after a situation has occurred. Thus, Clyde made himself enraged when his lover, Tony, stayed away from him for several days at a time after Clyde had been shown to be HIV positive. He tried to work on his feeling of anger and to change it to frustration when he was waiting for Tony and it was obvious that Tony was not going to show up. At first he did badly in this respect. So he let himself be enraged while waiting. But for the next few days, as he kept feeling furious, he used rational coping self-statements to make himself feel only frustrated and irritated but not enraged. He told himself, "Tony is treating me badly and that is very disappointing but not the end of the world. I hate it but I *can* stand it!" After a while, he was able to manage to feel appropriately frustrated instead of unhealthily furious about Tony's neglect. Finally, even when he was waiting for a promised visit from Tony and it became obvious that this was not going to happen, he was able to refrain from upsetting himself and to feel only displeased and not enraged. He did so well in this respect that he was then able to unangrily confront Tony and to agree upon a better kind of visiting arrangement that Tony was able to keep.

Shame-Attacking Exercises

REBT was the first major form of therapy to emphasize the importance of shame in the creation of human disturbance, to clearly show what it is, how it arises, and what can be done to minimize or eliminate it. I (AE) saw this when I first used REBT in the 1950's; and in the 1960's I created its famous shame-attacking exercise, which has now been used by tens of thousands of people all over the world, and which many of these people have reported as being very helpful.[5]

What we call shame—and, often, guilt—almost always arises from two Beliefs, one that is rational and one that is irrational and self-sabotaging. When you do almost any public act that, because of your social upbringing or for other reasons you consider wrong or foolish, you usually sensibly tell yourself, "I am doing this wrong and foolish act, and other people see that I am acting badly, and probably disapprove of me for my activity. I wish I were not acting this way and I definitely prefer that people not disapprove of me. Therefore, I'll try to stop acting like this and behave better from now on."

When you stay with this kind of rational Belief (rB), you feel sorry, disappointed, and regretful about your behavior and about the disapproval of others, and you try to correct your ways. So you are thinking, feeling, and behaving appropriately, and are making yourself into a socially proper creature. Fine!

However, under these same conditions, you frequently add another, demanding, irrational Belief (iB), such as, "I *should* not, *must* not act this way! I *absolutely need* the approval of those who are seeing me behave badly. How terrible that they think I am such a clod! Unless I stop this immediately and refrain from acting shamefully again, I am a complete fool and people should rightly boycott me!" As you process this irrational Belief, you immediately feel ashamed, humiliated, embarrassed, and self-downing. You tend to worry about continuing this "shameful" act. You obsess yourself about it. Sometimes, just because you actively keep in mind the "horror" of doing it, you compulsively repeat it again and again.

As we have been showing in this book, you can always actively Dispute your iB's that lead to feelings of humiliation and self-downing. Don't just question why your act was "wrong" or "foolish"—because you really may have brought on yourself several social and other disadvantages by performing it. But by all means Dispute your musts, your terribilizing, your dire need for others' approval, and your overgeneralizing—until you change your iB's and get back to feeling sorry and regretful about some of your *behavior*, but not overwhelmingly ashamed of *yourself*. You can also use reframing, rational coping self-statements, and a number of the other REBT techniques we have been describing in this book to overcome your feelings of shame, humiliation, and self-downing.

More precisely, you can also use REBT shame-attacking exercises. To do this, you think of some act that you would be ashamed or embarrassed to do—and then you deliberately do it, preferably several times, and risk public disapproval. Now, watch it! Don't do anything that would harm another person—such as slapping her in the face or cheating him out of money. And don't do anything that would likely get you into trouble—such as telling your boss or supervisor that she is no damned good, or walking nude in public. Only do something that you consider foolish and ridiculous and that others would not like, but that would merely lead to laughter or scorn but not to real penalties.

Some practical things you can "shamefully" do, for instance, include not tipping waiters or cab drivers when they have given poor service, because you would feel embarrassed not to tip them. Or asking a stranger to lend you some money. Or wearing a suit or dress that you have had in the closet for years because you think it is too garish to wear. Or wearing informal clothes to a formal gathering where people would stare and look askance at you.

Some not so practical, but rather foolish and "shameful" things you can do include asking a shoemaker if he fixes broken radios; wearing two socks of different colors; singing aloud when you are walking on the street; announcing the stations, in a loud voice, when you are riding on a train or in the subway; reading an obviously sexy book or magazine when sitting on a bus; or loudly asking for very small condoms in a drug store.

We find that when our REBT clients do these shame-attacking exercises, and especially do them several times, they soon begin to lose their feelings of shame and humiliation. For they see that many of the people they think will disapprove of them hardly notice what they are doing. Many of their observers are good humored and friendly. The "terrible" things that they were sure would happen never actually occur. When people do laugh at them they are able to take this unseriously. They increase their assertiveness and enjoy doing so. They get over some of their worst inhibitions. They actually start having fun doing some of the "shameful" things that they keep doing. They especially stop putting themselves down for acting "stupidly" and "foolishly."

Norma was exceptionally ashamed to tell anyone that she had lung cancer and might well die of it because, although she had smoked very little in her whole life, she was sure that everyone she told about her cancer would assume that she had been a heavy smoker for years and that she foolishly refused to stop smoking until it was too late. But she also felt quite ashamed of her secrecy, especially with some of her best friends, to whom she had at first lied and said that she had cancer of the spleen instead of cancer of the lungs.

Norma never came for psychotherapy but was greatly helped by reading *How to Stubbornly Refuse to Make Yourself Miserable About Anything—Yes, Anything!* and did several of the exercises in the book.[6] She finally got around to doing the shame-attacking exercise, which she at first avoided. She told her friends some things about herself that she had previously been ashamed to tell them, including the fact that she had been bulimic during her adolescence and kept her weight down by binging and then vomiting after each meal.

When Norma saw that she was able to tell these "awful" secrets, and that no one seemed to be unusually shocked or boycotted her, she risked telling her close friends about her lung cancer and completely overcame her shame of doing so. She then felt relieved because she was able to stop lying and to get much closer to some of her friends with whom she had been secretive.

So look closely at some of the things that you are quite ashamed to disclose to others. Don't, again, get into any real trouble by doing so; but do, at first, at least one "shameful" act that you know will only bring on some disdain but no serious penalties. Force yourself to do it, preferably a number of times, until you decrease your shameful, self-downing feelings.

Don't change your view that some acts that you may do are really wrong and immoral, and in that sense "shameful." Continue to believe, for example, that if you sexually seduce a child or physically abuse someone, your behavior would be immoral and therefore "shameful." But show yourself that even then you would not be a completely rotten, shameful *person*. You can refrain from doing such unethical acts by strongly convincing yourself how wrong they are, without also believing that you are a complete louse for thinking about or doing them.

Forceful Coping Self-Statements

As we showed in Chapter 9, if you discover your irrational Beliefs (iB's) and devise rational coping self-statements and say them to yourself several times, you will often be able to change them and develop an Effective New Philosophy (E). But we have found that some people only lightly tell themselves these coping statements. They unthinkingly parrot instead of solidly pondering them. Therefore, these people never really are convinced of their own coping statements. Or they temporarily subscribe to them but after a while find that they lose their effectiveness.

Sheila, for example, learned some REBT and told herself many times when her brother, Jim, came down with AIDS, "It's not really terrible and awful that Jim has this vicious disease. It's most unfortunate and sad. But AIDS has to exist when it exists, and my constantly worrying about Jim having it will not do me or him any good. So I'd just better accept it, live with it, and do my best to help ease his burden while he's still here."

For a while this coping philosophy worked quite well and Sheila only occasionally felt very upset about Jim and his grave illness. But then as he started to waste away and it was obvious that he couldn't last for more than a few months, she fell back to her awfulizing, told herself that AIDS was so bad that it absolutely shouldn't exist, and became so depressed that she could hardly be with Jim at all.

When she told her REBT group members what was happening and how depressed she was becoming, they supported her feelings of sadness and grief. But they tried to show Sheila that her depression went beyond these appropriate feelings and that she was saying her rational coping self-statements to herself only lightly and was much more powerfully repeating her self-defeating shoulds, demands, and awfulizing. They worked out with Sheila a set of very strong coping statements and recommended that she set aside several times each day to go over them, and record some of them and bring her recording in to the group sessions so the other members and the therapist could see how powerfully she was telling them to herself.

Sheila did this and the first two times she played her tape to the group almost all the members agreed that the content of her coping statements was good but that she was voicing them much too lightly. So she went over them again and began to repeat them and to record them much more strongly. She then was able to tell herself coping statements like: "Yes, AIDS is a vile and deadly disease. But Jim ABSOLUTELY SHOULD HAVE IT AND SUFFER WITH IT because that's the way things ARE with him. He DOES have the disease; and he WON'T get rid of it, no matter what he, I, or anyone else does. I CAN, yes I definitely CAN live with this grim reality, and I CAN BEAR TO BE WITH HIM, even when I see him suffering so much. I WON'T die of being around him; and I WILL help him by being with him as he approaches the end. THIS TOO SHALL PASS! Both of us, Jim and I, CAN STAND IT. TOO DAMNED BAD, BUT WE CAN!"

As she went over these powerful coping statements again and again, and really thought about them and saw that they could help her, Sheila truly made herself believe and feel them. She never felt good about Jim's disease and about his suffering. But she truly was able to bear thinking about it and to live with it. After Jim died she was happy that she had done so well with him during the last days and that she had almost completely been able to stop her awfulizing. Her therapy group was happy for her, too.

Forceful Recorded Disputing of Irrational Beliefs

In Chapters 6, 7, and 8 we have shown how you can find your irrational Beliefs (iB's) that accompany your emotional and behavioral disturbances and actively Dispute them. But, as we have just shown in the previous section of the present chapter, you may do Disputing and arrive at an Effective New Philosophy in a namby-pamby, ineffective manner, so that you come up with the right answers but don't really believe them. When you lightly hold rational Beliefs (rB's) but strongly hold irrational ones (iB's), the latter will help you to feel and act in a disturbed manner.

Tom, for example, strongly believed that he was a very stupid person because he had been told by his doctors six years ago that he had high cholesterol, that it might well lead to serious heart problems, and that he had better cut down on his fat intake. But he loved his bread and his potatoes, and several of his other foods with large amounts of butter; and although he cut down on butter slightly after his doctors had warned him against it, he still consumed much more than was wise. When his wife pointed out the great dangers of his eating habits he joked about it and insisted that all four of his grandparents had indulged in fatty foods and lived into their nineties, so what was the sense of his cutting down?

When he was forty-five, Tom had a serious heart attack, came close to dying, was left in a weakened condition, and told that he probably had, at most, two years to live. So he beat himself miserably: "How could I have been so idiotic to ignore my doctors' warnings? How stupid! I'm obviously a cretin, and it serves me right. If I had listened, I would probably have lived healthfully and happily to my nineties. How asinine! I guess it's poetic justice if I die soon, since I am so goddamned foolish that I really deserve to die! What's the use of going on like this when I continually have acted so senselessly?" Tom's wife and teen-age son kept agreeing with him and pointing out how selfish he had been to keep up his fatty diet at what now proved to be their great expense. Their criticism didn't help him.

Tom learned how to do REBT in his cardiac self-help group and seemed to be Disputing his irrational Beliefs often and well. But nothing was working, and he came back to the group every week with the same flagellation for his incredible stupidity. Finally, one of the group members who was doing very well with her REBT and was not castigating herself (though she, like Tom, had refused to diet and to exercise for several years before she had a near-fatal heart attack), suggested to him that he use the technique of forceful tape-recorded Disputing, which was invented in the 1970's in the course of one of my (AE's) group therapy sessions. A woman in my group was only lightly Disputing her anger and was therefore coming up with seemingly good E's (Effective New Philosophies) that just didn't seem to be helping her give up her frequent feelings of rage. So on the spur of the moment, I invented Forceful Recorded Disputing of Irrational Beliefs.

You use this REBT method by taking a cassette recorder and taping one of your main irrational Beliefs, such as Tom's, "Because I was clearly told to cut down on eating fats and oils, and because I stubbornly persisted in eating almost as much butter as I had done for the past thirty years, and because I brought on my own heart attack as I absolutely should not have done, that was completely idiotic, and I am obviously a stupid, rotten person!"

Right after you record this self-defeating idea on a cassette, make sure that you spend the next several minutes vigorously and powerfully Disputing it and record this Disputation on the same cassette. Then listen to the tape several times, have some of your friends or group members listen to it, and see if your Disputing is really forceful and convincing, or whether it is rational but is ineffective because you are saying it in a weak, namby-pamby manner. If you and other listeners judge that your Disputing is technically okay but that it is really weak, redo the recording, perhaps several times, until you make your Disputing much stronger and until you start convincing yourself that it, and the Effective New Philosophy to which it leads, are right on the mark. If you do this several times, you will develop powerful Disputes and convincing answers, and you will then tend to give up your irrational Beliefs.

Tom used this REBT method of forcefully Disputing his iB's and played several tapes to his self-help group. But all the members at first agreed that his Disputing was not powerful or convincing. He would keep asking himself, on

the tape, "Granted that my behavior in eating so much butter after I had been warned several times by my wife and my
doctors not to do so was idiotic, does that mean that I, a
whole person, am a blathering idiot and that I do not do anything intelligently?" And he would answer, "No, it only
means that I sometimes act very foolishly, because I am a
fallible human. But even a hundred stupid acts, like eating
too much butter, do not make me a foolish person, because I
also do many intelligent, sensible things, and therefore had
better not put myself down entirely because some of my acts
are unintelligent and asinine."

Tom's group agreed, however, that although his Disputing and his answers were technically correct, the manner
and the tone of voice in which he was saying them were
weak and unconvincing. He'd better keep the same content,
they said, but make his arguments and his answers much
stronger.

So Tom worked on this. He went back to his Disputing
and he changed it to: "Yes, my stubbornly persisting in eating so much butter really was idiotic, because I had the
knowledge, which I refused to accept, that my diet was most
likely going to be harmful. But does that stupid behavior
REALLY make me a blathering idiot? It shows that I acted
unintelligently but am I so UNIQUE in that respect? Didn't
Albert Einstein SOMETIMES act stupidly? Does acting unintelligently at times TRULY prove that I do not do ANY-
THING intelligent and that I'LL NEVER be able to do so?
And how about my savagely beating myself for my foolish
behavior? Is THAT kind of self-downing intelligent? Will it
ever GET ME anywhere? Will it undo the foolish acts I have
done? Will it make my heart and my clogged arteries ANY
better? Or will it, most probably, actually HARM me? Sure I
BEHAVED STUPIDLY. But does that make ME hopelessly
stupid for all time?"

As he worked out these strong Disputes and put them
on his cassette recorder, Tom began to come up with some
powerful and much more convincing answers and Effective

New Philosophies, like these: "Of course my idiotic behavior never makes me a BLATHERING IDIOT. Only a person who SOMETIMES acts idiotically—as, damn it, ALL of us humans FREQUENTLY do. I'm certainly NOT unique in this respect, but actually quite ORDINARY. If I NEVER acted idiotically THAT would really be UNIQUE! Yes, I think I can safely say that ALL humans, including me and Albert Einstein, SOMETIMES act unintelligently. SOME-TIMES, hell—VERY OFTEN! My acting unintelligently NEVER proves that I do not do ANYTHING intelligently, or that I'll NEVER be able to act well. And my savagely beating myself for my foolish behavior ISN'T at all intelligent—but is JUST as stupid as the behavior itself. It WON'T get me anywhere—except into more and more trouble. Beating myself for acting stupidly will most likely help me act MORE stupidly! It won't make my clogged arteries any better, and probably will help me make them a lot WORSE. Yes, it will do me much more HARM than GOOD and will APPRECIABLY ADD to the harm that I have already done myself. So it, my self-blaming, is really idiotic! Let's face it: I DID behave stupidly, foolishly, asininely, ridiculously. But all that NEVER NEVER NEVER makes me hopelessly stupid for ALL TIME!"

As Tom repeated this kind of strong, resolute Disputing and kept going over and over his powerful answers to his Disputes, he improved considerably, stopped practically all his self-berating, and spent the next several months showing other members of his self-help group how to become powerful instead of namby-pamby disputers of their irrational Beliefs, and how to solidly convince themselves of rational Beliefs to which they at first only weakly subscribed.

So if you are telling yourself what seem to be sensible Effective New Philosophies, at point E, look at your Disputing and at your E's more closely. See how weak some of them really are even when they are technically correct, and do your Disputing and your answering of your own Disputes much more vigorously and vehemently, until you really convince yourself that your iB's are ineffective, that you can truly change them, and that your use of a cassette recorder can help you do so. Also, if you do not like the recording technique, you can write down your irrational Beliefs and strongly Dispute and answer them on paper—until, in this manner, you again are able to come up with rational, self-helping answers that you truly believe.[7]

Rational Roleplaying

J.L. Moreno, back in the 1920's when he was still in Austria, originated an emotive method of psychotherapy which he called psychodrama or roleplaying. He would play out with people, often in public, some of their early traumatic experiences, especially with family members, and then act as their father, mother, brother, or sister, and get them to play themselves and to learn to react differently in the roleplay than they had felt and acted in the past. They thereby often began to understand themselves better, to work through some of their past experiences, and to release themselves for better functioning in the present, Raymond Corsini, Fritz Perls, and a number of other psychotherapists then adapted and added to Moreno's methods and made various kinds of roleplaying into therapy procedures.[8]

REBT uses its own kind of roleplaying for several purposes: (1) To help people get in touch with their past and present feelings, especially when they tend to suppress or repress these feelings and some of the Activating Events that go with them. (2) To do behavior rehearsal, and thus to show people how they are behaving ineffectively in the present and how they can learn to behave more effectively. (3) To look at what people are thinking in the course of the roleplay, thereby to clearly zero in on their irrational Beliefs that go with their disturbances, and to change these Beliefs.[9]

Let us illustrate with the case of Jenny. Jenny was quite unassertive with her doctors and her friends, even though she had little to lose by being assertive, because her inoperable cancer of the brain was spreading and it looked like she would not last for more than several months. But she still refused to ask her doctors questions that she thought might offend them. She pretended to want her friends to do practically nothing for her, because she feared that if she asked them to do almost any little thing she would turn them off, they would presumably hate her, and then they would refuse to come see her at all.

Jenny was too sick to come to a therapist's office but had REBT phone sessions with one of our supervisees. This therapist, a social worker, used REBT roleplaying with Jenny in several ways in the course of her therapy:

1. The therapist roleplayed Jenny's main physician while Jenny played herself. In the course of this roleplaying it became obvious that Jenny rarely spoke up to the physician because she was afraid that any kind of assertiveness would put him off, and that he would stop treating her because she was so much of a bother to him. Jenny's great feelings of anxiety and self-downing were clearly revealed in the course of this roleplaying; and where she had previously noted to the therapist that she was unassertive and had a history of being unassertive with most people, it now became clear that she felt panic right before she thought of being assertive with someone and possibly displeasing them, and that just as soon as she acted passively and unassertively her panic temporarily disappeared. It also became obvious that immediately after behaving unassertively, she felt very ashamed of her passive behavior and of herself for indulging in it. So her roleplaying with her therapist revealed the extent of her unassertive behavior and the great feelings of panic and shame that she felt regarding it.

2. Jenny's REBT therapist took the role of a physician that Jenny was being unassertive with and let Jenny play herself. It then became clear that, with this physician, Jenny was feeling very anxious, was saying things that she really didn't want to say, and was later berating herself for not speaking

up properly to him. When these feelings were evident, Jenny's therapist stopped the roleplaying and asked, "What are you telling yourself right now to create your anxiety?" Thus, when the therapist, playing Jenny's physician, said, "What was that important question you wanted to ask me?" and when Jenny then became hesitant to say anything, her therapist asked, "You seem to be anxious right now. What are you telling yourself to make yourself anxious?" Jenny replied, after thinking about it for a moment, "I'm telling myself that you're likely to take offense if I ask you what I want to know. You'll hate me for asking, and that will be awful. I'm thinking, 'I must not offend him! I need his complete approval!' "

When Jenny felt ashamed after she had been unassertive, the therapist again asked, "What are you telling yourself right now to make yourself ashamed?" Jenny answered, "I'm telling myself that I should have asked the questions I wanted to ask and should have been much more assertive, and I'm a rotten, weak person for not doing what I should have done!" During the roleplaying, then, Jenny's irrational Beliefs about needing her physician's approval and about being no good for being unassertive were clearly brought out; and these were actively Disputed, right then and there, until Jenny saw how foolish they were and began to give them up.

3. When some of the roleplaying was completed, and Jenny had not answered her physician (played by the therapist) adequately, the situation was replayed, and Jenny was encouraged to create new ways of talking to him. Thus, instead of saying to him, as she had first done in the roleplaying, "Oh, I can't think of any good questions to ask you now. Maybe I will think of some later," she was led to say, "You know, I really wanted to ask you about this medication that you've given me and that seems to have bad effects on me. Is it supposed to bring on the side effects that I experience? Might it not really have some dangers for me?"

In these ways, then, Jenny benefited from her roleplaying with her REBT practitioner. You also can do some role-playing with your therapist, with your friends, with members of your self-help group, and with other suitable individuals. In the course of doing so you can discover what your disturbed feelings and actions really are. You can find your irrational Beliefs that tend to create them and you can learn how to Dispute these Beliefs. And you can see what you can do to change your self-defeating actions and rehearse better ways of behaving.

Therapy Groups and Self-Help Groups

One of the best ways to help yourself feel better, when you are panicked or depressed about a fatal illness or almost anything else, is to be involved in some close human relationships, with selected individuals and with groups. Such relationships occupy you, get you involved with something outside yourself and your own problems, and may supply you with the kind of vital absorbing interest that we mentioned previously in this book. Friends and relatives, of course, may prove helpful in many ways, especially when you have a serious illness and do not have your usual energies with which to take good care of yourself.

Individuals and groups, however, also have their disadvantages, especially if you are perfectionistic, demanding, and utopian. For other people, like yourself, have their distinct limitations and personal difficulties. For good or bad reasons they hardly always come through with the help that they promise. They often urge you to follow their questionable and bad advice. They may actually lead you into harmful activities, such as too much drinking, eating, and antisocial behaviors. So as you become involved with others, you had better observe your own tendencies to follow them too much, to completely need their approval, and to make yourself enraged when they fail to do what you think is the right thing.[10]

If you watch your overinvolvement and your overreactions to people, you will almost always find that they are underlain by some of your irrational Beliefs (iB's). Thus, you may become overinvolved because you strongly believe that you *absolutely need* people to approve of you, that you *must not* antagonize them in any way, and that you *can't* take care of yourself *at all* without their help. You become hostile against your associates when you think that they *have to* act in one way and *absolutely must not* act differently. If you find, then, that you are having trouble relating to others, look for these kinds of dysfunctional Beliefs, find them, Dispute them, and change them to healthy, Effective New Philosophies.

You may find self-help groups quite helpful, especially when you or one of your friends is stricken with a fatal disease—if you find the right kind of group. One of our clients, Tim, had an advanced case of AIDS and joined a self-help group with other AIDS-afflicted individuals. But he discovered that all the other members of his group were obsessed with complaining about their cruel fate and making themselves feel better for a short while by their self-pity. They did nothing to acknowledge that they were at least in part needlessly depressing themselves and that they could do otherwise. So, after going for a few sessions, he quit that group and joined one of our regular REBT therapy groups, in which he was helped to give up his feelings of depression and to build a happier, more productive life before he died.

Self-help groups for people with fatal diseases should preferably know about and use REBT and other therapy methods. But even if they don't, you may find them helpful because the other members have similar problems to yours, they are usually out to encourage, support, and help you in any way they can. They often form warm personal relationships with you. They may provide you with useful information about your illness. They may encourage you to work for a cause, especially the cause of educating the public about your illness and helping to raise money and support for research purposes. You can find information on suitable self-help support groups through your physicians, nearby hospitals, community mental health centers, or advocacy organizations.

Therapy groups for people with your illness may be available in your community and would be worth investigating. We, naturally, favor REBT therapy groups, but some other groups may also be helpful. Therapy groups tend to have all the advantages of self-help groups, and to be run by a trained professional who keeps the group on track, shows the members how to use effective therapy methods, and intervenes in case there are disruptive individuals among the group members.

Group counseling, either professionally led or through a self-help format, can be exceedingly helpful for the person with a potentially fatal disease. Groups can work to counter many of the same dysfunctional emotions that individual therapy can. But groups offer some unique advantages for the person living with a mortal illness.

As described earlier, fatal illnesses frequently result in both perceived and real isolation. Thoughts of persecution and betrayal are common. Such feelings will tend to become pronounced if you have a severe illness, and have been plagued by emotional problems prior to becoming ill. Participating in a group helps in re-orienting oneself to the new reality of living with a life-threatening illness.

People with terminal illnesses are part of the society that often abandons or even condemns them, and cannot completely ignore its prevalent attitudes and values. You may find yourself accepting many self-depreciating beliefs, thereby creating feelings of shame and worthlessness. The group creates a micro-society in which acceptance is offered. This is especially true in Rational Emotive and other humanistically oriented groups in which all humans are considered acceptable and not rated as good or bad.

Commonly, if you are battling terminal illness you may unreasonably believe that your problem is unique, and that you have been specially chosen by the universe to suffer. This belief and feeling is "confirmed" because people frequently have been deserted by many people they thought they could count on. The group offers two solutions to this problem. You work with other people suffering similar crises and they offer you the support that may have been denied by others. This process of working with others on a common goal of acceptance and serenity will help diminish the feeling of unique suffering and unfairness.

Self-Help Group for Persons with AIDS Run on REBT Principles

One of the authors of this book (MA) started a self-help group for Persons with AIDS (PWA's) in 1986. It met weekly for one and a half hours a week at the Gay Men's Health Crisis Center in New York and still continues at this writing.

Let me (MA) describe some of the core members of this group. There were several members who participated for short periods who are discussed only in passing. The only stated purpose of the group was that it was open to all PWA's who wanted to work on practical and emotional problems.

Jon-Michael was an office manager at a university history department prior to going on disability leave as a result of testing positive for HIV. He had come to New York eighteen years earlier from a small town on the west coast. He described his youth as unhappy. He was fat, unattractive, and gay in a town with no gay community. In his early twenties Jon-Michael lost a hundred pounds and set off for New York. His weight loss made him attractive in a very masculine way. Being nearly six feet, four inches tall, and imposing in manner, he decided to cultivate the leather look, a style he maintained until shortly before his death. Despite his aggressive affectations, he was really interested in writing and literature, interests which he vigorously pursued while on disability. He published two plays and several short stories, over the two and a half years of his illness.

As distinctly masculine as was Jon-Michael, Michael was gentle and effeminate. He was an attorney who stopped practicing law several years prior to becoming ill. Law requires an assertive and persistent style, something Michael did not possess. He was easily offended and angered. A recurring issue for Michael was the hostile rejection by his family. They did not appreciate his being gay, and they viewed his AIDS as a consequence of his "self-destructive" life style. His younger brother made it clear that Michael was unwelcome around his niece and nephew. The rage he frequently expressed toward those close to him alternated with self-loathing views. Michael was in constant emotional pain and anger.

Gustavo had come to the United States from Cuba as a child. Despite his Latino origins his parents accepted his homosexuality. Perhaps this was a result of his quiet, unassuming style. He was a hard person to criticize. Gustavo virtually always was complimentary and positive, and seemed to lack the ability to be offended. Laconic to a fault, he was still able to convey both affect and thought when he wished. And in spite of his illness, it became clear that he was extraordinarily urbane. He had traveled to almost every country in the western world and, in his words, had done pretty much everything he had ever wanted to do. And by the age of thirty he had lived with his forty-five-year-old-lover for twelve years, which led to one of Gustavo's greatest fears. He was not at all afraid of dying, but was only afraid of leaving alone the man he loved so much.

Louis, in contrast, was strictly working class. A printer, he never attended college, nor had he traveled extensively. His parents were second-generation Italians who had spent their entire lives in Brooklyn. Louis looked and sounded like one would expect of someone of his background. Despite this, he was an artist who spent his spare time making mobiles and unusual sculptures. His dream was to leave the print shop and to earn his living through his art. Bearded, stocky, and forty-two, Louis was the very opposite of the gay stereotype. Underneath his avowed stoicism was his agonizing fear of becoming incapacitated.

Kevin was thirty-one when he began attending the group, but he could have passed for twenty-one. He seemed in a perpetual state of shock, which followed his diagnosis of having AIDS. He felt constantly depressed, with intermittent bouts of panic. Kevin was employed in an entry level job in an advertising agency while working at night on an MBA. All this ended when he came down with a series of infections that led to the discovery of his being HIV positive. He left work, determined to continue school. His physical malaise and severe depression aborted that effort in mid-semester. His face was mottled with viral warts, which he unsuccessfully attempted to disguise with a beard.

One group member who presented a particular challenge was Terrence. Two months prior to joining the group he had been exceedingly close to death as a result of herpes meningitis. He survived at great cost to the cortex of his brain, and was left with almost no short-term memory, was easily distracted, and had very little impulse control. His handicapped state aroused the other group members' worst fears: to be demented, erratic, and impulse-ridden. As one group member put it, Terrence was a caricature of what he must have been.

Prior to his illness, Terrence was a computer operator and programmer—a job he lost within two weeks of returning to work after recovering from the meningitis. He would rave on and on about how he would sue his firm for bias. But it was quite clear that Terrence could no longer operate a computer. His lack of insight into his condition was both a salvation and a cruel joke. If he had been aware of how much of himself he had lost he would have suffered intolerably. Yet his blindness to his new limitations kept him compulsively and pitifully trying to do the things he used to do. He would accomodate himself to his daily failures by inventing lies and projecting errors onto others. He kept claiming that he was treated unfairly, or that the equipment he was to operate was somehow different from the way it was supposed to be, or that something else was wrong.

When Mark joined the group he was the very prototype of the young corporate attorney. His grooming and Brooks Brothers suits would have given him entry to corporate headquarters anywhere. But underlying his professional demeanor was the desperation of a person in an inescapable trap. He had just been discharged from a hospital after a three-week stay, he had pneumocystis carinii, an opportunistic infection associated with AIDS.

Alan was the last of the core members to join the group. He was tall and slender and appeared several years younger than his age of twenty-seven. He was beginning the fourth year of medical school when he joined the group, and was facing the first in a series of illnesses that made him question the importance of his goal, that of becoming a psychiatrist. He had been diagnosed as being HIV positive in the second year of medical school and had resolved to fulfill his dream to be a physician, despite the well-meaning exhortations of many friends not to waste his time since he would never live to finish. Alan had a vital mission in his medical work and feared debilitation more than death. He sought group therapy to get help with the daily problems that might impede his completion of his goal. In his final year of medical school he began interviewing for admission to a psychiatric residency. During the beginning of this process he was stricken with esophageal lesions which left him gaunt and emaciated. He declined from 6'1" and 160 pounds to 115 pounds. To mask his condition, he donned a bulky sweater under his sport jacket, and proceeded with his interviews. He was accepted as a psychiatric resident at a major New York hospital.

These were the core members of the group, although there were several others who participated for brief periods.

Most of the members had been in some type of psychodynamic psychotherapy prior to beginning this AIDS group. In the early meetings I (MA) gradually discouraged talk about childhood "explanations" of their current distress, and brought out their current feelings and beliefs. The early meetings tended to center around the latest treatments for HIV and the merits of traditional versus alternative health care. By the fourth meeting one member had died. This was Jay, an accountant who had gotten sick at the height of his career, and felt that he would be a rotten failure if he retired as a result of the illness. The group focused on his demand that he had to keep pursuing his work; and he resolved, with its help, to withdraw from his job responsibilities without putting himself down. Unfortunately, he died three days later.

I announced to the other group members that he had died. None of them could remember who he was. Despite all my references to the previous week none acknowledged anything more than a vague memory of Jay. Remarkably, some two months later Louis made a reference to him during a discussion of the merits of leaving work to go on disability. The rest of the group had no problem remembering him then. When their anxiety level had diminished, Jay could be discussed. The issue of anxiety is an important one in group therapy of persons with AIDS and other life-threatening ailments. Denial and dissociation, which are usually seen as self-defeating, may be adaptive for people facing a high probability of imminent death. Their therapist had better respect and accept this. To challenge it may force fatally ill individuals to think of something that well people rarely contemplate. And how many well people would not feel panicked if they thought all the time of dying?

By the eighth meeting the members had grown close and cohesive. Instead of discussing treatment comparisons they brought out problems of panic, loneliness, and anger. Michael became the focus of the group, when he began to condemn his brother and sister-in-law for isolating him. He believed that they did not want him near their children. He angrily complained that his family had always ostracized him for being gay, and now he was being rejected for being sick.

The group first identified with and supported him in his feelings of hurt. Then Louis pointed out his *demand* that his brother treat him in the way he *wanted* to be treated only served to make him feel lonely and angry. This rational observation led to a discussion of how people take their appropriate feelings of sorrow and frustration, when they are alone and disapproved of, and how they make them into self-defeating feelings of self-downing and rage. Jon-Michael told of his long-term anger at his family.

Their discussion of family problems started them ruminating about significant people in their lives who had betrayed them by not providing enough support during their illness. Every group member, save Kevin, had a painful story to tell about a family member who had let him down. Kevin was living with his parents, whose only "offense" was to smother him with concern.

The goal of therapy at this point was to show the group members that their demands (rather than their strong *desires*) for understanding and support would only serve to make them intensely hostile and enhance the misery associated with their illness. They were implicitly demanding that significant people in their lives absolutely *should* understand their suffering and be kind to them. I pointed out that there was no universal rule dictating that significant others *must* always be supportive and understanding. Instead, their loved ones were just as limited by their ignorance, selfishness, and indifference as are most fallible humans. Alas! But not *awful* and horrible.

Their irrational demandingness became clearer as they observed each other's reactions. Each group member would point out the angry demands made by each of the other members on their loved ones while still angrily persisting in their own commands. Eventually, most of them began to see that their main relief would come from accepting (though not liking) the weakness of those that they saw as cruelly and unfairly abandoning them.

This became apparent when Michael began to denounce his brother, sister-in-law, and parents for not adequately supporting his needs. With a depressed anger, he whined that they were unfair and insensitive. He said that they were always that way, but now that he was sick they definitely should be more compassionate. Before he could go on too long, other group members joined in to complain how they too had been hurt or abandoned, by family or lovers. All had one or more horror stories. Another member, Brad, told how none of his siblings even acknowledged his existence, and attempted to keep family gatherings secret from him. Alan complained that his family treated him as though he were a crippled child. Despite the fact that he was a physician, they would condescendingly tell him how to take care of himself and how to limit his activities.

Finally, Jon-Michael joined in, and began to tell how his brother and two sisters avoided him at all costs, but he stopped that line of discussion in mid-sentence and said "But who cares! That's why I left California, I could never relate to them." He began to admonish the group for upsetting themselves so much over how their family and friends behaved. "Now I have Tim, and I don't really give a shit what my family does." He turned to Michael and said, "Stop complaining so much and stop expecting them to take care of you."

Michael reacted angrily and stated that he could complain as much as he wanted. But the tone of the discussion had changed. All of the complaining members had realized the futility of demanding that family treat them well or fairly. They also saw that none of them was alone in this complaint, so they began to care less.

In most group discussions, Terrence barely participated. He would sit and stare, occasionally making a comment which only marginally related to the ongoing discussion. He precipitated a ritual-like event in which he would light a cigarette, only to be immediately chastised by group members for violating a nonsmoking rule of the group. This occurred every week. He would, without acknowledging the criticism, put out his cigarette. After several sessions he began to act increasingly inappropriately. He would abruptly walk out when another member was talking, would arrive late, or would interrupt with an irrelevancy when someone had the floor. His behavior became so bad that several of the group members asked to speak to me alone to request that Terrence leave. All had previously accepted his behavior because of his apparent severe brain damage. But it seemed that he was too impaired to be appropriate for group therapy. I agreed but suggested that medication might make Terrence more manageable. Terrence was referred for a psychopharmacological evaluation, and was put on Prozac, an anti-depressant.

To the surprise of the group, within the next two weeks Terrence underwent an extraordinary change. He still was severely impaired, but his depression had clearly been exacerbating his bizarre behavior. He stopped smoking in group. His manner changed from emotionless and robotic to almost cheerful. And for the first time he began to articulate his anguish. He told of the pain of not being able to do the things he used to do, of difficulty in movement and of the problems with his lover resulting from his disabilities. Kevin, who suffered some similar losses in functioning, was the most effective in showing Terrence that he could still have a meaningful, though different, life.

One of the most compelling group sessions dealt with suicide, in a session that took place three months after the incident with Terrence. Michael had recently died, with relatively little suffering, from a viral infection. Mark was getting quite ill suffering from an MAI, an illness similar to tuberculosis, and Kaposi's sarcoma. And Gustavo had been recently diagnosed as having a cytomegalovirus infection in his retina. The treatment for this involved the insertion of a permanent catheter surgically implanted in his chest. This was required for the frequent infusions of the only antibiotic capable of slowing the growth of this blindness-producing virus.

The session began with superficial discussions of the weekly activities of several members. After about fifteen minutes Gustavo quietly insinuated himself into the discussion. "They want to put in a Hickman catheter, but I don't think so," he stated softly and unemotionally. All of the group members knew exactly what this meant. His CMV infection was spreading and the only treatment required prolonged infusions of a potent new drug through a catheter permanently and visibly implanted in his chest.

After a few moments of silence I ackonwledged the great distress of such a diagnosis, but asked why he would not want to do all that he could to maintain his health. Gustavo responded with an equanimity coming from his truly realizing that "horror" is our own creation. He said, "I have done everything I've ever wanted to do. I've traveled all over the world. I've done well selling my paintings. . . . I simply do not want to suffer."

Gustavo was telling the group he planned to kill himself. This frightened the sicker members of the group more than the ones who showed few symptoms. They were hearing Gustavo say there is no hope. As members of the group got sicker, they depended on the others to help them dispute the pessimism that chronic illness often produced. So Gustavo's pronouncement that he had decided on suicide appeared to be an endorsement of hopelessness.

I intervened and asked Gustavo if he was suffering right then. He replied he wasn't. I then asked him if he wasn't in fact saying, "I want to die because I might suffer." Gustavo responded indirectly by stating that he did not want to be disfigured by the catheter. Mark, who already had such a catheter, immediately joined in by stating that he too had thought it would be the most horrible thing he could imagine. However, after getting one he said, "It was uncomfortable at the beach, but other than that I rarely think of it."

Kevin pointed out that Gustavo did not have to get the catheter implanted at all. Gustavo replied, "If I don't get the medicine, I'll go blind." I agreed, but asked if he was blind now. Gustavo conceded that he wasn't but he had blurry vision in one eye. "Would you kill yourself if you knew it wasn't going to get worse?" I asked. Gustavo responded that he wouldn't. Mark saw where I was going and asked, "Gustavo, why don't you wait to see what happens, maybe you won't need the ganciclovir?" For several more minutes most of the other members exhorted Gustavo to wait until he was really impaired before seriously considering killing himself.

Gustavo, who at first seemed annoyed at being the center of attention for so long, began to appear reassured by the other members' intense concern about his continuing to live. This more than any factor swayed him to agree to go on living for the immediate future. When he agreed that he would postpone suicide, the group began a general discussion of ending one's life. Kevin and Jon-Michael were the only members that said they would not consider it under any conditions. All of the rest said that they had considered it at various points in their illness. Louis explained that he had thought of suicide many times but dreaded ending up in a near vegetative state as a result of a "botched attempt."

Gustavo calmly interjected, "If you have a catheter it's very easy to die, just inject a poison right in." The leader asked what poison he was thinking of. Gustavo admitted he was not sure. Louis continued his line of thought and said, "That's what I mean. You could pick the wrong poison and end up brain-damaged." Alan surprised some of us when he stated, "If you use a sufficient dose of potassium chloride you will almost certainly die."

The discussion about suicide continued for the rest of the session. Alan explained in detail how any member could kill himself with little risk of surviving impaired. By the end of the session all of the members showed that they wanted to live despite the pain, discomfort, and tension associated with having AIDS. I discovered that for most people with a life-threatening illness suicide represents two things: a final attempt to control one's fate, and an ultimate escape route from what can feel like an overpowering trap. What Alan realized and pointed out is that just knowing that this means of departure from pain is available is sufficient to bring some relief. Several others agreed.

Sadly, all but one of the original members of the group I led died before this writing. However, the group continues with new members who help each other find meaning in life while facing death. Each of the members described above remained active in social and professional affairs until shortly before his death.

Reverse Roleplaying

Because people who try to use REBT Disputing frequently do so, as we noted before, in a weak manner, and because they had better vigorously and forcefully Dispute their irrational Beliefs (iB's) that accompany their disturbed feelings and behaviors, we have found it useful to do reverse roleplaying with disturbed individuals. Thus, I (MA) will take some of my clients' dysfunctional Beliefs that they see but still refuse to change, and I will play the role of these clients, will hold firmly and stubbornly to their iB's, and will give them practice in talking me out of these irrational Beliefs.

You can use forceful reverse roleplaying by having one of your friends or group members strongly stick to some of your irrational Beliefs, and refuse for a while to surrender them, while you attempt to talk this person out of your own Beliefs. Oscar did this with his iB, "People who know that I only have a few months to live absolutely must devote a great deal of their time to me, because I won't be around very long and they will live a long, happy life after I am gone. So the least they can do is to devote considerable time to me right now and they are heartless bastards if they don't!"

When Oscar saw that he had this idea, refused to give it up, and thereby felt very angry at practically all his friends, he got his sister, April, to play himself and to persistently and strongly hold on to this idea while he, again playing himself, did his best to talk her out of it. At first he made little headway, because April did a good job of standing her (his) irrational ground. But as she did so, he began to see more and more clearly how foolish his irrational Belief was and he was able to change it to, "Even though people know that I have only a few months to live and that they may live a long, happy life after I am gone, they obviously don't have to devote a great deal of their time to me. I wish that they would see it my way but I can't make them do so. The more I insist that they think and act mainly in my interest, the more I'm likely to turn them off and encourage them to devote *less* time and energy to helping me. Now, how can I stick with my *wishes* and refuse to change them into godlike *demands*?"

When he started to really believe this Effective New Philosophy, Oscar lost his anger and got along much better with his friends. You can similarly use forceful reverse role-playing to explore and to help you change some of your own self-defeating thinking, feeling, and acting.

Using Humor

From its inception in 1955, REBT began to use humor as one of the main ways to help people combat their irrational thinking and their accompanying disturbances. For when they resort to absolutist musts, shoulds, oughts, demands, awfulizing, I-can't-stand-ititis, and false generalizing, they frequently lose their sense of humor and think, and even say to others, absurd ideas that, if looked at humorously and ironically, they would often surrender.

Thus, when you are disturbed, you frequently tend to believe almost unbelievable thoughts like, "Because I really want people to treat me nicely, they absolutely have to do so!" "Because I would get better results if I performed well at school or at my job, I at all times must do so!" "Yes, life should be often difficult for the ordinary people of the world but never for a Special Person like me!" If you look at these silly ideas humorously, you would probably soon see that they do not hold water and are really ridiculous, and you may then fairly easily be able to change them.

So REBT shows you how to reduce some of your irrational Beliefs to absurdity, to laugh at them, and to see how ironic it is that a presumably sensible person like you keeps holding these self-destructive notions. It tries to help you explode your overly serious ideas with irony, whimsy, and other forms of laughter. In so doing, REBT helps people to refuse to take themselves, other people, and the world too seriously and to put their self-destructive ideas into perspective.

Since 1976 REBT has been using a number of rational humorous songs that counterattack people's misperceptions and irrationalities. At the Institute for Rational-Emotive Therapy's psychological clinic in New York we give all our clients, among other materials, a group of rational humorous songs, which they can sing to themselves when they are emotionally upset and thereby interfere with their dysfunctioning.[11] Here is a group of these songs that you can use with some of your own disturbances. Happy singing!

Perfect Rationality
(Tune: Funiculi, Funicula! by Luigi Denza)
Some think the world must have a right direction,
And so do I! And so do I!
Some think that, with the slightest imperfection,
They can't get by—and so do I!
For I, I have to prove I'm superhuman,
And better far than people are!
To show I have miraculous acumen
And always rate among the Great!

Perfect, perfect rationality
Is, of course, the only thing for me!
How can I ever think of being
If I must live fallibly?
Rationality must be a perfect thing for me!

Love Me, Love Me, Only Me!
(Tune: Yankee Doodle Dandy)

Love me, love me, only me
Or I'll die without you!
Make your love a guarantee,
So I can never doubt you!
Love me, love me totally—really really try, dear.
But if you demand love too,
I'll hate you till I die, dear!

Love me, love me all the time,
Thoroughly and wholly!
Life turns into slushy slime
'Less you love me solely!
Love me with great tenderness,
With no ifs or buts, dear.
If you love me somewhat less,
I'll hate your goddamned guts, dear!

You for Me and Me for Me
(Tune: Tea for Two, by Vincent Youmans)

Picture you upon my knee,
Just you for me, and me for me!
And then you'll see
How happy I will be, dear!
Though you beseech me
You never will reach me—
For I am autistic
As any real mystic!
And only relate to
Myself with a great to-do, dear!
If you try to care
You'll see my caring soon will wear,
For I can't pair and make our sharing fair!
If you want a family,
We'll both agree you'll baby me—
Then you'll see how happy I will be!

I Wish I Were Not Crazy!
(Tune: Dixie, by Dan Emmett)
Oh, I wish I were really put together—
Smooth and fine as patent leather!
Oh, how great to be rated innately sedate!
But I'm afraid that I was fated
To be rather aberrated—
Oh, how sad to be mad as my Mom and my Dad!
Oh, I wish I were not crazy! Hooray, hooray!
I wish my mind were less inclined
To be the kind that's hazy!
I could agree to really be less crazy.
But I, alas, am just too goddamned lazy!

Lyrics by Albert Ellis,
copyright by Institute for Rational-Emotive Therapy, 1977,
1991.

Notes to Chapter 11

1. Ellis, 1988a; Ellis, Abrams & Dengelegi, 1992; Ellis & Velten, 1992.
2. Rogers, 1961; Ellis, 1988a.
3. Ellis, 1962, 1965, 1972c, 1973b, 1976c, 1977a; Ellis & Harper, 1975; Ellis and Whiteley, 1979.
4. Ellis, 1993c.
5. Ellis, 1969b, 1973a, 1985c, 1988a, 1990a.
6. Ellis, 1988a.
7. Ellis, 1962, 1973a, 1988a; Ellis & Abrahms, 1978.
8. Moreno, 1990; Perls, 1969.
9. Ellis, 1988a; Ellis & Abrahms, 1978; Ellis, Abrams & Dengelegi, 1992; Ellis & Velton, 1992.
10. Ellis, 1992d.
11. Ellis, 1977b, 1977c, 1981, 1987c.

12

Behavioral Methods
of Coping with Fatal Illness

As we have been emphasizing in this book, REBT includes quite a number of cognitive, emotive, and behavioral
methods of helping yourself, when you are in or out of therapy. It is particularly behavioral, because I (AE) followed the
early experiments of John B. Watson, the pioneer behaviorist, and used *in vivo* desensitization on myself, when I was in
my late teens, to overcome my neurotic fears of speaking in
public and of approaching young women I was interested in
dating. By forcing myself, no matter how uncomfortable I
was, to make myself first speak in public, and then keep
speaking and speaking, I completely overcame my phobia
within a few months. Then, being more interested in dating
women than I was in public speaking, I tackled that problem
and, once again, made myself talk to one hundred women in
a row in the Bronx Botanical Gardens during the month of
June, when I had finished my Junior year in college, and I
showed myself, despite my steady rejections, that I didn't
have to put myself down or make myself depressed over my
total failure to date any of them.[1]

So REBT, from its inception in 1955, has always favored many behavioral methods of psychotherapy, particularly *in vivo* desensitization. To use this method you
acknowledge that you have some senseless fears, you use active Disputing to show yourself that you will not die and not

suffer disaster if you act against them, and you then painfully and steadily force yourself to do what you are horribly afraid of doing—such as speaking in public, approaching potential dates, playing a sport badly, writing a novel, or otherwise risking failure and rejection that you usually desperately avoid. We shall discuss in this chapter how you can use this technique and a good many other behavioral methods of overcoming your emotional disturbances.[2]

Doing What You Are Irrationally Afraid of Doing

Usually, when you are irrationally afraid of doing something that would be advantageous for you to do—such as writing a business report or asserting yourself with friends—you have ego anxiety. You are then telling yourself, at point B in the ABC's of human disturbance, (1) rational Beliefs (rB's), such as, "I may fail at this task and be disapproved of by others, and I wouldn't want that to happen"; and (2) irrational Beliefs (iB's), such as, "Therefore, I *absolutely must not* fail and be rejected. So I can't risk doing this thing, for my not doing it will prevent my doing it poorly and being rejected." If these are your rational and irrational philosophies, you will not only fail to do this thing—that is, you will be phobic about doing it—but you will also avoid even thinking about doing it, because you will then make yourself feel anxious.

Another reason for your being afraid of things that are really not dangerous may be your low frustration tolerance or your discomfort anxiety. Thus, you may find it uncomfortable to go to high places, to ride in trains, or to speak in public, and may have some good reasons for feeling uncomfortable. You may then tell yourself, "I don't like the discomfort of riding in trains, but it won't kill me. So I won't go out of my way to ride in them but when there is no other good means of transportation, I'll bear the discomfort and take a train."

You may also, however, irrationally tell yourself, "Because I don't like the discomfort of riding in trains, I *absolutely must not* ever suffer this discomfort. It's *awful* and I *can't stand it*. Unless I am dragged kicking and screaming onto a train, I shall never go on one."

You sometimes, then, can have both ego anxiety and discomfort anxiety about doing something, and either or both of these feelings keeps you away from doing it. Frequently, however, you know full well that your phobia is irrational, so you put yourself down for having it: "I *must not* have this phobia and let other people see that I have it. I am a *weak, silly person* for allowing myself to indulge in it!" You can also have discomfort anxiety about having an irrational fear: "It's hard for me to conquer my phobia, and it *shouldn't be* so hard! It causes me all kinds of discomfort and I *must not* have this unnecessary discomfort. How awful it is for me to be plagued by this phobia!"

Both your primary and your secondary disturbances regarding irrational fears consist of your demands and commands for success and for comfort and may be Disputed, just as you can Dispute your other demands, by using the general principles of REBT. However, sometimes these fears are so profound that your Disputing doesn't help too much, and you still won't give up your phobias.

Suppose, for example, one of your close friends or relatives has AIDS and wants to come live with you for a while. You know, lightly or "intellectually," that there is very little chance of your acquiring an HIV infection from your friend as long as both of you take simple precautions so that your body fluids and blood do not come into contact with each other. But you still have such a great fear of acquiring AIDS that you refuse to let your friend stay with you, even for a short while. Then you may castigate yourself for being such a coward and for giving into your irrational fear.

Even with a simple elevator phobia you may feel so terrified about going into elevators that you never enter one, no matter how many times you tell yourself that nothing bad will ever happen if you enter an elevator and that you are being utterly foolish when you avoid riding in one. You are therefore panicking yourself about your panic. You know that you will feel panicked if you force yourself into an elevator; and you keep strongly telling yourself that feeling panicked is *awful* and that you *can't bear* it. So you never "risk" entering a single elevator.

To make things worse, every time you refuse to take this great "risk," you keep telling yourself something like, "If I go into this elevator, I am sure that I will be panicked and that something terrible will then happen to me. So I *have to* stay out of it!" These self-statements then make you *more* afraid of entering elevators than ever. So your avoidance makes your fear of elevators mount and mount!

When you have a profound phobia about anything, you usually are even afraid to *think about* doing this "horrifying" act. The mere thought of doing the thing you are phobic about once again makes you panicked. So you end up by (1) not thinking about your phobia, (2) not risking overcoming it, and (3) not going for any kind of therapy that might help you overcome it. Now you are triply cooked!

Joseph Wolpe, one of the fathers of behavior therapy, worked out a simple method to overcome a phobia that is called systematic desensitization. You can use this method by first imagining the thing you are afraid to do—such as getting on an elevator. But you imagine doing so, say, a year away. Then, if you feel anxious about this image, you relax, using Jacobson's progressive relaxation or some other relaxation techniques. Your relaxing will distract you from and interfere with your fear and may temporarily remove it.

Then you imagine going into the elevator, say, nine months from now, and again relax if you are still anxious. You keep imagining going into the elevator, six months, three months, and a few days from now, and you keep interfering with your anxiety by relaxing. If you keep doing this, you may finally lose your fears of elevators and actually be able to go in them. Why? Because, at least in imagination, you are facing your fear rather than running away from it. When you keep facing almost any fear you have a tendency to become desensitized to it and to see that it is actually not as fearful as you are making it out to be.[2]

You may employ Wolpe's method of systematic desensitization; but the trouble with it is that in order to see if it actually works you will finally have to bite the bullet and try to expose yourself to the thing that you fear. Otherwise, how will you ever know that your imaging technique actually is effective? You won't.

REBT therefore advocates, often from the start, your use of live exposure or *in vivo* desensitization. To use this method you gradually expose yourself to living with your friend or to taking a dreaded elevator, and you can do this a little at a time. Thus, you can let your friend with AIDS visit you for a very short while, then for a longer period of time, and finally for a week or two. Or you can get into an elevator when it is stationary, then take it up for one floor, then for two floors, then for three floors, until you find your fear of elevators wanes. You may even begin to enjoy riding in them!

REBT also recommends, when you are courageous enough to do so, to use implosive exposure—that is, to quickly expose yourself to one of the worst of your phobias and to do so many times in a row, until you thoroughly get over your fear.[3] One of our clients, Suzanne, was so afraid of all infectious diseases, including AIDS, that she wouldn't talk about them, wouldn't read about them, and kept, if she could, a long distance away from anybody who even had a common cold. She became so phobic in this regard that she couldn't keep any kind of regular job, because she would have to be in too close contact with a number of people, even in a small office, who might well have an infectious disease.

Suzanne was first shown how to use REBT to convince herself, over and over again, that most diseases, including AIDS, are really not that transmittable if she took common precautions. She also worked on herself to give up the irrational idea that if she did catch a disease like a common cold, it would surely lead to horrible complications—such as pneumonia—and that she then could not survive.

Suzanne tried Wolpe's imaginal systematic desensitization and it worked to the extent of allowing her to be able to think about a communicative disease without feeling utterly panicked. But she was still afraid to go near anyone who had or who might possibly have a disease. So in desperation—for she still was not able to hold any regular job—she first made herself take crowded subway trains five days a week and go from one train to another, until she went on at least ten a day. When she had done this for two months and only contracted one cold, which lasted five days and then disappeared, she began to see how silly her fears were and to feel relaxed when she was on a subway train. She then made herself volunteer for hospital duty and for another three months take many patients from their beds to other parts of the hospital where they would undergo various tests, and then take them back to their regular wards again. She contracted no ailment whatever, learned a great deal about taking precautions when she was around AIDS and other infectious individuals, and got entirely over her disease phobia.

At one of her last therapy sessions, Suzanne said, "I don't know if I could have done any active exposure to get over my phobia if I had not done a lot of REBT Disputing first. But I got myself to see, by doing strong Disputing, that even if I did catch almost any disease, except of course AIDS, I would most likely survive it. I also saw that my phobia itself was about the worst 'disaster' I could have, because it thoroughly incapacitated me, while having a real disease would not handicap me that much. Once I saw that, I realized that I could gradually expose myself to people who might be diseased, but I decided that course would probably take forever. So I made myself, as you remember, go on subway trains many times. Then I made myself take the volunteer job at the hospital. Those were the two best things I ever did for myself in my entire life, because now I am really free of that stupid phobia, and intend to keep myself free of it forever! Continual exposure was the right thing for me. Once I forced myself to keep doing it, it saved me enormous amounts of time and effort."

Using Reinforcements

As we have noted before in this book, REBT is highly behavioral as well as cognitive and emotive, and therefore often uses reinforcement or operant conditioning to help people change their self-defeating ways. Reinforcement principles have been supported by literally hundreds of experiments, largely following the theories of B.F. Skinner, the famous Harvard psychologist, who found that when you wish to succeed at a task—such as to hit a golf ball into a hole— and you actually perform it satisfactorily, you tend to keep repeating this task. When you fail and keep failing at it, you tend to give up and stop trying to do it.[4]

By the same token, when you find a task difficult to do—such as asking someone for a favor—you are much more likely to do it when you reward or reinforce yourself *after* you perform it. Thus if you allow yourself to have a good meal or to watch TV only after you perform this task, you will be more likely to do it than when you do not reward or reinforce yourself. Because people are often more prone to resist doing difficult tasks, such as giving up an addiction or stopping their procrastination, when they are not quickly reinforced for doing so, principles of reinforcement are often used to help them overcome their resistance.

Suppose, for example, that one of your close friends is suffering with a fatal disease but is refusing to take proper medical care of himself and is therefore not taking his medication or doing the physical exercises that his physicians strongly recommend. If you want to help this friend change his destructive behavior you can make an agreement with him that you will only visit him and do certain things for him *after* he regularly follows medical instructions. If the reinforcements that you use with your friend when he follows your agreement are sufficiently meaningful and rewarding, he will probably follow medical procedures when you keep reinforcing him—and may stop following them when you no longer reward him as you said you would.

Similarly with yourself. Suppose that you avoid doing some of the REBT homework that you have set for yourself. Or you keep promising an ill friend to see her regularly but then keep failing to keep this promise. If you will set yourself a meaningful reward or reinforcement that you allow yourself only *after* you have done one of the things you are avoiding, you will tend to find it easier to do.

Getting yourself to do some task that you are avoiding by arranging to reinforce yourself after you have done it often works. But it also has its disadvantages and limitations. Maimonides, the great Jewish scholar, pointed out several centuries ago that if we teach children to read good books only on condition that we will approve of them or give them some specific reward when they read, that will probably help them do more reading—but they will then do it mainly for the reward and not for the intrinsic pleasure that they can find in reading and learning. In fact, some of them may become more averse than ever to reading, because they realize that they are being forced to do it by external reinforcements rather than for their own desires.

When you reinforce someone for doing a difficult task by giving her approval for doing it, this kind of reward may have another disadvantage: The person you are reinforcing may decide that she *absolutely needs* your approval, and that she is *worthless* if she doesn't get it. So she may also actually reinforce her dire need for approval and thereby harm herself. If you use approval as a reinforcer, for yourself or for anyone else, try to see that the reinforced person doesn't increase her dire need for approval.[5]

Billy, one of our clients who had terminal cancer, was at first awfulizing about his condition and was insisting that because he hadn't done anything to bring it on—hadn't smoked, or eaten the wrong foods—he *shouldn't* have come down with cancer of the bladder. When he used REBT Disputing to try to surrender these irrational Beliefs (iB's), he was able to overcome them and to feel much better. But he disliked having to go back to vigorous Disputing when his iB's returned so he fell back to feelings of severe depression.

To help himself Dispute more regularly, Billy only allowed himself to listen to classical music, which was the great love of his life, after he spent at least a half hour a day of forceful Disputing. This kind of reinforcement worked, and he was able to continue uprooting his disturbed philosophies until the end of his life, two years later. Everyone marveled that he lasted that long, considering how bad was his physical condition. But he insisted that his steady Disputing, and the lack of emotional upsetness which it created, was the main reason for his living much longer than anyone expected him to live.

The Use of Penalties

Reinforcements work very well with children—who will do almost anything if you reward them with M&Ms!—and with adults who are not too severely addicted to self-defeating behaviors. But they often fail with people who have deep-dyed disturbed habits. Heavy smokers, for example, are not likely to give up their three packs of cigarettes a day if, when they do so, they use reinforcements like food, reading, or music. For they feel so pained and horrified when they are deprived of cigarettes that the reinforcements they allow themselves when they abstain are not pleasurable enough to compensate for their addiction.

It has therefore been found, in REBT and other forms of behavior-oriented therapy, that setting stiff penalties is sometimes required if people are to surrender their deeply ingrained destructive habits. Robbie, for example, was addicted to crack and heroin and acquired an HIV-positive infection through the use of contaminated needles. He was told, shortly after his infection was discovered, that his continuing to take drugs was the worst thing he could do and would impair his immune system and bring on AIDS faster. That, as you may well imagine, didn't stop Robbie's use of crack and heroin. In fact, he used his dismal future as an excuse, and insisted, "Since I'm doomed to get AIDS anyway, and since my life is going to be much shorter than it otherwise would be, I might as well keep indulging in the greatest pleasure I have—the highs I get from crack and heroin."

Three of Robbie's best friends, who knew REBT and were determined to get him to give up drugs, realized that they would have to arrange a severe penalty that he would experience immediately after taking crack or heroin. They had difficulty figuring out what such a penalty could be and how to make sure that Robbie actually used it. They finally came up with the idea that every time they discovered that he used crack or heroin they would make him send $250 in cash to a fundamentalist religious group in which he had been raised and whose ideas and practices he now thoroughly abhorred.

When, on a few occasions, Robbie went back to taking crack or heroin, his friends made sure that they quickly got him to give them $250 in cash, which they immediately sent to the religious group he hated, with a note saying that he greatly favored their work and wanted to help them promote it. After seeing that Robbie exacted his penalty three times, they succeeded in getting him to discontinue his use of crack and heroin.

So the setting and the enacting of severe penalties can work—for yourself or for any of your close associates who want to change an obnoxious habit but who will not ordinarily go through the pain of withdrawing from it. What penalties shall you set? That depends on you and the particular person that you are trying to help. Some of those that we have discovered are effective include sending money, as Robbie did, to an obnoxious cause; burning a hundred dollars or more every time you indulge in your destructive habit; forcing yourself to have sex with someone you dislike; talking at length with a boring person; eating a large portion of some food you detest; spending several hours at a very unpleasant task; making yourself unnecessarily lie, steal, or do some other unethical act that you abhor; refraining from following an observance that your religion considers very important; pointing out to some of your best friends their behaviors that you really detest; and letting unethical people get away with things that you would normally make a real effort to stop them from doing.[6]

Staying in an Uncomfortable Situation

People who have low frustration tolerance (LFT) quickly cop out of uncomfortable situations, without trying to correct them or to get over their horror of them. Thus, they leave good jobs because one of their co-workers is nasty to them and arouses their anger. Or they stay up late reading or looking at television because they are afraid to talk with their mates about relationship problems. Or they desert their families without trying to solve economic or other difficulties that, if they worked at it, they might solve.

In cases like these, REBT tries to help people stay in an uncomfortable situation until they stop upsetting themselves about it and then try to rectify it. Jules, for example, wanted a steady relationship with another gay male because he felt that it would be more satisfying in the long run than the brief relationships he usually had and because it would be much safer in regard to acquiring any sexually transmitted disease (STD). But he couldn't bring himself to talk intimately to his partners and he had low frustration tolerance about any of the failings that he soon found that they had. So, although he kept telling himself that he would do his best to find a steady lover, he picked the "easy" path of going from one brief encounter to another.

When Jules began to have REBT sessions, he worked

on his frustration intolerance when one of his partners did or said "wrong" things. Instead of running away from this partner, as he usually quickly did, he stayed with him, put up with the hassles that ensued, and fought against his irrational Beliefs (iB's) that he *couldn't stand* any such problems, that they *absolutely must not* occur, and that it was *completely awful* when they did occur.

With his partner, Sal, Jules finally strongly Disputed his iB's and came up with the Effective New Philosophy, "Yes, Sal really has his failings. He often avoids having sex, he says very stupid things, and he spends too much money. What a nuisance! But when he is ready to have sex he's damned good at it. I can easily ignore and live with some of the stupid things he says. And I can let him spend as much of his own money as he wants, without going along with him and spending too much of mine. So in some ways he's a nuisance. But who the hell isn't? If I really want to learn to settle down with anyone, I can accept Sal pretty much the way he is and show myself that I definitely *can* stand the hassles I have with him, and that they're merely *inconvenient* but hardly *awful*. I *wish* they wouldn't occur, but they *must* occur as long as Sal is Sal. So I'd better focus on his good, and not on his bad, points and see if I can make the best, rather then the worst, of my relationship with him."

Jules worked at believing this Effective New Philosophy, and for the next year was able to stay with Sal and to largely enjoy their relationship. He calmed down in the process, and got rid of his low frustration tolerance and his anger against Sal. Later, when he unangrily ascertained that Sal was hardly the best partner for him and that he could most probably find a better one—but one, of course, who still had his failings and limitations—he broke up with Sal and started a new relationship with Arthur. Arthur also had his problems and difficulties; but the low frustration tolerance that Jules decreased while he was with Sal put Jules in good stead with Arthur, and he was able to maintain a satisfying relationship with his new partner for the next several years.

Consider, therefore, any situation that you are in, at school, at work, in your family life, in your neighborhood, or elsewhere. Acknowledge—which you probably will have no trouble doing—its real disadvantages and limitations. But also look at its advantages. As you focus on the hassles, notice how you are disturbing yourself about them—making yourself very angry, depressed, panicked, or self-pitying. If this is the case, find your irrational Beliefs (iB's) with which you are creating your needless disturbance and actively Dispute them until you change them to rational preferences. For example: "My boss *doesn't* have to treat me kindly and fairly, though I really wish that he would do so." "My mate is a real pain in the ass in many ways, but she has her very good points, too. And I don't *have to* make her give up her bad ones!"

While you notice that you are unhealthily angry and horrified about the situation you are in, temporarily make yourself stay right where you are. Don't cop out and run away. Don't insist that your unfortunate Activating Experiences *absolutely have to be* changed. No, put up with them until you no longer feel very upset about them. Then, when your horror about the situation has vanished or moderated, make a hedonic calculus about the advantages and disadvantages of the situation.

A hedonic calculus means that you spend some time— perhaps a week or two—listing all the advantages of staying in this situation, of which you may be able to find quite a few, and then rate each one of these on a scale of 1 to 10. Thus, staying with a partner who is sexually good for you may rate 9 or 10 on this scale of advantages; or, if sex doesn't matter to you that much, it may only rate 2 or 3. Anyway, rate all the advantages of staying in the situation and then add these ratings up, to see how much they total.

Then you do the same for the disadvantages of the situation you are in. Rate each one, again from 1 to 10. Thus, staying with a partner who spends too much money may rate, in your view, a 6 or a 7. So, again, you take all the disadvantage ratings and add them up, to get a total.

If the total advantages of your staying in your present situation come to, say, a score of 78 and the total disadvantages of your staying in it come to a score of, say, 52, you then seem to think it more advantageous than disadvantageous to stay. But remember, first change your "horror" of staying in the situation (or your "horror" of leaving it). Then you will be able to decide more sensibly whether to stay or leave.

Using Stimulus Control

When you want to break an addictive habit you will often find it easier to do so when you employ the method of stimulus control. For most of your habits—such as eating or drinking too much, avoiding the medical procedures that it would be wise for you to take, and indulging in fits of rage and self-pity—are often triggered by things you encounter regularly in your environment. If you can manage to avoid these things, you may more easily give up your destructive habits.

Eating too much, for example, may be triggered by your passing a fine bakery on the way home from work and you may be able to take a different route and thus avoid this trigger for your overeating. Avoiding "obnoxious" medical procedures may be triggered by your contacts with a physician whom you personally dislike. So you may avoid this trigger by avoiding this physician or by checking his instructions with a physician whom you do like.[7]

Controlling environmental stimuli so that you minimize your risk of having them "control" you is not an elegant way of changing your bad habits, because it does not necessarily change your irrational Beliefs that mainly trigger your poor behavior and only changes some of your Activating Events (A's) or triggers. Thus, if you pass a fine bakery on your way home from work and the sight and smell of it "triggers" you to buy more cake than you ordinarily would buy, it is not really the bakery that "makes" you buy the cake, but your irrational Beliefs (iB's), such as: "Now that I am reminded, by passing this bakery, that the cake it sells is unusually delicious, I not only would *like* to have some of it, but I *need* it and *can't stand* being deprived of it! How *awful* if I have to pass it every day and not buy and eat its delicious cake!"

If, then, you merely arrange to take another route home and never pass this bakery, you still have the tendency to create these iB's, and you will probably have them, and act on them, when you pass other bakeries that have delicious cake. Or you may go out of your way to find other bakery stores—or even order cake by phone! So it would be nice if you actually allowed yourself to pass the good bakery every day and used the sight of it to practice facing your irrational Beliefs and actively Disputing them and giving them up. Then you would be less likely to buy cake—or other kinds of food—that sabotage your diet.

To be practical, however, you can use stimulus control to avoid "triggering" some of your bad habits. At the same time, you can discover your irrational Beliefs (iB's) that "trigger" these habits and then work hard at changing them for more preferential Beliefs. Such as, "The sight of this bakery reminds me that its cakes are delicious and I would prefer to buy and eat them. But I don't *need* what I *want, never have* to give into my preference, and can avoid buying a cake no matter how many times I pass this and other bakeries."

Florence had scleroderma and knew that she would continue to be in pain, would be quite restricted, and would eventually die of it. She was bitter because a number of her best friends, once they found out that she was stricken, seemed to avoid contact with her. As far as she could tell, some of them were afraid that she was contagious, which was not true. Others feared that she would ask them for too much help. Still others thought that visiting her was too grim. And some others knew they couldn't enjoy the activities, such as playing tennis, that they previously enjoyed with her.

All these reasons, Florence felt, were illegitimate. Her rational Beliefs (rB's) were that it was most unfortunate that so many of her former friends avoided her, but that was to be expected when she had such a serious illness. Her irrational Beliefs (iB's) were: "Considering how close we used to be with each other, and the things we enjoyed together, they *shouldn't* be avoiding me now. After all, if they had my condition, I wouldn't be avoiding them, would go out of my way to visit, and would try to help them in every way. Why can't they treat me the same way that I would surely treat them? How terrible that they do this! They're only fair weather friends, and really are pretty rotten people!"

Because Florence felt so bitter and angry whenever one of her former friends would write her how sorry they felt about her condition and then never call her or come to visit her, she stopped reading much of her mail. "It's too painful to read what those hypocrites write!" she told herself and put her mail in an unread pile.

She also got a telephone answering device, so that she could screen out her calls and refuse to answer the phone when one of her "hypocritical" friends called and she "knew" that the call would be brief and would not be followed up with any visit. So Florence became something of a hermit. Her use of stimulus control methods at times worked well, because she saved herself from much bitterness and rage by not reading the letters and not having phone conversations with her "offending" former friends. Soon they stopped writing and calling, so she no longer had to go out of her way to avoid contact with them.

When, however, Florence joined a self-help group whose members consisted of several other people with scleroderma and similar diseases, she found that most of them were not as bitter and angry as she was, even when they had similar experiences with their friends. Some of them had different attitudes about their loss of social contacts than she had; and one of them had read several books on REBT, especially Warren Johnson's *So Desperate the Fight*, and showed Florence how she was using REBT to overcome her self-damaging feelings about being afflicted with her fatal disease.[8]

So Florence started using REBT, too, had several sessions by phone with a psychologist who helped her understand and work with it, and began to see that her former friends had the right to act toward her in a less friendly manner. She lost her rage and bitterness, started to read her mail and answer her phone calls, and was able to maintain good contact with several of her friends who did devote some time to her and who gave her help and support. She also made some new friends in her self-help group and when they, because of their physical and emotional limitations, disappointed her on several occasions, she was able to accept this, not incense herself about their actions, and continue good relationships with them.

Using Skill Training

The behavioral aspects of REBT often include a good deal of skill training. Thus, in the 1950's and 1960's, I (AE) saw that emotionally disturbed people often have skill deficits. Sometimes, because of their disturbances, such as social phobias, they do not acquire the skills that other people acquire and practice. Sometimes, because of their skill deficits—such as attention deficit disorder, hyperactivity, dyslexia, stuttering, and lack of physical coordination—they became (or, in REBT terms, made themselves) disturbed.

One of my early REBT clients, Cynthia, had a nervous stutter and limped from a childhood accident to her hip, felt that she was too handicapped, and avoided social functions (while her younger and much less attractive sister became something of a social butterfly). Cynthia withdrew and made herself inaccessible and then, as you might expect, severely condemned herself for being socially inept.

I had little trouble in helping Cynthia to dig up some of her underlying irrational Beliefs (iB's), such as: "I *have to be* as socially competent as my sister. I'm just *no good* if I can't meet and talk to people. Because I know that I could improve socially if I didn't keep myself phobic, I'm clearly worthless for giving in to my fears and not making myself overcome them."

As Cynthia looked at these iB's and kept Disputing them, she became much less disturbed and began to plan to have more of a social and dating life. But she still had no particular skills. So I showed her several methods of encountering new people, talking to them, encouraging dates, becoming more intimate, having suitable sex relations, and acquiring other social skills. I often give workshops at the Institute for Rational-Emotive Therapy in New York on Creative Encounters and on Social Skills Training, and I taught Cynthia many of the methods that I teach in these workshops.

Also, beginning with my book, *How to Live With a Neurotic*, in 1957, and continuing with a series of other writings, a number of REBT materials have included considerable skill training.[9]

In 1963 the first edition of *The Intelligent Woman's Guide to Dating and Mating* had a chapter entitled, "How to Be Assertive Without Being Aggressive," which, along with the books of Andrew Salter and Joseph Wolpe, was one of the pioneering writings in the field of assertion training. REBT continued its skill training and assertion training teachings in the 1970's by influencing Robert Alberti and Michael Emmons' *Your Perfect Right*, by Janet Wolfe's Ph.D. thesis on REBT and assertion training, and by producing many other pamphlets, books, talks, and workshops.[10]

Skill training and assertion training are especially important for individuals who are afflicted with a serious or fatal illness. Such people have limited energies and abilities and, because of these handicaps, often have skill deficits. Thus, they cannot socialize, dance, exercise, or do many other things as well as can physically healthy people. Because of their limitations, they frequently withdraw from many normal activities, do not get the usual practice at them, become less skilled than others do, and sometimes forget skills that they once had. Therefore, they had better have specific instruction, in the form of physical therapy, courses, individual instruction, workshops, psychotherapy, and other forms of skill training.

If you are suffering from a serious disease or physical handicap, look for your skill deficits. Some of them may not be remediable. If you are in a wheelchair you may not be able to walk, play tennis, or do many other acts that are easy for non-handicapped individuals to do. But some of your handicaps may be improved. You can usually learn to converse better, to be more assertive, and to take socializing risks—as long as you don't put yourself down for not having certain skills or not being able to completely overcome your deficits.

So use REBT to accept yourself with your limitations and, at the same time, work at improving them. To this end, use the kinds of things that we, as therapists, often recommend to our handicapped (and nonhandicapped) clients: skill training literature, audiovisual materials, talks, workshops, courses, and individual instruction.

Don't, however, conclude that you can accept yourself mainly *because* you acquire better skills than you previously had. This kind of conditional acceptance is better than self-downing. But as we keep emphasizing, it still rests on the false assumption that you can only feel self-accepting when you perform tasks well or outstandingly well. First accept yourself *un*conditionally—then also work on acquiring useful skills or improving those that you already have. Unconditional acceptance will help you continue to improve your skills while you are still doing badly and even while, because of your physical limitations, you may continue to do worse than non-handicapped individuals may do.

Try, also, to acquire social and other skills not merely so

that you will do better with other people but also because you can intrinsically enjoy many of the things at which you make yourself skilled. Thus, Christy Brown, when he taught himself to type out his poems with his two big toes on an electric typewriter, greatly enjoyed composing these poems and other writings, and did not merely do so in order to win the approval of others. And, as we noted in Chapter 9, you can make one or more of your skills into a vital absorbing interest—as Brown did with his poetry. That sort of preoccupation can immeasurably help you to lead a much happier life.

Regular and Paradoxical Homework

Let us remind you, once again, that the first two major insights that you can acquire while using REBT are: (1) "I mainly upset myself about some of the unfortunate Activating Events (A's) of my life, rather than just get upset by these events." (2) "No matter how or when I originally started to make myself disturbed about these unfortunate A's by telling myself, at point B, that they *absolutely should not* and *must not* occur and that it is *terrible* when they do, it is not my past experiences that still upset me today but my present irrational Beliefs (iB's) *about* these events."

Assuming that you are acquiring and using these valuable REBT insights, you had better go on to its third major insight: "In order to change my irrational Beliefs and the disturbed feelings and dysfunctional behaviors that often accompany them, insight is not enough. There is normally no way but much work and practice—yes, much work and practice—to keep thinking, feeling, and behaving to undo my disturbance."

If you understand and use Insight Number 3 you will, of course, have to do considerable homework. Just learning REBT in individual or group therapy, in a self-help group, or through talks, workshops, courses, literature, and audiovisual aids, is not enough unless you practice, practice, and practice it! So as you learn the REBT methods we have been describing in this book, make sure that you give yourself, or work out with others, some regular homework assignments and consistently carry out these assignments. As we have shown here in the previous chapters, your homework can consist of a good many different cognitive, emotive, and behavioral assignments.

The techniques and exercises that you can take from this book are almost all straightforward and merely require that you plan them and force yourself to keep doing them—sometimes, to some extent, for the rest of your life. But you can also use some paradoxical homework assignments, because, as Viktor Frankl, Milton Erickson, and a number of psychiatrists and psychologists have shown, paradox can work very well both to help make you disturbed and to reduce your disturbances.[11]

Thus, we often tell our clients the fable of the King who didn't want a favorite Prince to marry his daughter unless the Prince passed many difficult tests that the King's wise men had dreamed up. The Prince, to the King's chagrin, passed all these tests. So, fearing that he would have no excuse to stop the Prince from marrying his daughter, the King warned his wise men that he would have them decapitated unless they found at least one important task that the Prince could not do, and thereby make him forfeit the Princess's hand in marriage. The wise men were pretty desperate but they finally found a task that the Prince could not perform: "*Don't* think of a pink elephant for twenty minutes!"

Paradoxically, of course, if the prince then told himself, "I *must not* think of a pink elephant! I *must not* think of a pink elephant!" he would then be thinking of one. So he couldn't pass this task and forfeited the Princess's hand. Similarly, if you tell yourself, "I *must not* be panicked about trains!" you will most likely be panicked when you think about or get on a train. And if you tell yourself, "I *must not* have another grim nightmare!" you will very likely keep bringing on grim nightmares. Why? Because that is how most humans work: When they think that they *absolutely must* perform a task well, they make themselves so anxious about it that they usually perform it badly; and when they tell themselves that they *absolutely must not* think or dream about bad things, they almost always increase their thoughts and dreams about these feelings. Odd—but true!

If, therefore, you are afraid to fail at something, such as social encounters, and you give yourself the paradoxical assignment of making sure that you fail at befriending ten new people, you will most likely fail at most of them all right—but you will usually have some successes while you accomplish your failures. And if you paradoxically keep doing something that you are phobic about doing—such as riding in trains or in elevators—you will most likely become less fearful of doing this thing; while, as we previously noted, if you keep avoiding the trains or elevators that you are phobic about, you will probably intensify your phobias.

So see if you can give yourself some paradoxical as well as regular homework assignments. Now don't, of course, engage in truly dangerous acts. Don't, for example, lean out of high balconies or have intercourse with a new partner without using a condom and other forms of protection. But review some of your irrational fears—such as your fear that you will be a worthless individual if you fail at making a new friend—and deliberately act against them. Try, for example, making a number of new friends, and showing yourself that nothing terrible really happens when you fail in many of your tries.

Some of your paradoxical homework assignments can be done through imagination and visualization, as Thomas Stempfl, a behavioral psychologist, has shown. Thus, if you are afraid of spiders and frantically try to avoid them or even to avoid thinking about them or looking at photos of them, you can deliberately imagine yourself encountering a barrel of spiders, see yourself looking intently and consistently at them, and even visualize your handling them. If you keep doing this, you will have a good chance of desensitizing yourself to spiders, freeing yourself to think about them, and even later encountering real spiders with minimal feelings of anxiety.[12]

John was terribly afraid to visit his friend, Saul, who had AIDS, even though Saul assured him that many other people had visited and none of them had come down with AIDS or any other infectious disease and even though Saul also assured him that they would have no direct contact if John did visit him. But John stayed strictly away and would only talk to Saul on the phone, and at times even crazily thought that kind of contact would lead to his becoming infected.

John came to REBT treatment for his general anxiety and for this particular fear of visiting Saul and another of his friends, David, who had an HIV-positive infection. In the course of his REBT sessions, he learned how to Dispute his irrational Beliefs that he could easily acquire AIDS by visiting Saul and David, and he even learned how to Dispute his irrational Beliefs (iB's) that if he ever did acquire AIDS he absolutely couldn't stand it and couldn't have any pleasure whatever for the rest of his life.

His Disputing his iB's helped John considerably, so that he no longer obsessed about catching AIDS and stopped having nightmares about acquiring it. But he still didn't dare to visit Saul or his HIV-positive friend. So he paradoxically got a list of AIDS and HIV-positive victims, made sure that he visited twenty-five of them, even shook hands with several of them, and within a month of starting to do this he lost his AIDS phobia. He soon was able to visit Saul and David with no trouble, and did a good many helpful errands for both of them.

Notes to Chapter 12

1. Ellis, 1965, 1972d, 1990a, 1990c.
2. Ellis, 1962; Wolpe, 1991.
3. Ellis, 1983.
4. Skinner, 1938.

5. Ellis, 1983.

6. Ellis, 1965, 1988a; Ellis, Abrams & Dengelegi, 1992; Ellis & Velten, 1992.

7. Ellis, Abrams & Dengelegi, 1992; Ellis & Velten, 1992.

8. W.R. Johnson, 1981.

9. Ellis, 1963, 1965, 1973a, 1975a, 1976b, 1979b, 1980b, 1988a; Wolfe, 1992.

10. Alberti & Emmons, 1990; Ellis, 1975a, 1977a, 1979d; Wolfe & Fodor, 1975.

11. Erickson, 1981; Frankl, 1959.

12. Stampfl & Levis, 1967.

13

To Grieve or Depress Yourself? That Is the Question

Grief is one of the most painful and hurtful but often self-helping emotions. When we lose someone we love, depend on, or identify with, we will naturally suffer, sometimes a little and sometimes a great deal. We make people close to us part of our lives and when we lose them we lose part of ourselves. So when we lose them we grieve for our own loss of completeness.

Through grieving, you can mourn for the loss of a central part to your life; and if you accepted this loss as sad but irreparable you may move on to many other lovable people and things.

Grief doesn't merely stem from the death of a loved person. It can arise from any expected or actual loss. If you are fighting a mortal illness you easily grieve for the loss of the security and regularity that usually go with health. Or you may grieve for yourself, the person whose health and energy is waning. This kind of grieving is a natural and sometimes inevitable response to losing part of oneself.

If you are grieving about your or a friend's serious illness, it is important that you know the difference between the rational and healthy grief arising from personal loss and irrational (self-destructive) grief. The latter usually involves depression. If, for example, you are disfigured and lose some

217

of your attractiveness or social acceptability, your rational responses to this can be: "This is very frustrating, but I can still
live with this loss and lead an enjoyable life." You would then
feel appropriate grief. Your irrational response can be, "No
one will want to have anything to do with me, and that's
awful! I can't bear this loss and have any enjoyment!" You
would then feel depressed.

With demanding and absolutistic statements, like "This
deprivation *must* not occur, and it is *completely terrible!*"
you will usually feel depressed. Your feeling of real deprivation and sadness is natural and healthy. But your feeling of
horror and depression is common but unhealthy.

Although you may accept the losses that occur with
your gradual aging, sudden losses from severe illness can be
dramatic and startling. If you can anticipate and predict
these changes and losses, you can make potentially stressful
events less noxious. This can be accomplished when you are
severely ill by becoming informed about the course, treatment, and probable outcome of your illness.

Understanding and anticipating your impairments will
allow you to see them as the normal progression of your illness. You will tend less to see them as punishments from
God, or acts of unfairness of the universe directed at you.
You will then usually feel sad and regretful, but not depressed and embittered.

When you know your days are limited, you will normally feel quite sad about the impending loss of your own
existence. Even most of us who are not ill commonly grieve
about our eventual end. We look ahead to a time in which
the world will go on without us, and feel sad or deprived.
Even when we are aging we may grieve about the "approaching" end of our lives. We often tell ourselves "How
sad that my youth is gone forever," "How unfair it is that I
am growing old while others are still young." This is normal
sorrow. But we also may depress ourselves with self-destructive statements like, "I can't stand getting older. How terrible!" So it is not surprising that, if you are facing a terminal

illness, you may healthfully grieve at the unhealthful loss of self that mortality represents.

Anticipatory grief about your dying is not pathological if it is limited to a poignant sadness, or a frustration at the unfairness at having to face your end sooner than you would prefer. But when you make yourself severely depressed, enraged, or horrified about dying, you are indulging in demands on reality with which it will simply not comply.

Thus, you are demanding that the world must not be so unfair as to shorten your life. Or you are insisting that it absolutely should not treat you so unfairly as it actually is treating you. Marvelous musturbation!

To demand that a person you lose by death absolutely must not, should not have died, and that you can't stand her or his demise, is highly dramatic—but also silly. So is the command that you have to live as long as you want to. This irrational Belief (iB) will make you enraged, panicked, or all of the above. By whining about your (or anyone else's) impending death, you are fighting a battle that you, or anyone else, can't win. All of us die. Few facts are less challengeable. Despite our awareness of this reality, we usually are relatively unconcerned about our inevitable demise. Why? Because we have made the implicit—and highly sensible—decision to accept it.

What is the greatest difference between someone with cancer, AIDS, or some other life-threatening illness and a person in good health? Duration of existence. As one of our clients with AIDS once said, "My fuse is shorter." If you choose to view it this way, you will find yourself less depressed and angry than if you see yourself as entirely different from a healthy person. Listen for your demands, and your horrifying, if you are dispirited rather than grieving about your unfortunate state. Look for your demands for fairness ("Why me!"). Observe whether you are damning God, your doctors, or other people you believe to be at fault for your illness.

Find your horrification of your illness. Acknowledge

that it is your irrational Beliefs (iB's), philosophies, and atti-tudes that underlie your disturbed emotions. If you find them and actively challenge them, as we have been showing in this book, you will find yourself spending less time de-pressing yourself, and more time making the most of the op-portunities for enjoyment that you still have.

Many people are fortunate enough to survive without ever having a life-threatening illness, but few never have a loved one with a fatal ailment. Grief, therefore, is almost an inevitable part of life. However, if you panic and depress yourself when expecting someone's death you almost always harm yourself and others. Anticipatory grief—which is usu-ally anticipatory panic—leads to needless suffering while your loved one is still alive. You then bring on terror, depres-sion, and often severe withdrawal.

Paradoxically, you then tend to hurt the people for whom you are doing advanced grieving. You keep them at an emotional distance, you see them as already gone, so you make them less a part of your life. However, of course, they are still alive and can be left feeling rejected, depressed, and angry.

If you have someone you love who is dying, examine what you are saying to yourself about your expected loss. If you are panicked or depressed, you are probably saying things like "I cannot bear to lose my friend," or "This loss shouldn't happen and when it does, it will be terrible!"

If you find yourself making irrational self-statements like these, actively Dispute them. Show yourself that you and everyone you love is dying, some just more rapidly than others. Show yourself that you can stand to see a loved one pass away, because you always stood the idea that he or she would die. To say it is horrible that your loved one is dying prematurely is mistaken because you have no basis to know when someone should die. Of course, if someone is terminal when very young, this is sad and unfair, but sad and unfair events should sometimes exist. Accepting this unfair reality will allow you to have the closest possible relationship with your dying friend.

You may easily make yourself guilty when you are losing or have lost a close relative or friend. You may obsess about whether you have done enough for this person, or if you have done or felt the "right" things. This kind of guilt is virtually never useful or justified. If you cared for the person you probably did everything you could have done. To say that you should have helped the person more than you did is almost the same as saying that you should have been a different person. Everything you did, said, and felt was a function of your basic personality and you could not then (though you may be able to now) behave differently.

Moreover, you are always a fallible human, always imperfect, always prone to err and at times transgress. It is also extremely irrational to blame yourself for information you obtain after the fact. Before and after the time your loved one was sick you acted with the information that was then available. And you acted according to your feelings and perceptions at that time. It follows, then, that everything you did was exactly what you should have done!

Anger or rage at your beloved's illness is also destructive. Thus, you may enrage yourself at his or her dismal state or at some of the people you expected to help more while your loved one is dying. Rage means that your wish for this person's good health is raised to a destructive demand. When you feel rage you are damning doctors, friends, or others who you feel let you or your loved one down. You are insisting that they should have acted differently. They acted according to their characters and temperament. Demanding that they be different from the way they are will only create your own emotional disturbance. Work on accepting that people are the way they are and they have no imperative to behave according to your rules of living, no matter how "right" your rules may be. Making yourself angry and betrayed will serve to isolate and alienate you.

Sometimes you direct your anger at the dying or dead

person you love. If you are feeling this way, you are demanding that he or she must not let you down by dying. How arrogant! Do you believe that people you care for absolutely should do more to prolong their lives? Did they arrange to die too soon? Are they rottenly unfair for leaving you alone? Do they have to be more kindly toward and considerate of poor you? What nonsense!

Larry, a successful twenty-nine-year-old executive, was very attached to his father and suffered from anticipatory panic when he saw the father going downhill after he had a stroke. Realizing that his father's condition was hopeless he still insisted, "I must help him and save him! I can't let him suffer and die!" Because Larry was helpless to do what he absolutely "must" do, he made himself deeply depressed. "I need him, need him and can't bear living without his love and support!"

Larry at first saw a psychoanalyst, who listened to his painful childhood and present desperation for fifteen sessions, said practically nothing, and left him more depressed than ever. When, after a few more months, his father died, Larry was at first relieved because he at least was able to give up his demand that he save his father from suffering. But he still felt severely depressed, withdrew from enjoyable activities like playing tennis, and barely was able to function on his job.

A friend who had benefited from REBT practically dragged him into therapy and Larry found almost immediately that he liked his therapist actively conversing with him, unlike his previous analyst's compulsive passive listening. With his therapist's help he was soon in touch with his demands while his father was dying—"I must help him and save him!"—which led to his anticipatory panic. And he clearly saw his continuing insistences after his father's death: "I still need him! I can't bear being without his love and support for the rest of my life! What good at all is my remaining alive, when he is completely dead?"

While actively Disputing this necessitizing, Larry lifted his depression, resumed his enjoyable activities, and went back to his absorbing work. He still grieved about the real loss of his father. But he no longer demanded that this loss must not exist and accepted it as very unfortunate and depressing—but not "disastrous" and "horrible." While panicked and depressed, Larry's sensitive body acted up—as so many people's do when they incessantly overstress themselves—and he experienced severe headaches and dizziness that at first made some of his physicians fear that he had a brain tumor. All his physical symptoms ceased—as they sometimes do—when REBT helped him overcome his self-defeating panic and depression and resume his appropriate feelings of grief for the loss of his father.

Grief can take many forms and can persist for extended periods. If you have lost someone, and suspect that you are suffering more than other people in bereavement, if you grieve too long, by all means check with a professional. Prolonged, severe grief, or grief resulting in physical problems may well really be serious depression. If so, that can be diagnosed and treated with REBT.

14

Living with Dying: Those Who Rationally Faced Fatal Illness

You can often best confront your (or one of your friends) dying by learning from people who have reacted sanely and sensibly to this ordinarily grim experience. So let us look at the coping strategies of people—some of them famous—who have avoided the awfulizing, obsessing, and social withdrawal to which terminally ill people frequently succumb. Some of those we are about to describe fully enjoyed the remaining time that they had, and, remarkably, they appear to have lived longer than they otherwise would have lived, because reducing one's stress may lead to improved immune function and longer survival.

Most of the people we will now describe have never studied REBT, nor been helped by an REBT therapist. Yet all of them appear to utilize many of the principles we have discussed in this book. How come? Probably because REBT methods are so good for coping with serious adversities that some problem-solving people naturally figure them out and use them. Yes, some aspects of REBT are "common sense" solutions to life's problems.

The virus that results in the particularly catastrophic disease, AIDS, has afflicted more than one million people in the United States. Among those infected have been several well-known individuals, who have exemplified the attitude toward terminal illness that we present in this book. Arthur Ashe is among the better known of these people.

A champion in tennis, he won three of the sports' most prestigious tournaments. His greatest accomplishment occurred in 1975 when he won the Wimbledon championship. Within four years of this high point in his career, his failing health forced him to retire.

Ashe was only in his mid-thirties and, having kept up his physical condition, he decided to re-enter professional tennis after a brief retirement. Sadly, what he did not know was that the arteries leading to his heart had become choked with atherosclerotic plaque. The heart attack he suffered, shortly after beginning his comeback, brought his tennis career to a painful and abrupt close.

But his difficulties kept growing. His physicians told him the only hope for a normal life would be through quadruple by-pass surgery. This complex, life-threatening procedure required that Ashe have portions of arteries in his legs removed to replace those that fed his heart. His great loss of blood necessitated a transfusion. This ordeal was repeated in 1983, when he was forced to undergo a double by-pass operation.

Ashe recovered and lived in relatively good health for the next five years. His career as an athlete was over, but he responded by setting new goals. His new life and career were shattered one morning when his hand stopped working. It began with a numbness and progressed to complete paralysis. Tests revealed it was not a stroke, as he believed, but a parasitic infection caused by toxoplasmosis, a pathogen quite rare—except in the case of AIDS. Apparently, the transfusions he received during his second by-pass operation contained HIV, the AIDS-causing virus.

Arthur Ashe avoided anguishing about the unfairness of his being stricken by choosing to view his illness as a biological event rather than an act of providence. In fact, he stated that racism was a greater burden on him than AIDS: "My disease is the result of biological factors over which we, thus far, have had no control. Racism, however, is entirely made by people, and therefore it hurts and inconveniences infinitely more."[1] And even with racism, which he disliked so intensely, he acted to change it rather than just resent it.

Ashe saw that he could avoid depressing himself if he consciously worked at changing the way he viewed his situation. He realized that depression is commonly a result of "brooding on circumstances, especially circumstances one cannot avoid or over which one has no control."[2] Instead of brooding, he decided to make his life as meaningful as possible. That would enable him to face the "absolute end." Naturally, his fame, wealth, and social connections helped him to meet his goals, which included starting a foundation, political activism, and using his access to the media to further his causes. However, his celebrity cost him the personal privacy that he had worked hard to maintain during the early years of his illnesss. As with other misfortunes, he acknowledged this burden without making himself resentful or enraged. He deeply disliked the rumors that sprang up about his sexuality and drug history. Having his private life forced into the public domain was very painful for him. But he managed to avoid hating those he believed to be responsible.

Arthur Ashe reported apprehension and discomfort from his illness, but according to all reports he avoided enhancing his adversity by awfulizing, complaining, blaming, or panicking over what would happen next. He not only continued living his life fully but expanded his range of activities. He could have easily withdrawn into bitterness and resentment. After all, it certainly was unfair that the blood he was given was contaminated with HIV. Indeed, it would be easy to understand a person's rage at surviving two open-heart surgeries at a relatively young age only to get AIDS. But Ashe wisely counteracted the self-defeating emotions that could have made his last years bitter and miserable: "I can't avoid the fact that AIDS is a terminal disease. No doubt science will one day come up with a vaccine or even a way to reverse the effects of AIDS itself in the human body. But that will be a cure for other people, too late for me. Meanwhile I keep sailing on this middle passage. I am sailing into the wind and the dark. But I am doing my best to keep my boat steady and my sails full."[3]

Dan Seman was neither famous nor glamorous. He had spent his life as an independent businessman, always setting a goal and going for it. This approach to life was exemplified in his marriages. In his late twenties he married Frances, a woman three years his junior. She was a quiet woman and her strong features made her subtly attractive. During the twenty-two years of their marriage they had two children, neither of whom had ever gotten to know Dan very well.

As their marriage went on, Frances, who seemed to have suffered from manic-deressive disorder, became increasingly eccentric and unpredictable. Dan had decided years earlier that he did not want to stay with her, but he waited until BettyAnn and Larry had grown before he told her he wanted a divorce. His decision had been made easier by Muriel. She was a young art student he had met in the building in which he worked. Dan charmed her and a relationship began. Slender and aristocratic, she was as different from Frances as a woman could be.

Within three months of divorcing Frances, Dan married Muriel. This helped drive Frances to a suicidal state, and led Dan's daughter to disavow any relationship with Dan, who was now married to a woman younger than she was. Dan and Muriel were quite happy for the next nineteen years. Their relationship produced another daughter for Dan, and he flourished economically.

In the early 1970's Dan's fortunes began to wane. He lost virtually all of his assets, which had been concentrated in a couple of securities. Even worse, he was forced to retire from his executive position, and was replaced by a much younger man. Thus, he literally went from being wealthy to struggling to raise his next mortgage payment. Now in his early seventies, he would crowd onto the morning rush of the New York subway system to try to make a fresh start as a jewlery salesman. Every day the old man would commute over two hours each way to earn a fourth of what he had earned as a young man. He never complained or seemed to react to adversity; in fact no one, save Muriel, knew of his difficulties. Dan rarely apologized and he never complained. For two years he fought to re-establish himself, and he was winning until his body betrayed him. For several days he felt a discomfort—he never said pain—in his abdomen. At Muriel's insistence, he went to a large Long Island hospital for tests and was told it was pancreatic cancer.

He calmly asked the oncologist about the prognosis and treatment for his illness. Many physicians assume that, since older people have brief life expectancies, an even shorter one can't be too upsetting. So Dan was bluntly told that with aggressive chemotherapeutic treatment he could expect to live eight months . . . maybe even longer! Dan left the office and did not discuss what the oncologist told him until later that evening. He told Muriel, "Dr. Jarrod said that I don't have to do anything, just leave it alone." Thereafter he wouldn't discuss it or get any additional medical help. The only exception to his absolute denial was his acceptance of narcotics when the severity of his pain made it impossible for him to think of anything else.

During the progression of his illness he continued to work, forcing his way onto the crowded subway to sell jewelry. Every day he would haggle and cajole with customers while his cancer grew. He refused to slow down, even when the flat abdomen he had always taken pride in had grown to be bizarrely distended. When friends, who had not seen him for a while, were unnerved by his pallor and distended midsection, he dismissed their inquiries of concern by indicating that there was nothing wrong with him. Those who knew him said that this was the way he approached his illnesss: He refused to accept its existence. He maintained this posture for seven months, after which he rapidly grew ill and had to be hospitalized. He had made it clear to his wife and physician that he wanted no extraordinary care. He died, without a great deal of pain, within a week of admission.

Dan always knew he was dying. He made a conscious choice to make no changes in his life and to deny his illness—not its reality, but its ability to make him yield. Shortly before his death he said something to the effect that he never asked the world permission for anything he did, so he would not petition it for mercy. He lived his life until the last moment of mobility, spending only his last week in the hospital. Dan died at the age of seventy-three. Despite a lethal and debilitating illness, he experienced virtually no depression or bitterness. He accepted the vagaries of life perhaps because he accepted himself despite his own imperfections. His illness was just one more challenge. He met it as best he could.

Anatole Broyard had never dwelled much on his mortality. His joy in living was too great. He did, however, write a great deal on issues relating to dying and illness. His father's difficult struggle with bladder cancer had deeply shaken him. His talents as a writer permitted him to explore the process of dying through his poignant essays, and thereby accept it and fully appreciate living.

Broyard was an editor, literary critic, and writer for the *New York Times* for more than forty years. He had been spared actue illness for all of his sixty-nine years, until one day he experienced a sudden inhibition in his urine flow. It did not take very long for him to discover that he had prostate cancer that was spreading. Shortly afterward he made a decision: "When you learn your life is threatened, you can turn towards this knowledge or away from it. I turned toward it. I thought that time had tapped me on the shoulder, that I had been given a real deadline at last."[4] In his writings he explored the process of dying and, through this, he grew to know a great deal more about living.

As his illness progresssed, he began to lose functions he had always taken for granted. This served to give him a choice—to continually grieve at the loss of each ability, or to refocus and reframe. Broyard chose the latter. Like Arthur Ashe, he concluded that despair procreates more despair. It is a way of raging at a universe that won't bargain, or apologize. People who despair are much like those who righteously fight against an unbeatable foe; they frequently demoralize and defeat themselves. Broyard worked at finding alternatives: "When the cancer threatened my sexuality, my mind became immediately erect. If in the future the treatment should interfere with the mechanics of sex, I can imagine all kinds of alternate approaches. As John Dewey said, 'We never know what we might find until we are forced to look.' "[5]

Just as he refused to despair, he decided that anger at the unfairness of illness is irrational and futile. He said, "There is too much talk about anger among the sick and the books about them, and I think they should be cautioned against this. The feeling of being unjustly singled out is a cancerous kind of thinking and you can't get rid of it in Elisabeth Kübler-Ross's screaming room. I'm sixty-nine years old, and I've never been seriously ill in my life—what have I got to be angry about? I think sick people are more frustrated by their illness than angry and that they should think about ways to go on with their lives as much as possible, rather than proclaiming their anger like King Lear on the heath."

Broyard believed that facing a severe illness does not signify the apocalypse. He strove to go on being the same person he was before. The main difference he found is that ill people had best add fighting their illness to their life's plan. One technique Broyard found useful was humor. He mocked and caricatured his cancer. Each person has to find his or her own way of coping, but Broyard firmly believed that everyone *can* find a way to cope.

During the last months of his illness he chose to travel and continue working. He balanced the use of analgesics to minimize both his pain and loss of clarity. According to his wife, Alexandra, "Anatole died doing what he did best, commenting on life and his surroundings. And yes, he was alive, as he had hoped, when he died."

One of the authors met Lenny Dean when he sought medical care at a clinic in which the author worked. Lenny was an actor, he never made much money at it but that's the way he defined himself. His career had been limited to a few small parts in minor movies, a couple of commercials, and one major role in a documentary about would-be actors. Lenny was gay and flamboyantly so. In fact, his main source of income came from portraying women on telephone sex lines. One wonders how the many eager callers would have felt if they had known that their sexual fantasy woman really was a small fortyish bald man.

Lenny's lover of eight years was dying of AIDS when he was told that he, too, had the disease. Remarkably, he was not overly upset. He said, "Well, it's been going around, so I guess I got it too." Lenny was fully aware of the consequences of his illness, but accepted his symptoms without magnifying them.

Lenny was always concerned with the picayune. For two months he labored over what type of hairpiece he would buy. A well-known gay actor was visiting New York from California and Lenny was invited to a party he was giving. He didn't want to go there bald. Yet at the same time he failed to notice a rapidly increasing distension in his abdomen. When a friend pointed it out to him, he dismissed it as stemming from his overeating. It wasn't. He nearly died from pancreatitis. He had been taking a toxic drug for AIDS that was known to have that side effect. He recovered after two critical weeks in the hospital. His response to his close encounter with death was to decide to quit smoking.

Lenny seems to be a case of deep denial, but not really. He made a conscious decision to live every day without unduly worrying about his illness. He therefore picked the best health care professionals he could find and left all the medical decisions to them. Lenny took an active role in caring for himself in the same way a good chief executive manages

a large corporation: Find the best people, divide and dele-
gate many responsibilities, and then supervise the crises. He
divided the responsibility of his health care by engaging no
less than five different specialists, and he saw one of them
every week—more often if he had any new symptoms.

Death was not something he feared, he simply did not
think about it. He feared pain and indignity. He took precautions to minimize the likelihood of any great suffering, and
his managerial approach with his physicians helped lessen
the indignities many terminally ill people suffer.

Despite an increasing neuropathy that made walking
painful, Lenny walked half the length of the small city in
which he lived after being fitted with his new hair-weave. He
was beaming, he wanted everyone to see. He went to the
New York party and had a great time. It was as though he really didn't believe he was ill. But shortly before his death he
labored over how to tell his conservative brother that he was
gay and had AIDS. He said, "I'd better tell him now. I'd hate
for someone to tell him after I'm dead. . . . He'd really be
pissed then!"

Lenny did die, two months after telling his brother, who
fully accepted him and was closer to him during the last days
of his illness than he had ever been. Lenny never did experience much pain. During the last few months of his life, he
did everything he wanted to do, and really made the most of
his life. He even made a lot of his suitors happy while making sure they would not be infected.

In his autobiographic book *Life Work*, poet Donald
Hall proposes a solution to existential anxiety: Work! With a
proselyte's fervor, he proposes this solution to the dread that
can come with contemplating mortality. Hall is a writer who
had discovered his special passion in life, chronicling
through prose and verse his unique view of the world. This
mission precluded a significant portion of the despair that he
confronted when he discovered that he had cancer of the
colon. He wrote, after having half his colon removed, "When
I learned of my illness, I wept for myself and for my old

mother, for my children and grandchildren, and for Jane. And I wept to think that I would have to stop working."[6]

Hall recovered from his operation and was able to continue writing and to stay absorbed in his work, his passion. He focused on finding a meaning to his life, by writing of his past, his parents, and his legacy. By creating a continuity with his life and those who precede and follow it, he gave himself considerable solace.

Writing has always been Hall's vocation. He came from a family of New Englanders whose deep respect for the value of work was imparted to him. He recalled that "a year after my father's death, she [his mother] developed an ulcer. She went to a surgeon who said 'Work.' "[7] Hall's mother chose to follow the surgeon's recommendation and recovered without any additional medical care. This anecdote best characterizes Hall's philosophy, which helped him confront the recurrence of his cancer.

A couple of years after his first surgery, a growth was discovered on his liver. The cancer had metastasized. His initial reaction was fear and dread, then curiosity about what medical procedures he would now face. He knew that the liver can regenerate itself even after losing more than half its structure. But was the cancer localized enough for such surgery? He was lucky, it was. There was hope, not for cure, but for more time to write, to create. I (AE) have always recommended that people facing emotional distress find a vital, absorbing interest in life. Few people who pursue strong long-term interests have time to create the misery that saps the pleasure of their existence. Hall also came to this conclusion. His vital interest was his writing.

He survived the surgery, which removed a large portion of his cancerous liver, and he began chemotherapy, knowing his long-term chances for survival were not good. He wrote, "I am about to start chemotherapy. I read the medical literature concerning my disease and understand how poor my chances are to live more than a few years: maybe three, but what will the third be like? Will there be energy enough for work?"[8] Hall decided that that question was not the most relevant one he could ask himself. Instead he chose to continue his passion. He would write, and when doing so his fear of dying amazingly dimmed. He lived for the completion of each poem or story. He concludes *Life Work* by stating: "If little poems announce themselves I will open the door; they knock infrequently these days. But I will undertake no more long projects. I will do short stories, children's books, new short poems, maybe another essay. . . . Today if I begin a thought about 1995 I do not finish the thought. It is easier, and it remains pleasant, to undertake short endeavors which absorb me as much as any work can. There is only one long-term project."[9]

Stanley Jones was in many ways distinct from the other boys in his part of the Bronx. At first glance he was quite similar. He was a tall black kid with a confident walk, but as you got to know him the differences became more and more obvious. His voice was soft and his speech clearly articulated, something he had worked hard for. No ghetto talk for him, he wanted to go places, and heavily accented speech would be a trap. Stanley was not interested in gangs or street fights, or drugs. And unlike the other teen-agers, he never had a girlfriend. Not that the girls were not interested in him. He was far better looking than average and his calm, confident demeanor endowed him with additional appeal. The reason he didn't have a girlfriend was simple, he did not want one. He was attracted to males and had his first sex with an older man when he was sixteen.

Being gay was not the central theme in his life, however. His ambition was. In fact after his one teen-age love affair he put his sexuality aside until college. It was too dangerous and uncomfortable for him to keep a secret life, when he was trying to keep up his grades. So he completed high school near the top of his class and was accepted by every college to which he applied. He decided on what many considered the foremost campus in his state. Stanley took courses in several areas, most related to the social sciences. By his third year he was majoring in psychology, with the intensely focused goal of becoming a clinical psychologist. At twenty Stanley began living an openly gay lifestyle, now that he could do so without anxiety while living in the progressive college town. At that time he met his first lover, James—a man whose background was quite different from Stanley's. James came from a WASP family in eastern Long Island. He never worried about being gay, and was the vice-president of the campus gay and lesbian alliance.

They were an unlikely couple. Stanley was tall, black, laconic, and very proper—in contrast to short, blond, and gleefully gregarious James. Despite their dissimilarities, Stanley loved his little James very much. And unlike most of his gay contemporaries who delighted in sexual variety to bizarre extremes, Stanley only liked to sleep with James. Many of his gay friends at school thought Stanley somewhat prudish, but he considered himself temperate and disciplined. James saw Stanley as the centering force of stability in his life.

Stanley did very well, graduating in the late 1970's with a degree in psychology, and achieved one of his great goals by being accepted by a major Ph.D. program in clinical psychology in New York City. He was both excited and frightened about returning to New York City. He would face great temptation from the bars and the gay scene. But going to graduate school in New York was too exciting to pass up, he would simply practice self-discipline. James also enrolled in graduate school in New York, to begin work on a master's degree in fine arts . . . he planned to be an actor. For the first few months they lived together, but James had entered the world of show business with its many beautiful young men. He still felt strongly about Stanley, but he was young and in demand, and could not see himself wasting all this on only one person. So they split up, and Stanley focused on school, where he did excellently.

During the five years he worked on his doctorate, Stanley still avoided giving much time to the bars and gay clubs.

And unlike many of his peers in the mid 1980's he dated rarely and had sex infrequently. Stanley was unusually monogamous during this era of open and free sexuality. So when many gay men began to live in terror of AIDS, he was confident he would be all right.

With his family and new lover, Robert, proudly present at his commencement, Stanley—the first college graduate in his family—received the degree of Doctor of Philosophy in psychology. Shortly after graduation he accepted a position in a clinic working with children and adolescents, where he earned a reputation as a highly competent psychologist and administrator. Among his largely conservative co-workers, Stanley did not present himself as gay, but made no attempt at hiding it. He dressed meticulously and adorned his right ear with a diamond stud earring. He had learned a while back that shame only exists in the sufferer's head.

With effort and ambition, Stanley's career moved rapidly so that by age thirty-six he was appointed director of an entire children's psychiatric facility—the first psychologist to hold the position—and the first African-American gay man to hold it. Just two months after his elation at this achievement, Robert got sick. He had shown symptoms for some time, but both Stanley and Robert denied what they saw. They finally could not deny the diagnosis: Robert had AIDS.

The news left Stanley with a dizzying combination of fear and grief. "Could Robert have it and not me?" He was relatively sure of the answer but would not take a test, for more than a year. Meanwhile he made a decision that, no matter what he discovered, he would continue what he loved doing: working with kids.

Robert lived with AIDS for just one more year and died of a rapidly spreading lymphoma. Stanely had been with him every day, but managed to find time for all his responsibilities at the hospital. Only after Robert's death did Stanley have himself tested, and despite all his mental preparations the realization that he had the HIV virus hit him with a sickening impact. How unfair it seemed! Stanley lamented to himself, "I didn't sleep around, I wasn't like those other guys. . . ." But despite the shock and the hurt of the cruel unfairness, he was in his office the very next day. He realized that complaining about injustice made no sense. His illness was not part of a plan; and obsessing would not explain it or make it go away. He concluded that getting AIDS was no more unjust than any of the many cruelties inflicted on the kids he worked with. He had always helped the children from broken and abusive homes by encouraging them to accept themselves despite all the indignities they had borne and to accept the world despite its apparent cruelty. He now applied this philosophy to himself.

For the next three years Stanley felt few effects from the virus. Of course each cough or sore throat encouraged a surge of panic that would momentarily paralyze him. But he would say to himself, "It won't kill me today, and I have responsibilities." Death scared him, and he hated the idea that at some point he would no longer be here, but he discovered something essential to emotional well-being. A condition can only be very upsetting if one keeps awfulizing about it! Stanley chose to focus on his work and the very satisfying task of taking mentally ill children and helping them get back into the world. The hospital began more than a dozen new treatment programs for troubled kids, and it became one of the foremost psychiatric facilities for adolescents in the country.

Recently, Stanley has begun to cut back his schedule because of the gradual worsening of his illness. He hates the fatigue and constant infections. But he no longer fears dying. He focuses on his legacy—all the kids he has helped or influenced, and the hospital whose procedures and methods all have his mark. He says that he always knew he would die, but he has accomplished more in his thirty-eight years than anyone else in his family had in seventy. He says he is satisfied.

Stephen Jay Gould's career has been the dream of every academic. He earned his Ph.D. at Columbia University and within a few years he was a Harvard University professor. He made significant contributions to the field of evolutionary biology. He lectured on issues ranging from philosophy, religion, the history of racism to neo-Darwinism. His own research resulted in radical changes about the principles of evolution. Gould proposed that evolution is not a gradual and continual process, but occurs in torrents followed by quiescent periods of adjustment. He is a prolific author who has written in technical and popular fields. Many of his technical books have even sold well to people outside of his field.

At thirty-nine he received a MacArthur Foundation grant that awarded him $38,400 a year for five years to do with as he pleased. This grant is reserved for especially creative and talented individuals irrespective of field of endeavor or expertise. He was the recipient of an American Book Award, a National Magazine Award in 1980, and even made the cover of *Newsweek*. His greatest talent was in his perseverance, as well as in his working hard at being competent at many things. Above all he enjoyed what he did and tried to avoid limits in his life.

Unfortunately, like all humans, he is limited by the workings of his body. And this went awry at the age of forty-five. During a routine examination of his prostate, a lump was found. Exploratory surgery was performed, and the lump was found to be mesothelioma, a highly malignant cancer of the lining of the abdomen and chest cavity. When advised of the illness, he asked his physician about the prospects. The response, although presented as optimistically as possible, showed a bleak outlook. The "odds" he was given were not good. Mesothelioma has no specific cure, and the typical survival time is eight months after diagnosis.

Gould did not accept this probability. Instead he went to the Harvard medical library, researched this illness, and drew some inventive conclusions. The ways physicians calculated odds of survival were based on statistical errors. They tended to be practitioners, not research scientists, and they had flawed statistics. He re-worked his physician's guesses and came to a quite different conclusion: He had a very good chance of living!

Gould concluded that his "odds" were far better than the experts believed. He factored in his age, health history, and other personal data and calculated that with the right treatment he would be among the infrequent survivors. This could have been a sophisticated type of denial, or indeed a genuine discovery. But in either case, it helped him enter treatment with a state of mind that really helped. His optimism did not make the course of his treatment any easier. But he took an active role and helped select a treatment plan. This included radiation therapy to shrink a remaining tumor, another surgical procedure, and ultimately an experimental form of chemotherapy.

These treatments led to peritonitis, which nearly killed him. He recovered but not before he had lost much of his hair and shrank from 180 to 120 pounds. Those close to him were certain that he would die, but he never complained or stopped being optimistic. He chose to view his illness as another problem in biology. Death was never the issue; he wished to stay alive because he loved living. He wanted to see his sons grow up and he wanted to keep studying fossils, shale, and natural history.

Gould reports that his illness taught him no fundamental truths about life, except that he liked living and would work hard to avoid giving it up. Rather than protesting the unfairness of his cancer, it gave him a sense of urgency, he said. He would work even harder at writing and researching. If he had less time to live, he would use it in the most constructive and enjoyable ways possible.

At this writing Gould is still living, more than eleven years after his first operation. Since then he has written several books and hundreds of essays and articles.

Of the vast number of people who awaken each day to confront a life-threatening illness, among the best known is Earvin "Magic" Johnson. A professional basketball player of international repute, he had acquired great wealth and the adoration of literally millions of fans, only to discover in one stunning moment that he was still just a man. Shortly after arriving in Utah for a game, he received an emergency call from his physician informing him that he must return to Los Angeles. He was told he had "failed" his insurance physical. He left Utah and returned to Los Angeles immediately. Naturally, he considered all the horrifying possibilities on the way there, but he could not have been prepared for what he was told: He had been infected with the HIV virus.

After the period of disorientation that comes when a familiar world suddenly seems different and dangerous, he came to understand the meaning of this diagnosis. He did not have AIDS but the virus that caused it. This meant that his life expectancy was shortened but it did not mean he was sick. In fact, the initial medical reports revealed that he showed few ill effects from the virus.

Possibly it is easier to face any crisis if you are wealthy, famous, and provided with tremendous emotional support. Indeed, Earvin "Magic" Johnson had all that. But no amount of wealth, fame, or adulation could stop the virus from destroying his immune system and ending his life sooner or later. Johnson still had to face this painful reality. He did so by announcing that he was retiring from professional basketball upon advice of his doctors and by publicly revealing his condition and its origin.

Before the press had a chance to speculate on how he contracted the virus, Johnson discussed the behavior that had increased his risks. Like many professional athletes, he had been very sexually active. He had several relationships with women in almost every city where he played basketball. It simply did not occur to him that this could be dangerous. Sex with large numbers of eager, attractive young women had long been a "perk" of international class athletes. Johnson believed himself to be less promiscuous than some of his peers, but he was active nonetheless. He explained: "People make all kinds of choices in their lives. Some drink. Some smoke. Some eat too much. That wasn't mine. My pleasure was being with women."[10]

His greatest source of enjoyment had turned into his greatest source of pain. But he chose to eschew shame and guilt. On the day after his retirement announcement he appeared on a live television show in which he discussed his infection, how he got it, and what others had to do to avoid it. He was asked by the host if he ever said, "Why me?" He answered that he did so initially but it did not take him long to understand how he got ill. AIDS was not different from any infectious illness: If you are exposed to the pathogen you usually get it, that's the answer. Magic Johnson accepted responsibility for his behavior, viewed his illness as a consequence but not a punishment, and felt that there was no one to blame and no need to apologize. He acknowledged that his battle with HIV would be easier for him than for many sufferers. Johnson was famous and rich, he was referred to as the first "mainstream" celebrity with AIDS; that is, he avoided some of the stigma of the ordinary "risk" groups.

To his credit, he used his position to obtain a seat on a national AIDS commission—a post he held only briefly, resigning in protest over his perception that the federal government was not committed to a full effort to fight the disease. Johnson decided he could best serve the crusade to help those living with AIDS by serving as an example—while playing the game he loved. So he returned from his retirement to represent the United States in the Olympics. Here was this man with a fatal illness playing basketball with what was touted as the best team in the history of the game. This "dream team" easily won the Gold Medal.

His performance at the Olympics led Johnson to conclude that his illness need not prevent his return to the Los Angeles Lakers in the National Basketball Association. But some players feared that they could contract the virus from blood shed while playing with or against him, so Magic Johnson retired from NBA basketball again—perhaps a little more painfully this time.

Like many people whose illnesses force them to limit their normal activities, Johnson made the rational decision to devote himself to something else. Lamenting the end of his athletic career would have served only to create misery, but looking to something new creates hope—hope for new pleasures, challenges, and achievements. Business was one of Johnson's goals and he decided to start a new career as a businessman. His optimism and enthusiasm about his new career led some to say he was in "denial." His response was: "One thing that really makes me mad is when people say that I'm in denial about having HIV. Maybe they think that way because I continue to be upbeat and optimistic, but I'm not going to crawl into a hole. The truth is, I don't have bad days. I don't wake up in the morning and think I am going to get AIDS. I don't have bad dreams about it. When I dream, it's usually about playing basketball. And when I wake up from that dream, I'm ready for that game. There have been moments of sadness about the virus, but not many. I've always been that way, thinking positive, with a bright outlook on life. And since this thing has happened to me, I've met dozens of other people who are living with HIV, just like me."[11]

Magic Johnson, at this writing, continues to live his life joyously and productively. Whether it be his nature or his personal philosophy that has helped maintain his equanimity since the grim verdict, he stays active trying to demonstrate to others that a shortened life span is not a reason to stop living.

Perhaps the most compelling example of a person facing death without succumbing to the horrors of the pain, alienation, and emotional distress is seen in the case of Anthony Godby Johnson. Anthony completed his autobiography *A Rock and a Hard Place* shortly before his death at fifteen. In it he told of being less than ten years old when his parents began to use him as a sexual commodity. They literally would sell their young son for the amusement of pedophiles. Anthony recalled that their abuse might have been endurable had they tempered it with even occasional affection. But, sadly, they never did. Instead, they seemed to assuage their guilt by working to convince Anthony of his worthlessness. To show any affection at all might mean that he did not deserve their sadistic treatment. So he lived a childhood of constant torment. His parents told him their beatings and deprivations came only because he was bad, and that he had sex with adult men because *he* wanted it.

Anthony ended his nightmare with his parents by calling a suicide hotline. He did not expect to be rescued, but hoped that someone would understand why he felt he had to die. But events moved rapidly and he was removed from his parents' domination by volunteer workers, who not only got him help, but actually adopted him themselves. His new parents, "mom" and "pop," gave him the kind of home he had dreamed of. They treated him with love and respect. For the first time in his life he felt safe, but the damage was done. Anthony was suffering from fifty-four badly healed bones; he had advanced syphilis and acute malnutrition. In addition, his body showed damage from his excessive use of aspirin. His parents never provided this child any medical care so he treated all of his pains, bruises, and diseases with large amounts of aspirin. It was Anthony's use of aspirin and his generally poor health that led to the paralyzing stroke he suffered at eleven.

With the help of his new parents he overcame most of the ill effects of the stroke. Pop would get him up early each day and they would exercise his immobile left side. A few months of this therapy left him with only a slight limp and some weakness on his left side. Anthony described this adversity in passing. But then how could he see this one new adversity as terrible after all that he had suffered? The worst now was over. He was back in school, doing well. Mom and pop were loving and supportive. Anthony got to travel, to experience the world in the way other children do—the way that had been cruelly denied him.

He had been tested for HIV, which was necessary as a

result of the extent of his sexual abuse. The results were negative from tests repeated over two years. Anthony had been spared from this most severe affliction. Or so it seemed. As he began to catch up with all the living he had missed, his happiness was plagued by strange symptoms. He would frequently awake bathed in sweat. Fatigue was almost continuous. And finally his greatest fears were confirmed when he contracted the opportunistic infection, PCP pneumonia. He had AIDS and he was thirteen.

Anthony fully understood what this diagnosis meant. Of course he was afraid of dying and afraid of pain. Yet he consciously decided to find meaning in his life, and in the world that had shown him so much cruelty. The Make a Wish Foundation provided him with a computer so that he could write his story and he spent the last months of his short life writing his autobiography. In it he provides insights into those desires of humans that can make a life worthwhile— even if shortened by illness. Anthony told of a teacher who had been one of the first people to show him love and concern during the years with his parents. One day this teacher disappeared. He understood when he heard other teachers gossiping in contemptuous tones, saying that the kind teacher was dying of AIDS. Anthony wrote: "He'd lost his job when his HIV-positive status was found out. One of the first to get caught by the 'gay plague,' he had gotten almost no support from family or co-workers. Those who weren't afraid of him were disappointed in him." Anthony recalled crying because no one remembered that this man was special. He grieved because this teacher probably died without ever knowing how special he was.

Shortly after this loss, Anthony told of an encounter with an intoxicated homeless woman on the New York subway: "I looked across the subway car at the stoned-out woman again. Our eyes met and I smiled. Surprisingly, she smiled back. Maybe no one had told her she was special. That's what love was—letting people know that you would hold them because they were special."[12]

This was Anthony's most compelling answer to the fear of death, knowing that he, like all people, is special and worthy of love. He discovered that all humans have worth and meaning, even though some contest this. A further discovery of Anthony was that most cruelty comes from fear and ignorance, and that these can be cured. During the last months of his life, in which he encountered more callous and insensitive people, he also found people who demonstrated selfless concern for others and strong moral composition. There was consolation, perhaps even hope for humanity, with people like the caring ones he found. As he got more ill he fought the natural inclination to complain by concluding that although his suffering was severe it was not unique. His pain was not an act of retribution, but a part of life.

Anthony found a great deal of peace in knowing that his life had meaning. He concluded that his name would "indicate in a solid way that, for however short a time, Anthony Godby Johnson was here. I want my humanity and imperfections to come through. I'd like to know that I was a strand in the web of life."[13]

As we approach the end of writing this book, the famous physician, biologist, and writer, Lewis Thomas, whose unforgettable *The Lives of a Cell* and other books have sold millions of copies, has been slowly dying for five years of Waldenstrom's disease, an abnormal proliferation of lymphocytes and plasma cells which keep the body's immune system in order. As reported in a recent interview with Thomas by essayist Roger Rosenblatt in the *New York Times Magazine*, Thomas, now eighty, experiences "a deep, invading weakness" but is by no means inactive or miserable. He keeps reminding his interviewer that "there's really no such thing as the agony of dying . . . I'm quite sure that pain is shut off at the moment of death." How? Thomas's explanation is that the body, when about to die, releases peptide hormones from cells in the hypothalamus and pituitary gland that attach themselves to cells that make us, when not dying, feel pain.[14]

Taking this view, Thomas uses his walker mainly to push things out of the way, takes to his wheelchair, or lies in bed. But, as Rosenblatt puts it, "Because Thomas is forced to maintain a sedentary state these days, his mind takes on a special prominence, like the Wizard of Oz's disembodied head—though, in fact, Thomas seems to have lived in his mind most of his life."[15]

Just as he did since he graduated *cum laude* from Harvard Medical School at the age of twenty-four, Thomas rejects the thought of an afterlife, doesn't believe in God, and still vigorously espouses the wonder he can find in the observable fundamental benign mysteries of nature. As he notes to Rosenblatt, "In the building of a termite hill, there comes a point when most, if not all, of the uprights are in place. And the word gets around the termites that it's time to turn the arch. And they all begin to turn the arch. And at just about the same time. And it turns out to be architecturally just the right time to do it, if you're going to have the right kind of ventilation and air-conditioning in the hill. But I don't think there's anybody calling the shots from some central platform, and saying, 'Turn the arch.' "[16]

As for solacing himself with wishes about immortality, Thomas says, "Once we get better at living together, I think the question of an afterlife will not seem so important. And once we acquire that as a habit of living in our dense populations—the habit of peace-making—I don't think that we'll feel the need for ideas like immortality."

Also: "It may be as important for us to die as it is for plant life to die. So we die and live in our successors. I'll tell you, I wouldn't want to live forever, even if I could. Science is tending in the direction of that possibility, keeping people alive for 140 to 150 years. An appalling prospect, when you think that people will age and be fragile that much longer, and what it takes for society to take care of aging bodies. For me frailty is a lot harder to bear than dying."[18]

In contemplating the usefulness of some of the things he has written and thought, Thomas goes peacefully on

through his dying days—still absorbed in the study of ety-
mology, cells, people, and other living things. No self-pitier,
he! (Shortly after this was written, Lewis Thomas peacefully
died.)

The Commonalities

All of the people described in this chapter, none of
whom had REBT or other sensible forms of therapy, had
several philosophies in common. This allowed them to confront fatal illness with a minimum of distress, anxiety, and
despair. Interestingly, it is not so much what they did, but
what they stubbornly refused to do—to make themselves utterly miserable.

None of these people chose to view their illness as a
unique punishment from God or the cosmos. All viewed it as
an undesirable but natural aspect of living. Without demanding that unfair situations absolutely should not, must
not occur, they refused to make themselves angry. There was
no one to blame, not God, not their doctors, not the person
who donated tainted blood. No one. By perceiving their in-
firmities as events that were not purposely inflicted on them,
they refrained from feeling victimized. They headed off intense rage and depression that many seriously ill people
often bring on.

A second characteristic of the people portrayed here is
their insistence on taking an active role in their treatment.
They did not obsess over their illness, and may have even ignored certain aspects of it, but all rationally selected the best
treatment they could obtain. This is true even with Dan,
who chose minimal treatment when he understood that
standard treatments would disable him without meaningfully
increasing his life expectancy. Anatole was told early in his
illness that castration would be the most effective treatment
for his type of tumor. He refused. He quite rationally decided that the advantage of castration over the hormonal
treatments did not compensate for the great reduction in the
quality of his life that he felt castration would cause.

All these people kept living to the fullest extent that

they could. They accepted that their illness shortened their lives but did not immediately end it. They wrote, worked, traveled, celebrated, and loved. They refused to let their illness become their vocation. They took care of themselves, but refrained from making their care the only core of their lives.

Notes to Chapter 14

1. Ashe, 1993, p. 126.
2. Ashe, 1993, p. 208.
3. Ashe, 1993, p. 59.
4. Broyard, 1992, p. 3.
5. Broyard, 1992, p. 27.
6. Hall, 1993, p. 62.
7. Hall, 1993, p. 112.
8. Hall, 1993, p. 113.
9. Hall, 1993, p. 124.
10. E. Johnson, 1992, p. 249.
11. E. Johnson, 1992, p. 339.
12. A. Johnson, 1993, p. 90.
13. A. Johnson, 1993, p. 185.
14. Rosenblatt, 1993.
15. Rosenblatt, 1993.
16. Rosenblatt, 1993.
17. Rosenblatt, 1993.
18. Rosenblatt, 1993.

15

Toward Unconditional Acceptance

If anything is unacceptable to men, women, and children it is the knowledge that they or their loved ones are seriously ill and may (or definitely will) soon die. The very word *human* implies your being alive, consciously *knowing* that you are and *feeling* alive, and realizing that, in all probability, you will for some period of time remain active and vibrant.

Of course, as Ernest Becker observed, you always "know" that your life span—and that of your loved ones—is limited.[1] But you "know" that quietly, unobtrusively, and pretty much in the back of your mind. You "know" it without often thinking about it. Protectively, and sensibly enough, you focus on your present—and on your future.

Actively *thinking* about death is a shock. So why not avoid doing so? Fine, ordinarily. Go right ahead and think of other things. Good! But hardly when you are *seriously* or *fatally* ill. Or one of your loved ones is. Can you *then* stop reflecting about death and dying? Not very easily. Not very sanely. You can almost completely turn off your mind. But had you better? Probably not. There is no final or surefire answer to this important human problem. Because there is no final human. You are a unique individual. What is best for you, whenever great difficulty arises, is never exactly what is best for others. Nor is what's best for you today necessarily what will be best for you tomorrow and the next day. Humans, including you, change and grow. They do not have total free will but they do have some choices.

To help you face the problem of remaining unterrorized and undespairing when faced by death and dying, Rational Emotive Behavior Therapy (REBT) offers you the answer of acceptance: To courageously and gracefully accept what you can't change.

This is not a perfect answer. You may not always want or choose acceptance. When you do choose—or accept—it you may at times fall back to nonacceptance and to panic and depression. Don't give up, don't tell yourself that it is hopeless, nor that you are hopeless. Difficult, yes. Hopeless, no. You can always return to accepting acceptance.[2]

To summarize some of the main things we have been saying in this book, here are the important aspects of unconditional acceptance that you can keep working to achieve when you or your loved ones are confronted with almost any kind of living—or dying—problem.

General Acceptance

The basic theory of REBT can be summarized in one word: acceptance. For it says that you and other people are born and reared to be easily disturbable, and you largely disturb yourself by constructing strong goals, values, desires, and purposes, which help keep you alive and add to your happiness. You then raise these into grandiose, absolutist demands, commands, shoulds, oughts, and musts—which often help to prematurely kill you and make you needlessly miserable and disturbed. Therefore, REBT holds, if you will only accept—not like but accept—fortunate and unfortunate reality, you can first minimize both your disturbances and your disturbability and, second, actualize yourself and make yourself happier.

But, alas, it is very difficult for you to accept yourself, to accept other people, and to accept grim reality. You, like others, are almost allergic to doing so; and even when you see that doing this would be beneficial and healthy, you still often refuse to do so. Or you temporarily do so, and then quickly go back to your godlike shoulds, oughts, musts, and demands. REBT tries to help you achieve several kinds of acceptance, which we shall now describe.

Accept Human Fallibility

All humans are human, and no one is infallible or superhuman. They agree to certain rules that they accept from their society and that they devise for themselves, agree that it would be better if they followed rather than went against these rules, and then they often break them. In families and in relationships, they usually agree to live together, share finances, be nice to each other, and do one set of things and refrain from doing another set. Then they often act against these rules, and usually feel badly about doing so. But that does not stop them from breaking the same rules again. No matter what they decide to do, by themselves or with others, they frequently don't do; and whatever they decide to refrain from doing, they still frequently do.

To be happy with yourself and with your partners, you'd better fully accept your own and their fallibility. No, not relish this fallibility; and no, not stop trying to be less fallible and trying to help others be less fallible. But never demand that you, or your mates, or close relative and friends be perfect. Never!

Accept Human Demandingness

All normal humans prefer, wish, and desire. Without doing so, they would not be able to survive; and they certainly wouldn't arrange to be happy. But just about all humans also have a tendency, an innate and learned strong tendency, to often demand, command, and insist that their desires be fulfilled and that their dislikes be avoided. They not only strongly *want* to perform well, be loved by others, and be comfortable; but they also easily and frequently construct arrant absolutist *demands* about their wants. They foolishly—and devoutly—believe that because they want good things, meaning things that they define (along with most members of their society) as "good," they *necessarily must* have them, that it's *awful* when they don't, that they *can't stand* deprivation, and that they are no good, other people are no good, and the world is no good when they are seriously deprived of their strong "needs."

This seems to be the biosocial nature of humans—to have strong desires, goals, and values that are both biologically predisposed and socially learned, and then often to raise these to imperative, absolutist demands. Unless you accept this almost universal condition of men, woman, and (especially!) children, you are going to demand that demanders not be the way they indubitably are—and your demands will frequently get you into trouble. Your friends and relatives, in particular, who are seriously or fatally ill may well be unusually demanding. Accept, accept, accept!

Accept Uncaringness and Unlovingness

Children and adults are born and reared with strong tendencies to care for others, particularly their family members, and to be attached to, and often madly in love with, these others, But they are also born and reared with strong tendencies to be uncaring, disinterested in others, unloving and at times antagonistic, hostile, and cruel. No matter how much they like or love you, people will often be absorbed in themselves, neglectful, and preoccupied with other people and things. They can easily care for you, and even strongly love you, for decades, or until the day they die. Nonetheless, their active absorption in you and their catering to your wants and dislikes may be exceptionally intermittent, inconsistent, and often entirely lacking. If you find one person in your entire lifetime who is not this way, you are extremely lucky. If you find several, it is a miracle! Seriously and fatally ill individuals may at times be unusually kind and loving—and at times almost completely into themselves. So may you, as their caretaker, vary considerably in your loving feelings. Don't be surprised by them—or by you!

Accept the Proneness to Human Disturbability

In one way, none of us is responsible for our own emotional disturbances. First, we are all born with a strong tendency to become needlessly upset over our relatively small frustrations and hassles; and this innate tendency may well have preserved the human race tens of thousands of years ago, when the hassles and dangers of living were enormous and when, unless we felt very anxious and/or angry about obnoxious and dangerous humans, animals, and environmental conditions, we probably would never have survived long enough to beget progeny to carry on our race.

Second, we all are prone to be beset with thousands of trials and tribulations, some of them very serious during our lifetime, including assault, rape, incest, accidents, diseases, and handicaps. So we are biosocially very disturbable; and practically none of us, including kings and millionaires, avoid fairly frequent bouts of depression, panic rage, and self-pity.

Third, as humans, we are normally quite conscious of many of the serious problems—economic, social, political, artistic, and recreational—that may befall us; and we know, even when we refuse to closely honor this knowledge, that we all have to die. So serious concern (sometimes called angst) seems to be the human condition; and it is easy for most of us to jump from this kind of "rational" concern to "irrational" overconcern, or to severe states of anxiety or panic. Environmental and biological factors predispose all of us to some degree of emotional disturbability.

Fourth, practically all of us are taught to be more disturbed than we probably need be by our families and our culture. Our parents are unduly alarmed about us when we are very young, because they know how vulnerable we are to disaster and death, and they communicate their overwhelming anxiety to us. Our schools and our religious groups instill us with many sensible and not so sensible fears. Our mass media, especially our films and TV presentations, teach us to be vulnerable to rejection and failure, and to put ourselves down when we do poorly and to mightily scare ourselves when we are faced with dangers.

On many counts, then, environmental *and* biological factors predispose us to some degree of emotional disturbability, even when we lead "normal" lives. When, in addition, we or our loved ones are seriously ill or dying, our own and their disturbability easily—and naturally—increases. Expect, heed, and *accept* this.

Accept Some Degree of Responsibility for Your Own Disturbance

All the biological and social causes of our disturbability are bad enough. But to make matters much worse, we seem, says REBT, to be biologically prone to easily disturb ourselves. For what we largely learn from our parents and our culture as goals, wants, desires, and preferences, and the rules that they and we build around these preferences are reasonably good and self-helping. In any social group, if the individuals in it are not to live in chaos and not to continually fight with each other, a set of rules, mores, regulations, and laws has to be devised and taught to most of its members. Thus, just about all communities have rules and standards about child raising, work, money, politics, sports, and rule-making. So, because we live in communities of people, we all tend to learn these rules, and to learn that it is highly preferable to follow them most of the time. For if we go against them—and, for example, raise our children "badly," steal, fail to work, or kill others—we usually are strongly censured and penalized. Thus, we are scorned, jailed, divorced, refused food, disenfranchised, and kept from playing in sports. So it is distinctly to our advantage to follow most of the rules of our community and only occasionally or mildly ignore them.

We are taught, then, that it is highly preferable for us to do well and undesirable for us to do badly; and if we rigorously stay with these preferences, we will get in little social and individual trouble. For if you tell yourself, "My group tells me that I'd better be nice to other people," you can choose (1) to be nice to them and get favored by your group; or (2) not be nice to them and win your group's disfavor. Rarely, however, will your group literally kill you or entirely boycott you if you win its disfavor. It will merely disadvantage you in certain ways, and thereby encourage you to go back to acting by its rules. So social rules, set by your family and by your community, penalize you if you refuse to follow them but rarely saddle you with utter destruction or death.

When, moreover, you go against these rules and get yourself penalized, you normally only feel sorry, disappointed, and regretful about such penalties (or lack of advantages) and these appropriate, self-helping feelings encourage you to change your ways to try to follow the rules better the next time you encounter them. So being penalized or disadvantaged is bad; but it hardly seriously upsets you, as long as you decide to live with these disadvantages or to do something to change your ways and to reduce them.

Being, however, a "natural" absolutist-inclined human, you frequently choose to seriously upset yourself by taking your desires and preferences to do well and to be approved by significant others and making them into grandiose demands. Thus, you may tell yourself, "I *absolutely must*, under virtually *all conditions* and *at all times*, perform well and win the approval of significant others—else I am a rotten person who deserves no good in life!" Or you may convince yourself, "I *absolutely must not* be deprived of money or other material things that I want, and that my society tells me are good—or else it's *awful*. I *can't stand it*, and the world is a *horrible, depressing place* for me to live in!"

REBT says, then, that for the most part your feelings of severe anxiety, depression, rage, and self-pity are not only the result of your being born and reared to have these kinds of feelings. Instead, you are mainly inclined, as a human, to feel very disappointed, regretful, and annoyed when you fail and when things do not go your way; and those negative feelings are good or advantageous, because they encourage you to go back to the unfortunate Activating (A's) events of your life and either to change them or to accept them and live with them. But you have your *own* tendency, which is partly biological, to take just about any of your strong desires, wishes, and goals and to *make them, construct them,* into grandiose, Jehovian commands.

The three basic demands that you frequently make are:

1. "I *absolutely must* perform quite well and be approved by significant others or else I, a *total person*, am no damned good and am undeserving of an enjoyable life!" This demand mainly leads to your feeling severe anxiety and depression when it is not fulfilled.

2. "Other people *absolutely must* treat me kindly and fairly or they are *rotten individuals* who deserve to be damned and punished!" This demand leads to anger, fury, rage, feuds, fighting, wars, and genocide.

3. "The conditions under which I live *absolutely must be* comfortbale and undangerous, else it is *awful*, I *can't stand* it, and life is *hardly worth living*." This arrogant demand leads to low frustration tolerance, depression, and self-pity.

REBT says that even though you are born with a tendency to disturb yourself, and even though you model some of your serious disturbances after the teachings of your parents and your culture, you still have a real choice. You can choose—yes, choose—to take your goals, standards, and values—many of which you derived from your social upbringing—and raise them or *not* raise them to godlike demands on yourself, on others, and on the world. If you choose to think and feel grandiosely, construct absolutist musts, shoulds, oughts, demands, and commands, about and around your strong preference, then you had better accept that this is your choice, admit your own responsibility for making it, and work hard at giving up your self-constructed demands and at changing them back into strong preferences and desires. Strong ones? Yes, because they make your life more interesting.

So let yourself have strong likes and dislikes. Don't *just* be stoical and avoid powerful feelings. However, no matter how strongly you feel and believe, "I really, really *want X* and will feel highly displeased and sorry if I don't achieve it!" you can always look at your implicit *demand* that may easily underlie this want. If you find it, you can convince yourself, "But I *don't have to have* what I want, and I can still be happy, though not as happy, without it. Now let me see how I can get what I want. If I can't, too bad, it's not the end of the world. Tough! I can still lead a good life." Even when you are faced with your or a loved one's serious illness or death you can still accept your self-disturbability *about* this grim reality and choose to feel very sad and sorrowful but not panicked and depressed about it.

Accept Nonabsoluteness and Nondemandingness

Once you accept the reality that you largely construct and create—rather than are just given—your own emotional and behavioral disturbances, you had better accept the fairly obvious (but damned hard to acknowledge) reality that absolute necessity doesn't seem to exist in the world and that demanding that it does will get you nowhere—except disturbed. For no matter how much you desire some things and no matter how much it would be preferable for you to get what you *want*, you clearly don't absolutely have to get this desire fulfilled.

Contingently, you often do. Thus, if you want to live you must breathe, and if you want to breathe, you must have a sufficient amount of oxygen to take into your lungs. But these contingent necessities depend on your *desires* to live and breathe—both of which you *choose* to have and neither of which *has to be* fulfilled.

Obviously, you don't *have* to breathe, and you don't *have to* do just about anything. If you *choose* to live, then you must do a few things—such as breathe, eat, and defecate. But you—and the whole human race—can choose not to live, choose not to breathe, choose not to look at TV, etc. Once you do choose to do X, then Y may well be necessary to accomplish doing it. So Y is a contingent necessity, and X still may not be chosen at all.

If you will stick to the goals, values, and desires that you choose, but if you never—yes, never—demand that your preferences absolutely *must* be achieved and that your displeasures absolutely *must not* exist, you will find great difficulty in making yourself disturbed. Then, once you stop seriously upsetting yourself you will hardly achieve eternal bliss, but will have a much better chance of living with your problems—even serious ones like severe illnesses and extreme restrictions—and finding some satisfactions. Will you be happy *about* real pain and disability? Hell, no. Can you be happy *in spite of* it? Yes, if you give up arrant demandingness.

Acccept Yourself Unconditionally

The three main forms of nonacceptance people choose—and foolishly stick themselves with—are: (1) Self-downing: Blaming oneself for one's poor performance and one's unlovability; (2) Anger and rage: Blaming others for their poor behavior, especially to oneself; and (3) Low frustration tolerance: Blaming the world for having rotten conditions that it *absolutely should not* and *must not* have.

As for Number 1, you can always choose to unconditionally accept yourself—and thereby reduce the ravages you create with Number 2 and Number 3. For if you blame yourself for your inadequate behavior, you will also tend to damn others and damn the world when they provide you with unsatisfactory conditions. Blaming yourself, moreover, is one of the prime disruptors of relationships: If you think that you as a person are inadequate and undeserving, you will not even try very hard to work for a good relationship because you believe and feel that (1) you do not deserve it and (2) you presumably are incapable of achieving it. You may also feel that you *deserve* rotten conditions, including serious illness, and that you *should* suffer with them.

Unconditional acceptance of oneself is achieved, using REBT, either inelegantly or elegantly. Inelegantly, you realize that self-damning is a definitional choice: You *decide* that you are worthless because you function poorly in some important respects and you *define* yourself as a "bad person" for having these important defects. But because this is so, you can just as well (but, alas, not just as easily) define yourself as a "good person" by insisting that "Just because I am alive and human, I am good—*whether or not* I behave well and *whether or not* I am loved by significant others." You can see that this definition of yourself will work better than the opposing one: "Because I do poorly and am not approved by significant others, I am no good." So you merely choose to affirm it and stick with it, even though it is a pragmatic solution and though you cannot prove, empirically or otherwise, that you really *are* "good" or "bad."

Because this solution to the problem of rating your self, your being, or your totality is definitional, you can devise the more elegant solution of not giving yourself a global or total rating or evaluation *at all*, but *merely* and *only* rating your deeds and traits. Thus, you can say, "My acts are 'good' when they lead to results that I and my social group deem desirable; and they are 'bad' when I and my social group view them as undesirable. So I will only rate my acts and performances and will refuse to rate my self, my being, or my essence at all. Now how do I perform more good and fewer bad deeds?"

If you really accept either this inelegant or this elegant view of your self and thereby unconditionally accept yourself, you are well on the way to REBT's next element of acceptance: unconditionally accepting others.

Unconditional Acceptance of Others

To unconditionally accept others, and particularly your intimates with serious or fatal diseases, you use the same two solutions just described in accepting yourself. Inelegantly, you convince yourself, "I choose to see my relatives and friends as good persons just because they are alive and human, *whether or not* they perform well or are lovable. If I damn *them* for their behaviors and think that *they* are bad because their *acts* are bad, I wrongly overgeneralize—because they have millions of behaviors, some good and some bad, and they keep changing these behaviors from day to day and year to year. Moreover, my damning them as persons will get me nowhere, because it will only encourage them to damn me back for my poor behaviors and we'll go round and round in a hate-begets-hate circle. So if I am to build good relationships with others, which I would definitely like to do, I'll unconditionally accept them with their un-ideal or even rotten behaviors. Then I'll have a better chance to converse with them and perhaps induce them to change some of their behaviors."

For a more elegant solution to accepting others unconditionally you can tell yourself: "I will do my best not to give other people, especially when they are seriously ill, *any global* or *total* rating, for that is always inaccurate. So I will only rate and measure their *performances* and *traits*; and when they behave desirably, according to my standards and to social standards, I shall say, '*That* is good' and when they behave poorly, I shall say, '*That* is bad.' But I shall always do *my* best to avoid saying, '*They* are good' or '*They* are bad.' 'They are *persons who* at times act badly and are *persons who* at other times act well.' " This REBT-inspired kind of unconditional acceptance of others, even when they behave poorly, will appreciably help you to relate well to some of your most difficult friends and relatives—as seriously and fatally ill ones often tend to be.

Acceptance of Unchangeable Frustrations and Harsh Reality

Once you have begun to work at unconditionally accepting yourself and others, you can also start working at accepting, while still actively disliking, unchangeable frustrations, and the harsh realities of your life—including serious ailments. As noted above, hassles and frustrations are the inevitable lot of just about all humans—and, especially, disabled ones. When you are helping ill people, you have to agree with them about scheduling visits, meals, entertainment, and a hundred other things. Obviously, you often cannot get them to do what you want or even to let you do what you want; and obviously you will often want to prevent them from doing what they want and to block their forcing you to do what you don't want to do.

The solution to this problem of avoiding unnecessary frustrations is, as Reinhold Niebuhr said, to try to change the difficult things that you can change, to accept those that you can not change, and to have the wisdom to know the difference. To accept, of course, does not mean to *like* what you accept; and sometimes you can strongly dislike it and still accept or tolerate it.

To accept what you don't like means, according to REBT, to accept without disturbing yourself. For, as Paul Hauck has shown, when something goes wrong, especially in a relationship, you have three basic solutions to the problem: (1) do nothing; (2) work for change; and (3) leave the situation. But, remember, you can do all three of these things with or without feeling emotionally disturbed (e.g., anxious, depressed, or enraged). Real acceptance means your accepting the difficulties of life (and of relationships) without disturbing yourself about them:[3] telling yourself, for instance, "I definitely don't like what is happening to me in this situation and I shall do my best to change it. But whether I succeed or not in this respect, even if I only achieve a poor solution, I shall accept that it's too bad, quite unfortunate, and a real pain in the neck. But it's not *awful* or *terrible*; I *can* stand it; and I'm determined to make myself as happy as I can be even if the situation turns out badly. Tough! But I can still find ways to enjoy myself and be a reasonably enjoying person." When you or a close friend is seriously ill, this kind of acceptance of harsh reality can make a crucial difference.

Acceptance of the Possibility of Nondisturbance About Frustrations

Our last point implies another kind of acceptance: That you accept the reality that, just as disturbing yourself about bad things is in large part your own choice, refusing to disturb yourself about them is also definitely your choice. If you are feeling intractable physical pain, this choice may not exactly be yours: Your pain may literally keep you from thinking about how you can refuse to seriously upset yourself about it or about anything else. But normally you do have a choice and can, as REBT shows, make yourself appropriately sorry, displeased, and disappointed about unfortunate events or, instead, make yourself terrified, horrified, and depressed about them. So fully accept that you have this choice and that you can almost invariably take it no matter how ill or disabled you or one of your loved ones may be. Once again, the choice is yours!

Notes to Chapter 15

1. Becker, 1974.
2. Ellis, 1988a; Ellis & Robb, 1993; Jacobson, 1992; Pietsch, 1993.
3. Hauck, 1973, 1974; Pietsch, 1993.

References

Note: The items preceded by an asterisk (°) in the following list of references are recommended for readers who want to obtain more details of Rational Emotive Therapy (REBT) and Cognitive Behavior Therapy (CBT). Those preceded by two asterisks (°°) are REBT and CBT self-help books and materials. Most of these materials are obtainable from The Institute for Rational-Emotive Therapy, 45 East 65th Street, New York, N.Y. 10021-6593 (212) 535-0822. The Institute's free catalogue and the materials it distributes may be ordered by phone or by FAX (212) 249-3582. The Institute will continue to make available these and other materials, and it will offer talks, workshops, training sessions, as well as other presentations in the area of human growth and healthy living, and list these in its regular catalogue.

°Adler, A. (1927). *Understanding human nature*. New York: Greenberg.

°Adler, A. (1929). *The science of living*. New York: Greenberg.

°°Alberti, R.F. & Emmons, M.L. (1990). *Your perfect right*. 6th rev. ed. San Luis Obispo CA: Impact.

Ashe, A. (1993). *Days of grace*. New York: Alfred A. Knopf.

°Baldon, A. & Ellis, A. (1993). *RET problem solving workbook*. New York: Institute for Rational-Emotive Therapy.

°Bandura, A. (1986). *Social foundations of thought and action: A social cognitive theory.* Englewood Cliffs NJ: Prentice-Hall.

°Beck, A.T. (1976). *Cognitive therapy and the emotional disorders.* New York: International Universities Press.

°Beck, A.T. (1991). Cognitive therapy: A 30-year retrospective. *American Psychologist, 46,* 382-389.

Becker, E. (1973). *The denial of death.* New York: Norton.

Beilin, R. (1981). Social functions of denial of death. *Omega: Journal of Death & Dying, 12,* 25-35.

°°Benson, H. (1975). *The relaxation responses.* New York: Morrow.

°Bernard, M.E. (Ed.). (1991). *Using rational emotive therapy effectively: A practitioner's guide.* New York: Plenum.

°°Bernard, M.E. (1992). *Staying rational in an irrational world.* New York: Carol Publishing.

°Bernard, M.E. & Wolfe, J.L. (Eds.) (1993). *The RET resource book for practitioners.* New York: Institute for Rational-Emotive Therapy.

Bolt, M. (1977). Religious orientation and death fears. *Review of Religious Research, 19,* 73-76.

°°Borcherdt, Bill (1993). *You can control your feelings.* Sarasota FL: Professional Resource Press.

Bourland, D.D., Jr. & Johnston, P.O. (1991). *To be or not: An E-Prime anthology.* San Francisco: International Society for General Semantics.

°°Broder, M.S. (1993). *The art of staying together: A couple's guide to intimacy and respect.* New York: Hyperion.

Brown, C. (1985). *Down all these years.* New York: Bantam.

Broyard, A. (1992). *Intoxicated by my illness.* New York: Clarkson Potter.

°°Burns, D.D. (1980). *Feeling good: The new mood therapy.* New York: Morrow.

Coué, E. (1923). *My method.* New York: Doubleday, Page.

°Crawford, T. & Ellis, A. (1989). A dictionary of rational-emotive feelings and behaviors. *Journal of Rational-Emotive and Cognitive-Behavior Therapy,* 7 (1), 3-27.

Danysh, J. (1974). *Stop without quitting.* San Francisco: International Society for General Semantics.

Dean, C. & Surtees, P.G. (1989). Do psychological factors predict survival in breast cancer? *J. Psychosom Research,* 33, 561-569.

De Bono, E. (1991). *I am right—you are wrong: From rock logic to water logic.* New York: Viking.

°°DiGiuseppe, R. (Speaker). (1990). *What do I do with my anger: Hold it in or let it out?* Cassette recording. New York: Institute for Rational-Emotive Therapy.

°Dryden, W. (1984). *Rational-emotive therapy: Fundamentals and innovations.* Beckenham, Kent: Croom-Helm.

°°Dryden, W. (1990). *Dealing with anger problems: Rational-emotive therapeutic interventions.* Sarassota FL: Professional Resource Exchange.

°Dryden, W. & Ellis, A. (1989). Albert Ellis: An efficient and passionate life. *Journal of Counseling and Development,* 67, 539-546. Reprinted: New York: Institute for Rational-Emotive Therapy.

°°Dryden, W. & Gordon, J. (1991). *Think your way to happiness.* London: Sheldon Press.

°Dryden, W. & Hill, L.K. (Eds). (1993). *Innovations in rational-emotive therapy.* Newbury Park CA: Sage.

°Dryden, W. & Yankura, J. (1992). *Daring to be myself: A case study in rational-emotive therapy.* Buckingham, England and Philadelphia, USA: Open University Press.

Dubois, P. (1907). *The psychic treatment of nervous disorders.* New York: Funk & Wagnalls.

Ellis, A. (1950). An introduction to the scientific principles of psychoanalysis. *Genetic Psycholofy Monographs,* 41, 147-212.

°°Ellis, A. (1957). *How to live with a neurotic: At home and at work.* New York: Crown. Revised ed., Hollywood CA: Wilshire Books, 1975.

°Ellis, A. (1958a). Rational psychotherapy. *Journal of General Psychology,* 59, 35-49. Reprinted: New York: Institute for Rational-Emotive Therapy.

°°Ellis, A. (1958b). *Sex without guilt*. New York: Lyle Stuart. Revised ed: New York, Lyle Stuart, 1965.

°°Ellis, A. (1960). *The art and science of love*. Secaucus NJ: Lyle Stuart.

°°Ellis, A. (1962). *Reason and emotion in psychotherapy*. Secaucus NJ: Citadel.

°°Ellis, A. (1963). *The intelligent woman's guide to manhunting*. New York: Lyle Stuart and Dell. Revised ed: *The intelligent woman's guide to dating and mating*. Secaucus NJ: Lyle Stuart, 1979.

Ellis, A. (1965). Workshop in rational-emotive therapy. Institute for Rational-Emotive Therapy, New York City, September 8.

Ellis, A. (1968). Is psychoanalysis harmful? *Psychiatric Opinion, 5,* (1), 16-25. Reprinted: New York: Institute for Rational-Emotive Therapy.

°Ellis, A. (1969a). A cognitive approach to behavior therapy. *International Journal of Psychiatry, 8,* 896-900.

°Ellis, A. (1969b). A weekend of rational encounter. Rational Living, 4 (2), 1-8. Reprinted in A. Ellis & W. Dryden, *The practice of rational-emotive therapy*. (pp. 180-191). New York: Springer, 1987.

°°Ellis, A. (1971). *Growth through reason*. North Hollywood CA: Wilshire Books.

°Ellis, A. (1972a). Helping people get better rather than merely feel better. *Rational Living*, 7 (2), 2-9.

°°Ellis, A. (1972b). *How to master your fear of flying*. New York: Institute for Rational-Emotive Therapy.

°Ellis, A. (1972c). *Psychotherapy and the value of a human being*. New York: Institute for Rational-Emotive Therapy. Reprinted in A. Ellis & W. Dryden, *The Essential Albert Ellis*. New York: Springer, 1990.

°Ellis, A. (1972d). Psychotherapy without tears. In A. Burton (Ed.), *Twelve therapists* (pp. 103-126). San Francisco: Jossey-Bass.

°°Ellis, A. (Speaker) (1973a). *How to stubbornly refuse to be ashamed of anything*. Cassette recording. New York: Institute for Rational-Emotive Therapy.

°°Ellis, A. (1973b). *Humanistic psychotherapy: The rational-emotive approach*. New York: McGraw-Hill.

°°Ellis, A. (Speaker) (1973c). *Twenty-one ways to stop worrying.* Cassette recording. New York: Institute for Rational-Emotive Therapy

Ellis, A. (1975a). *How to live with a neurotic.* Revised Ed. North Hollywood CA: Wilshire Books.

°°Ellis, A. (1975b). (Speaker). *RET and assertiveness training.* Cassette recording. New York: Institute for Rational-Emotive Therapy.

°Ellis, A. (1976a). The biological basis of human irrationality. *Journal of Individual Psychology, 32,* 145-168. Reprinted: New York: Institute for Rational-Emotive Therapy.

°°Ellis, A. (Speaker). (1976b). *Conquering low frustration tolerance.* Cassette recording. New York: Institute for Rational-Emotive Therapy.

°°Ellis, A. (1976c). RET abolishes most of the human ego. *Psychotherapy, 13,* 343-348. Reprinted: New York: Institute for Rational-Emotive Therapy.

°°Ellis, A. (1976d). *Sex and the liberated man.* Secaucus NJ: Lyle Stuart.

°°Ellis, A. (1977a). *Anger—How to live with and without it.* Secaucus NJ: Citadel Press.

°°Ellis, A. (Speaker). (1977b). *Conquering the dire need for love.* Cassette recording. New York: Institute for Rational-Emotive Therapy.

°°Ellis, A. (1977c). Fun as psychotherapy. *Rational Living, 12 12* (1), 2-6. Also: Cassette recording. New York: Institute for Rational-Emotive Therapy, 1977.

°°Ellis, A. (Speaker). (1977d). *A garland of rational humorous songs.* Cassette recording and songbook. New York: Institute for Rational-Emotive Therapy.

°°Ellis, A. (1978). *I'd like to stop but . . . Dealing with addictions.* Cassette recording. New York: Institute for Rational Emotive-Therapy.

°Ellis, A. (1979a). Discomfort anxiety: A new cognitive behavioral construct. Part 1. *Rational Living, 14* (2), 3-8.

°°Ellis, A. (1979b). *The intelligent woman's guide to dating and mating.* Secaucus NJ: Lyle Stuart.

°Ellis, A. (1979c). A note on the treatment of agoraphobia with cognitive modification versus prolonged exposure. *Behavior Research and Therapy, 17,* 162-164.

°Ellis, A. (1979d). Rational-emotive therapy: Research data that support the clinical and personality hypotheses of RET and other modes of cognitive-behavior therapy. In A. Ellis & J.M. Whiteley (Eds.), *Theoretical and empirical foundations of rational-emotive therapy* (pp. 101-173). Monterey CA: Brooks/Cole.

°Ellis, A. (1980a). Discomfort anxiety: A new cognitive behavioral construct. Part 2. *Rational Living, 15,* (1), 25-30.

°°Ellis, A. (Speaker). (1980b). *Twenty-two ways to brighten up your love life.* Cassette recording. New York: Institute for Rational-Emotive Therapy.

°Ellis, A. (1981). The use of rational humorous songs in psychotherapy. *Voices, 166* (4), 29-36.

°Ellis, A. (1983). The philosophic implications and dangers of some popular behavior therapy techniques: In M. Rosenbaum, C.M. Franks & Y. Jaffe (Eds.), *Perspective in behavior therapy in the eighties* (pp. 138-151). New York: Springer.

°Ellis, A. (1984). The place of meditation in cognitive-behavior therapy and rational-emotive therapy. In D.H. Shapiro & R. Walsh (Eds.), *Meditation* (pp. 671-673). New York: Aldine.

°Ellis, A. (1985a). Anxiety about anxiety: The use of hypnosis with rational-emotive therapy. In E.T. Dowd & J.M. Healy (Eds.), *Case studies in hypnotherapy* (pp. 1-11). New York: Guilford.

°°Ellis, A. (1985b). Intellectual fascism. *Journal of Rational-Emotive Therapy, 3* (1), 3-12. Reprinted: New York: Institute for Rational-Emotive Therapy.

°Ellis, A. (1985c). *Overcoming resistance: Rational-emotive therapy with difficult clients.* New York: Springer.

°Ellis, A. (1985d). Jealousy: Its etiology and treatment. In D.G. Goldberg (Eds.), *Contemporary marriage* (pp. 430-438). Homewood IL: Dorsey.

°Ellis, A. (1987a). The impossibility of achieving consistently good mental health. *American Psychologist, 42,* 364-375.

°Ellis, A. (1987b). A sadly neglected cognitive element in depression. *Cognitive Therapy and Research, 11*, 121-146.

°Ellis, A. (1987c). The use of rational humorous songs in psychotherapy. In W.F. Fry Jr. & W.A. Salameh (Eds.). *Handbook of humor and psychotherapy* (pp. 265-287). Sarasota FL: Professional Resource Exchange.

°°Ellis, A. (1988a). *How to stubbornly refuse to make yourself miserable about anything—Yes, anything.* Secaucus NJ: Lyle Stuart.

°°Ellis, A. (Speaker). (1988b). *Unconditionally acepting yourself and others.* Cassette recording. New York: Institute for Rational-Emotive Therapy.

°Ellis, A. (1989). The history of cognition in psychotherapy. In A. Freeman, K.M. Simon, L.E. Beutler, & H. Aronowitz (Eds.), *Comprehensive handbook of cognitive therapy* (pp. 5-19). New York: Plenum.

°°Ellis, A. (Speaker). (1990a). *Albert Ellis live at the Learning Annex.* 2 Cassettes. New York: Institute for Rational-Emotive Therapy.

°Ellis, A. (1990b). Is rational-emotive therapy (RET) "rationalist" or "constructivist"? In Ellis, A. & Dryden, W., *The essential Albert Ellis* (pp. 114-141). New York: Springer.

°Ellis, A. (1990c). My life in clinical psychology. In C.E. Walker (Ed.), *History of clinical psychology in autobiography.* Homewood IL: Dorsey.

°Ellis, A. (1990d). Special features of rational-emotive therapy. In W. Dryden & R. DiGiuseppe (Eds.), *A primer on rational-emotive therapy* (pp. 79-93). Champaign IL: Research Press.

°Ellis, A. (1991a). Achieving self-actualization. In A. Jones & R. Crandall (Eds.), *Handbook of self-actualization.* Corte Madera CA: Select Press.

°Ellis, A. (1991b). *Cognitive aspects of abreactive therapy.* Rev. ed.. New York: Institute for Rational-Emotive Therapy.

°°Ellis, A. (Speaker). (1991c). *How to get along with difficult people.* Cassette recording. New York: Institute for Rational-Emotive Therapy.

°°Ellis, A. (Speaker). (1991d). *How to refuse to be angry, vindictive, and unforgiving.* Cassette recording. New York: Institute for Rational-Emotive Therapy.

°Ellis, A. (1991e). Rational-emotive family therapy. In A.M. Horne & J.L. Passmore (Eds.), *Family counseling and therapy*. 2nd edition (pp. 403-434). Itasca IL: F.E. Peacock.

°Ellis, A. (1991f). The revised ABCs of rational-emotive therapy. In J. Zeig (Ed.), *The evolution of psychotherapy*: The second conference. New York: Brunner/Mazel. Expanded version: *Journal of Rational-Emotive and Cognitive-Behavior Therapy, 9* 139-172.

°Ellis, A. (1991g). Suggestibility, irrational beliefs, and emotional disturbance. In J.F. Schumaner (Ed.), *Human Suggestibility* (pp. 309-325). New York: Routledge.

°Ellis, A. (1991h). Using RET effectively: Reflections and interview. In M.E. Bernard (Ed.), *Using rational-emotive therapy effectively* (pp. 1-33). New York: Plenum.

°°Ellis, A. (Speaker). (1992a). *Addictive Personalities*. 3 Cassette recordings. New York: Institute for Rational-Emotive Therapy.

°°Ellis, A. (1992b). Comments on David Mills' *Overcoming self-esteem* (pp. 13-15). New York: Institute for Rational-Emotive Therapy.

°°Ellis, A. (1992c). Foreword to Paul Hauck (Ed.), *Overcoming the rating game* (pp. 1-4). Louisville KY: Westminster/John Knox.

°Ellis, A. (1992d). Group rational-emotive and cognitive-behavioral therapy. *International Journal of Group Psychotherapy, 42,* 63-80.

°°Ellis, A. (Speaker). (1992e). The rational-emotive approach to marriage and family therapy. Two cassette recordings. Norcross GA: The Resource Link.

°Ellis, A. (1992f). Rational-emotive approaches to peace. *Journal of Cognitive Psychotherapy, 6,* 79-104.

°°Ellis, A. (Speaker). (1993a). *Living fully and in balance: This isn't a dress rehearsal—this is it!* Cassette recording. New York: Institute for Rational-Emotive Therapy.

°°Ellis, A. (Speaker). (1993b). *How to be a perfect non-perfectionist*. Cassette recording. New York: Institute for Rational-Emotive Therapy.

°°Ellis, A. (1993c). Rational-emotive imagery: RET version. In M.E. Bernard & J.L. Wolfe (Eds,), *The RET source book for practi-*

tioners (pp. 8-2 to 8-10). New York: Institute for Rational-Emotive Therapy.

°Ellis, A. & Abrahms, E. (1978). *Brief psychotherapy in medical and health practice*. New York: Springer.

°°Ellis, A., Abrams, M., & Dengelegi, L. (1992). *The art and science of rational eating*. New York: Barricade Books.

°°Ellis, A. & Becker, I. (1982). *A guide to personal happiness*. North Hollywood CA: Wilshire Books.

°Ellis, A. & Bernard, M.E. (Eds.), (1983). *Rational-emotive approaches to the problems of childhood*. New York: Plenum.

°°Ellis, A. & DiMattia, D. (1991). *Rational effectiveness training: A new method of facilitating management and labor relations*. New York: Institute for Rational-Emotive Therapy.

°Ellis, A. & Dryden, W. (1987). *The practice of rational-emotive therapy*. New York: Springer.

°Ellis, A. & Dryden, W. (1990). *The essential Albert Ellis*. New York: Springer.

°Ellis, A. & Dryden, W. (1991). *A dialogue with Albert Ellis: Against dogma*. Philadelphia: Open University Press.

°Ellis, A. & Grieger, R. (Eds.) (1977). *Handbook of rational-emotive therapy. Vol. 1*. New York: Springer.

°Ellis, A. & Grieger, R. (Eds.), (1986). *Handbook of rational-emotive therapy. Vol. 2*. New York: Springer.

°°Ellis, A. & Harper, R.A. (1961). *A guide to successful marriage*. North Hollywood CA: Wilshire Books.

°°Ellis, A. & Harper, R.A. (1975). *A new guide to rational living*. North Hollywood CA: Wilshire Books.

°°Ellis, A. & Knaus, W. (1977). *Overcoming procrastination*. New York: New American Library.

°Ellis, A., McInerney, J.F., DiGiuseppe, R. & Yeager, R.J. (1988). *Rational-emotive therapy with alcoholics and substance abusers*. Needham MA: Allyn & Bacon.

Ellis, A. & Robb, H. (1993). Acceptance in rational-emotive therapy. In S.C. Hayes, N.S. Jacobson, V.M. Follette, & M.J. Dougher (Eds.). *Acceptance and change* Reno, NV: Context Press.

°Ellis, A., Sichel, J., Leaf, R.C., & Mass, R. (1989). Countering per-
fectionism in research on clinical practice. I: Surveying rationality changes after a single intensive RET intervention. *Journal of
Rational-Emotive & Cognitive-Behavior Therapy, 7*, 197-218.

°°Ellis, A. & Velten, E. (1992). *When AA doesn't work for you: A rational guide for quitting alcohol.* New York: Barricade Books.

°Ellis, A. & Whiteley, J.M. (1979). *Theoretical and empirical foundations of rational-emotive therapy.* Monterey CA: Brooks/Cole.

°°Ellis, A. & Yeager, R. (1989). *Why some therapies don't work: The
dangers of transpersonal psychology.* Buffalo NY: Prometheus.

°Engels, G.I., & Diekstra, R.F.W. (1986). Meta-analysis of rational
emotive therapy outcome studies. In P. Eelen & O. Fontaine
(Eds.) *Behavior therapy: Beyond the conditioning framework*
(pp. 121-140). Hillsdale NJ: Lawrence Erlbaum.

°°Epictetus. (1890). *The collected works of Epictetus.* Boston: Little,
Brown.

°°Epstein, S. (1993). *You're smarter than you think.* New York:
Simon & Schuster.

Erickson, M.H. (1981). *A teaching seminar with Milton H. Erickson.*
Edited with commentary with J.K. Zeig. New York:
Brunner/Mazel.

FitzMaurice, K. (1991). *We're all insane.* Omaha NE: Palmtree Publishers.

Forinash, M. & Gonzalez, D. (1989). A phenomenological perspective of music therapy. *Music Therapy, 8,* 35-46.

Frank, J.D. & Frank, J.B. (1991). *Persuasion and healing.* Baltimore
MD: Johns Hopkins University Press.

Frankl, V. (1959). *Man's search for meaning.* New York: Pocket
Books.

Freud, S. (1965). *Standard edition of the complete psychological
works of Sigmund Freud.* New York: Basic Books.

°Glasser, W. (1965). *Reality therapy.* New York: Harper & Row.

Goleman, D. (1993, March 21). A slow methodical calming of the
mind. *New York Times Magazine.*

Greenberg, L.S. & Safran, J.D. (1987). *Emotion in psychotherapy.* New York: Guilford.

Hall, D. (1993). *Life work.* Boston: Beacon Press.

Hartman, R.S. (1967). *The measurement of value.* Carbondale IL:University of Southern Illinois Press.

°°Hauck, P.A. (1973). *Overcoming depression.* Philadelphia: Westminster.

°°Hauck, P.A. (1974). *Overcoming frustration and anger.* Philadelphia: Westminster.

°°Hauck, P.A. (1992). *Overcoming the rating game: Beyond self-love—beyond self-esteem. Louisville KY: Westminster/John Knox.*

Hayakawa, S.I. (1965). *Language in action.* New York: Harcourt, Brace and World.

Hoelter, J.W. (1979). Religiosity, fear of death and suicide acceptability. *North Central Sociological Association (NCSA), 525.*

Hollon, S.D. & Beck, A.T. (1993). Cognitive and cognitive behavioral therapies. In S.L. Garfield & A.E. Bergin (Eds.), *Handbook of psychotherapy and behavior change.* Fourth edition. New York: Wiley.

°°Jacobson, E. (1938). *You must relax.* New York: McGraw-Hill.

Jacobson, N.S. (1992). Behavioral couple therapy: A new beginning. *Behavior Therapy, 23,* 491-506.

Janne, P., Reynaert, C., & Cassiers, L. (1990). [Denial and coronary disease. A reconsideration of the denial mechanism in psychosomatic diseases and particularly in coronary disease.] Deni et maladie coronarienne. Pour une reconsideration topique du mecanisme de deni dans les maladies psychosomatiques et la maladie coronarienne en particulier. *Annals of Medical Psychology, 148,* 165-178.

Johnson, A.G. (1993). *A rock and a hard place.* New York: Crown.

Johnson, E.M. (1992). *My life.* New York: Fawcett Crest.

Johnson, W. (1946). *People in quandries.* New York: Harper & Row.

°Johnson, W.R. (1981). *So desperate the fight.* New York: Institute for Rational-Emotive Therapy.

Katz, L. & Epstein, S. (1991). Constructive thinking and coping with laboratory-induced stress. *Journal of Personality & Social Psychology, 61*, 789-800.

°Kelly, G. (1955). *The psychology of personal constructs*. Two vols. New York: Norton.

Kim, C.J., Yoo, J.S. & Park, J.W. (1989). [The effect of crisis intervention by the visiting nurse with cancer patients.] *Kanho Hakhoe Chi, 19*, 63-80.

°Knaus, W. (1974). *Rational-emotive education*. New York: Institute for Rational-Emotive Therapy.

Korzybski, A. (1933). *Science and sanity*. San Francisco: International Society of General Semantics.

°Lazarus, A.A. (1977). Toward an egoless state of being. In A. Ellis & R. Grieger (Eds.), *Handbook of rational-emotive therapy*. Vol. 1 (pp. 113-116). New York: Springer.

°Lazarus, A.A. (1990). *The practice of multimodal therapy*. Baltimore: Johns Hopkins.

Lazarus, R.S. (1982). Thoughts on the relations between emotion and cognition. *American Psychologist, 37*, 1019-1024.

°Lazarus, R.S. (1991). *Emotion and adaptation*. New York: Guilford.

°Lazarus, R.S. & Folkman, S. (1984). *Stress, appraisal, and coping*. New York: Springer.

LeBaron, S. (1989). The role of imagery in the treatment of a patient with malignant melanoma. *Hospice Journal, 5*, 13-23.

Levy, J.J., Dupras, A., & Samson, J.M. (1985). Religion, death and sexuality in Quebec: Research note. *Les Cahiers de Recherches en Sciences de la Religion, 6*. 25-34.

°°Low, A.A. (1952). *Mental health through will training*. Boston: Christopher.

°Lyons, L.C. & Woods, P.J. (1991). The efficacy of rational-emotive therapy: A quantitative review of the outcome research. *Clinical Psychology Review, 11*, 357-369.

°Mahoney, M.J. (1991). *Human change processes*. New York: Basic Books.

°°Marcus Aurelius. (1890). *Meditations*. Boston: Little, Brown.

°Maultsby, M.C., Jr. (1971). Rational emotive imagery. *Rational Living, 6* (1) 24-27.

°Maultsby, M.C., Jr. (1984). *Rational behavior therapy.* Englewood Cliffs NJ: Prentice-Hall.

°°Maultsby, M.C., Jr., & Ellis, A. (1974). *Technique for using rational-emotive imagery.* New York: Institute for Rational-Emotive ·
Therapy.

°McGovern, T.E. & Silverman, M.S. (1984). A review of outcome studies of rational-emotive therapy from 1977-1982. *Journal of Rational-Emotive Therapy, 2* (1), 7-18.

°Meichenbaum, D. (1977). *Cognitive-behavior modification.* New York: Plenum.

°°Miller, T. (1986). *The unfair advantage.* Manlius NY: Horsesense, Inc.

°°Mills, D. (1993). *Overcoming self-esteem.* New York: Institute for Rational-Emotive Therapy.

Moreno, J.L. (1990). *The essential J.L. Moreno.* New York: Springer.

°°Nottingham, E. (1992). *It's not as bad as it seems: A thinking approach to happiness.* Memphis TN: Castle Books.

Peale, N.V. (1952). *The power of positive thinking.* New York: Fawcett.

Perls, F. (1969). *Gestalt therapy verbatim.* New York: Delta.

°Phadke, K.M. (1982). Some innovations in RET theory and practice. *Rational Living,* 17 (2) 25-30.

Pietsch, W.V. (1993). *The serenity prayer.* San Francisco: Harper San Francisco.

Richman, K.O. (1980). Religion and Death Anxiety. *Southwestern Sociological Association (SWSA), 1437,*

Rogers, C.R. (1961). *On becoming a person.* Boston: Houghton-Mifflin.

°Rorer, L.G. (1989). Rational-emotive theory: 1. An integrated psychological and philosophic basis. 2. Explication and evaluation. *Cognitive Therapy and Research, 13,* 475-492; 531-548.

Rosenblatt, R. (1993, November 21). Lewis Thomas. *New York Times Magazine,* pp. 50-53.

Royce, J.R. (1984). The factor-gene basis of emotionality. *Motivation & Emotion, 8,* 285-310.

°Ruth, W.J. (1992). Irrational thinking in humans: An evolutionary proposal for Ellis' genetic postulate. *Journal of Rational-Emotive and Cognitive-Behavior Therapy, 10,* 3-20.

°Safran, J.D. & Greenberg, L.S. (Eds.) (1991). *Emotion, psychotherapy, and change.* New York: Guilford.

°Seligman, M.E.P. (1991). *Learned optimism.* New York: Knopf.

°°Sichel, J. & Ellis, A. (1984). *RET self-help form.* New York: Institute for Rational-Emotive Therapy.

°Silverman, M.S., McCarthy, M., & McGovern, T. (1992). A review of outcome studies of rational-emotive therapy from 1982-1989. *Journal of Rational-Emotive and Cognitive-Behavior Therapy, 10,* (3), 111-186.

Skinner, B.F. (1938). *The behavior of organisms.* New York: Appleton-Century.

Spivak, G. & Shure, N. (1977). *Social adjustment in young children.* San Francisco: Jossey-Bass.

Stampfl, T.G. & Levis, D.J. (1967). Essentials of implosive therapy. *Journal of Abnormal Psychology, 72,* 496-503.

Tate, F.B. (1989). Symbols in the graphic art of the dying. *Arts in Psychotherapy, 16,* 115-120.

Taylor, S. (1990). *Positive illusions.* New York: Basic Books.

Templer, D.I., Cappelletty, G.G., & Kaufman, I. (1990). Exploration of death anxiety as a function of religious variables in gay men with and without AIDS. *Omega, 22,* 43-50.

Tillich, P. (1953). *The courage to be.* New York: Oxford.

°°Trimpey, J. (1989). *Rational recovery from alcoholism: The small book.* New York: Delacorte.

°Vernon, A. (1989). *Thinking, feeling, behaving: An emotional education curriculum for children.* Champaign IL: Research Press.

°Walen, S., DiGiuseppe, R., & Dryden, W. (1992). *A practitioner's guide to rational-emotive therapy.* New York: Oxford University Press.

°Warga, C. (1989). *Profile of psychological Albert Ellis.* Original version of the article published in *Psychology Today*, September, 1988. New York: Institute for Rational-Emotive Therapy.

°Warren, R. & Zgourides, G.D. (1991). *Anxiety disorders: A rational-emotive perspective*. Des Moines IA: Longwood Division Allyn & Bacon.

°°Wolfe, J.L. (1992). *What to do when he has a headache*. New York: Hyperion.

°Wolfe, J.L. & Fodor, I.G. (1975). A cognitive-behavioral approach to modifying assertive behavior in women. *Counseling Psychologist*, 5 (4), 45-52.

Wolpe, J. (1990). *The practice of behavior therapy*. (Fourth ed.) Needham Heights MA: Allyn & Bacon.

°Woods, P.J. (1992). A study of "belief" and "non-belief" items from the Jones irrational beliefs test with implications for the theory of RET. *Journal of Rational-Emotive & Cognitive Behavior Therapy, 10*, 41-52.

°Yankura, J. & Dryden, W. (1990). *Doing RET: Albert Ellis in action*. New York: Springer.

°°Young, H.S. (1974). *A rational counseling primer*. New York: Institute for Rational-Emotive Therapy.

About the Authors

Albert Ellis, born in Pittsburgh and raised in New York City, holds a bachelor's degree from the City College of New York and M.A. and Ph.D. degrees in clinical psychology from Columbia University. He has been Adjunct Professor of Psychology at Rutgers University, Pittsburg State College, and other universities and has served as Chief Psychologist of the New Jersey State Diagnostic Center and Chief Psychologist of the New Jersey Department of Institutions and Agencies. He is the founder of Rational Emotive Behavior Therapy and the grandfather of Cognitive Behavior Therapy. He currently is President of the Institute for Rational-Emotive Therapy in New York City, has practiced psychotherapy, marriage, and family therapy, as well as sex therapy, for almost fifty years and continues this practice at the Psychological Clinic of the Institute in New York. He is a Board of Advisors member of Rational Recovery Systems.

Dr. Ellis has published more than 600 articles in psychological, psychiatric, and sociological journals and anthologies and has authored or edited more than 50 books, including *How to Live With a Neurotic, Reason and Emotion in Psychotherapy, A New Guide to Rational Living, A Guide to Personal Happiness, The Practice of Rational-Emo-*

tive Therapy, and *How to Stubbornly Refuse to Make Yourself Miserable About Anything—Yes, Anything!*

Michael Abrams is a licensed psychologist in New York and New Jersey. He is a psychologist at Kingsboro Psychiatric Center in Brooklyn, New York and is Director of Psychological Medicine, a private group practice in Jersey City, New Jersey. He holds degrees in statistics, history, business, and psychology from New York University, Brooklyn College, and Queens College of the City University of New York. He is a fellow of the Institute for Rational-Emotive Therapy in New York.

Dr. Abrams spent several years as a therapist working with persons with AIDS and their families at the Gay Men's Health Center in New York. In addition, he has worked with numerous individuals with severe illnesses in his private practice. He is the author of several articles in clinical and physiological psychology and is the co-author of *The Art and Science of Rational Eating.*

Prior to becoming a psychologist, Dr. Abrams spent many years as a financial researcher at the New York Stock Exchange, Citicorp, and Merrill Lynch.

Index